NGOs and Organizational Change
Discourse, Reporting, and Learning

The organizational dynamics of non-governmental organizations (NGOs) have become increasingly complex as they have evolved from small local groups into sophisticated multinational organizations with global networks. Alnoor Ebrahim's study analyzes the organizational evolution of NGOs as a result of their increased profile as bilateral partners in delivering aid. Focusing on the relationships between NGOs and their international network of funders, it examines not only the tensions created by the reporting requirements of funders, but also the strategies of resistance employed by NGOs. Ebrahim shows that systems of reporting, monitoring, and learning play essential roles in shaping not only what NGOs do but, more importantly, how they think about what they do. The book combines original case studies and research with an extensive review of literature. It draws from multiple fields including organizational behaviour, social and critical theory, civil society studies, and environmental and natural resource management.

ALNOOR EBRAHIM is Associate Professor in the School of Public and International Affairs at Virginia Polytechnic Institute and State University (Virginia Tech). He is also founding Co-Director of the Center for Global Accountabilities.

NGOs and Organizational Change

Discourse, Reporting, and Learning

Alnoor Ebrahim

Virginia Polytechnic Institute and State University

CAMBRIDGE
UNIVERSITY PRESS

CAMBRIDGE UNIVERSITY PRESS
Cambridge, New York, Melbourne, Madrid, Cape Town, Singapore, São Paulo

Cambridge University Press
The Edinburgh Building, Cambridge CB2 2RU, UK

Published in the United States of America by Cambridge University Press, New York

www.cambridge.org
Information on this title: www.cambridge.org/9780521824866

First published 2003
First paperback edition 2005

A catalogue record for this publication is available from the British Library

ISBN-13 978-0-521-82486-6 hardback
ISBN-10 0-521-82486-9 hardback

ISBN-13 978-0-521-67157-6 paperback
ISBN-10 0-521-67157-4 paperback

Transferred to digital printing 2006

Cambridge University Press has no responsibility for the
persistence or accuracy of URLs for external or third-party
internet websites referred to in this publication, and does
not guarantee that any content on such websites is, or will
remain, accurate or appropriate.

Contents

List of figures	*page* vi	
List of tables	vii	
Acknowledgments	viii	
List of abbreviations	x	
Introduction	1	
1	The making of NGOs: the relevance of Foucault and Bourdieu	7
2	The NGOs and their global networks	21
3	NGO behavior and development discourse	34
4	Interdependence and power: tensions over money and reputation	52
5	Information struggles: the role of information in the reproduction of NGO-funder relationships	77
6	Learning in NGOs	107
7	Challenges ahead: NGO-funder relations in a global future	151
Notes	160	
References	170	
Index	179	

Figures

2.1 Districts in Gujarat, India with AKRSP (I) and Sadguru
    programs   *page* 22

4.1 AKRSP (I)'s expenditure by funding source, 1985–2000   54

4.2 Sadguru's expenditure by funding source, fiscal years
    1986–2000   57

4.3 Sadguru's expenditure by foreign funding source, fiscal years
    1986–2000   58

4.4 Organizational inputs, outputs, and outcomes   72

4.5 Basic capital flows between NGOs and funders   74

5.1 Information sources and flows   79

6.1 A cycle of learning steps   111

6.2 The environment of Sadguru and AKRSP (I)   115

6.3 A stimulus–response model of learning   116

Tables

2.1 Activities of Sadguru and AKRSP (I)   *page* 25

5.1 Logical framework for community management of natural
   resources project   88

6.1 Physical achievement in Sadguru, FY 1976–97   118

6.2 The evolution of Sadguru's water resource program   119

6.3 Physical achievement in AKRSP (I), 1985–96   131

6.4 Physical achievement, expenditure, and staffing in AKRSP (I),
   1985–96   132

6.5 Activities and practices added and dropped by AKRSP (I),
   1985–96   140

Acknowledgments

Many people have contributed to the pages which follow. I owe a particular debt to the staff and leadership of the organizations detailed in this book: the Navinchandra Mafatlal Sadguru Water and Development Foundation (Sadguru), the Aga Khan Rural Support Programme India (AKRSP (I)), and the Aga Khan Foundation (AKF) offices in New Delhi, Geneva, London, and Ottawa. In particular, I wish to thank Harnath Jagawat, Anil C. Shah, Barry Underwood, Apoorva Oza, and E. M. Shashidharan for being so gracious and generous not only during fieldwork, but also in communications afterwards. I am also grateful to the staff of the Development Support Centre in Ahmedabad, and to various members of the New Delhi offices of the Delegation of the European Commission, the Ford Foundation, and the Norwegian Agency for Development Cooperation.

At Stanford University, I wish to thank Leonard Ortolano, Ben Crow (now at University of California, Santa Cruz), Akhil Gupta, Haresh Shah, and W. Richard Scott. I am especially grateful to Len for his good humor, sincerity, and candid critiques. At Virginia Tech, I am thankful for the encouragement provided by my colleagues John Randolph, Joe Scarpaci, and Edward Weisband. For their steadfast support and friendship, I am indebted to Michael Goldbach, Sanjeev Khagram, Helga Wild, and Niklas Damiris. Also for their support, I would like to acknowledge Greg Browder, Earthea Bubanje-Nance, Nicole Carter, Rick Gelting, Katherine Kao-Cushing, Ernesto Sánchez Triana, Stephanie Ohshita, Jiang Ru, Mara Warwick, Jimin Zhao, Jill Nomura, and Duc Wong.

For their hospitality and kindness during fieldwork, I wish to thank Shankar and Lakshmi Narayanan, Sonal Mehta, and the Sethi family – particularly Gautam, Sujata, and the late Lalita – as well as Bhagat, Malti, and Heera.

Numerous organizations have contributed to this book in terms of funding, research assistance and logistical support. I wish to thank the Natural Sciences and Engineering Research Council of Canada, the Aga Khan Foundation, the American Institute of Indian Studies, the India Studies Program of the Shastri Indo-Canadian Institute (especially P. N. Malik), and the Government of India.

Many thanks to Nicole Kehler for preparing the index. Responsibility for the content of this book, however, rests solely with me.

My deepest gratitude is reserved for last: to my parents, Shirin and Sadrudin, and to my wife and partner, Maria.

Abbreviations

AKDN	Aga Khan Development Network
AKF	Aga Khan Foundation
AKRSP (I)	Aga Khan Rural Support Programme, India
BMM	Baseline Monitoring Mission
CIDA	Canadian International Development Agency
CMNR	Community Management of Natural Resources
DFID	Department for International Development (United Kingdom)
DRDA	District Rural Development Agency
DSC	Development Support Centre
EC or CEC	European Commission
EU	European Union
GOI	Government of India
ICEF	India–Canada Environment Facility
ILO	International Labour Organisation
IMF	International Monetary Fund
JFM	Joint Forest Management
JMM	Joint Monitoring Mission
LFA	Logical Framework Analysis
LI	Lift Irrigation
LICS	Lift Irrigation Cooperative Society
MERC	Management of Environmental Resources by Communities
NGO	Non-Governmental Organization
NORAD	Norwegian Agency for Development Cooperation
NRM	Natural Resource Management
PIC	Program Implementation Committee
PIM	Participatory Irrigation Management
PRA	Participatory Rural Appraisal
Sadguru	Navinchandra Mafatlal Sadguru Water and Development Foundation
SHT	Spearhead Team
USAID	United States Agency for International Development

Introduction

This book is about change in non-governmental organizations (NGOs). It explores how NGOs change over time and examines the forces, both local and global, that shape them. Following the end of the Cold War, there has been an increase in attention among the international aid community to civil society organizations and institutions, and especially to development-oriented NGOs. This growth in attention and funding to NGOs appears to have been motivated by a number of factors. On one hand, it has been driven by evidence of state failure in service provision and an attendant neo-liberal economic climate of state retrenchment. On the other hand, it has been inspired by a belief that NGOs are not only more efficient service providers than public agencies but that they are also more democratic and effective in reaching the poor, despite a dearth of supportive empirical evidence. As development aid is increasingly channeled through NGOs rather than through governments, there is mounting pressure on NGOs to expand and scale-up their work, sometimes to the extent of replacing state services.

The focus of this book is on relationships between NGOs and their international networks of funders. Understanding these broader linkages is crucial to making sense of how and why NGOs change. In exploring the impacts of international funding on NGOs, this book devotes special attention to organizational reporting and learning systems. It examines not only the tensions created by the reporting requirements of funders, but also the strategies of resistance employed by NGOs as well as long-term changes in organizational behavior. Focusing on two NGOs in rural western India, and a host of funders in North America and Europe, it shows that systems of reporting, monitoring, and learning play especially central roles in shaping not only what NGOs do but, more importantly, how they think about what they do. How organizational members think about and conceptualize their work has profound implications for their long-term development strategies.

The initial seed for this book was planted in 1991. As a young fellow in a program supported by the Canadian International Development Agency and the Aga Khan Foundation Canada, I had the good fortune to spend several months with one of India's most highly reputed development NGOs – the Aga

Khan Rural Support Programme, India (AKRSP (I)). This first visit sparked my research interests for years to come. It was at this time, during informal conversations with staff and managers, that I was introduced to the highly politicized world of reporting and monitoring. As is well known, many NGOs like AKRSP (I) are required by their international funders to institute reporting systems for the sensible purposes of financial accountability and for monitoring the impacts of their interventions. At the same time, however, monitoring systems are a source of considerable tension between NGOs and their funders, since funders often wish to see evidence of quick "success" in the programs they fund, even though poverty alleviation and social change are likely to be slow processes.

I have since returned to India a number of times in order to conduct research on NGOs. Most of the primary data for this book were collected between 1995 and 1999. This project examines relationships between international funders and two of India's most successful NGOs – AKRSP (I) and the Navinchandra Mafatlal Sadguru Water and Development Foundation (Sadguru). Both organizations have much in common: they are two of India's largest development NGOs, both in terms of staff and funding; they have solid international reputations in environment and development work, especially in land and water resource management; and they receive funding from a number of the same international sources.

The core of this book is an analysis of four factors that shape NGO behavior, and which are of significant import for NGO-funder relations in general: (i) global discourses on development and environment; (ii) an interdependence between NGOs and funders; (iii) reporting and monitoring systems and structures; and (iv) processes of organizational learning.

In particular, I present three key arguments. First, I contend that while international actors have played a central role in introducing specific development ideas and practices to NGOs (e.g. sustainable development, gender, and professionalism), NGOs are not passive recipients of these discourses and are actively involved in contesting and reshaping them. Second, I challenge the standard notion that NGOs are "dependent" on international organizations for funds. Instead, I demonstrate that there is an interdependence between NGOs and funders in which NGOs leverage funds by providing information on "successful" projects, thereby conveying a positive reputation on their funders. This resource exchange leads to a highly structured interaction between NGOs and funders that favors short-term and easily measurable activities at the expense of longer-term processes of social and political change. At the root of this interdependence between NGOs and funders lies the more fundamental and value-based issue of how "success" is measured. This is a central issue in the book, and has penetrating consequences for NGO-funder relations and for lasting social change. Finally, I link these reporting and monitoring processes to learning systems. While funders have enhanced learning by introducing NGOs to new ideas and technologies, they have simultaneously impeded learning by insisting on reporting and monitoring systems designed to meet their own information needs for demonstrating short-term success.

The cases described in this book provide a window through which to understand the concrete effects of global discourses, and reporting and learning systems, on organizational behavior. Thus, while many of the details presented in this book are about Sadguru and AKRSP (I), they tell a larger story about organizational change. These cases are broadly significant in a number of additional respects. First, the organizational networks of the two NGOs are made up of actors that interact with hundreds of other organizations in India as well as internationally. The networks include, for example, the European Commission (EC), the Canadian International Development Agency (CIDA), the United Kingdom's Department for International Development (DFID), the Aga Khan Foundation (AKF), the Ford Foundation, the Norwegian Agency for Development Cooperation (NORAD), and many public agencies.

Second, the case NGOs were the first in India to receive "bilateral" funds from the European Union (exceeding US $14 million). Since such grants are normally provided to governments, this allocation to NGOs marked an important global precedent in development funding. Given their experience, strong reputations, influential connections, size and considerable bargaining power, AKRSP (I) and Sadguru constitute a "crucial test" for NGO-funders relations – if these two NGOs experience tensions with and pressures from funders, then it is likely that the behavior of smaller, less powerful NGOs will also be affected by these tensions. In other words, the interactions I articulate for these cases potentially reflect a more general patterning of relations between NGOs and funders, with deep structural implications.

Third and finally, the development context which I describe in this book, and the changes in that environment over time, are not unique to the NGOs described here, but are part of a larger series of transformations in development thought and activity over the last three decades. For example, notions of integrated rural development, sustainable development, and gender and development have found their way to NGOs around the world, although their impacts and emphases have varied.

This book is organized into seven chapters. The first chapter lays a foundation for conceptualizing NGO-funder relations. Drawing from the work of two social and critical theorists – Michel Foucault and Pierre Bourdieu – I provide an introduction to concepts of *discourse, habitus,* and *capital.* These concepts are then linked to ideas about organizational behavior in order to develop a framework for thinking about structuration and change in organizations. Readers less interested in this analytical basis may proceed directly to the more empirical chapters.

Chapter 2 furnishes some background details on the two case study NGOs, as well as on their organizational networks. The chapter is intended to provide a layout of the organizational landscape and thus to serve as a reference for subsequent discussion. In chapter 3, which is the first of four core chapters in the book, I commence a mapping of the effects of global development discourses on Sadguru and AKRSP (I). I pay particular attention to the role of language in discourses on basic needs, participation, sustainable development, gender and development, economic liberalization, and civil society. I begin the chapter by outlining key elements of development discourse operating at the founding of each of these NGOs in the early 1970s and 1980s and follow subsequent changes in both development discourse and the behavior of the two NGOs. While this chapter emphasizes global influences on NGO behavior, it also demonstrates that NGOs are not simply passive recipients of these global ideas which are transmitted to them through international consultants or conditions in foreign funding. Instead, it shows that NGOs are frequently and actively involved in challenging, reshaping, and appropriating global discourses – especially on environment and sustainability – to suit their own needs and are sometimes even able to spark wider structural change at international levels.

The following two chapters examine the relationships between NGOs and funders, focusing on forms of resource exchange between organizations. Chapter 4 begins with a resource-dependence perspective, which focuses on the flow of financial resources from funders to the two organizations under study. I then broaden this perspective to include exchanges of other kinds of resources such as information and reputation which I demonstrate to be equally important in a struggle for power between funders and NGOs. An examination of these various kinds of resource exchange uncovers significant *inter*-dependencies between organizations, which lead to both cooperative and antagonistic behaviors. This marks the beginning of a "reproduction" argument, in which I claim that both cooperation and antagonism are responsible for reproducing (i.e. perpetuating) the roles and relationships between NGOs and their funders.

This argument is furthered in chapter 5 through a critical look at NGO reporting and monitoring systems. While NGOs may be dependent on international organizations for funds, funders also rely on the NGOs for information which demonstrates that their funds have led to "successful" projects. I show not only how NGOs use information to buffer their key activities from funder intervention, but in doing so, how they also end up reproducing tensions between NGOs and funders. The resulting emphasis on short-term and easily measurable activities occurs at the expense of longer-term and less certain processes of social and political change. This interdependence between NGOs and funders (which is highly structured through reporting and monitoring systems) points to the more fundamental and value-based issue of how "success" is measured. This is a pivotal concern that has profound consequences for NGO-funder relations and for lasting social change.

After examining organizational relations in terms of resource flows, I return, in chapter 6, to processes of change by looking at organizational learning in Sadguru and AKRSP (I). I show how the structured nature of NGO-funder exchange is evident in processes of organizational learning. The learning model, which I have adapted from various organization theorists, distinguishes between learning that is concerned primarily with improving organizational performance (i.e. single-loop learning) and learning which leads to changes in the basic relations of power and worldviews underlying organizational behavior (i.e. double-loop learning). Single-loop learning is very common in the case NGOs, but double-loop learning is rare. While this may not be surprising, since double-loop learning is rare in most organizations, it is of particular concern in development organizations interested in longer-term social and political change. Relationships with funders play an important role in enabling as well as impeding learning of both types. The final section of this chapter shows how funders have enhanced learning by introducing NGOs to new ideas and technologies, and yet have impeded learning through specific reporting and accountability systems.

Finally, in the concluding chapter, I revisit some of the larger questions raised in the book concerning the global context in which NGOs increasingly find themselves, the structured nature of their interactions with funders, and the limitations of change through organizational learning. I emphasize a recurring theme in the book – that monitoring and learning systems are a core part of NGO-funder relations and are pivotal to both constraining and enabling organizational change. I close with suggestions for meeting a key challenge that lies ahead: rethinking relationships and strategies of learning and reporting, so as better to achieve social and political change.

1   The making of NGOs: the relevance of Foucault and Bourdieu

In 1994, the European Commission (EC) granted over US $14 million to fund rural development and environment activities in western India. The grant, entitled "Community Management of Natural Resources," was to jointly support two of the country's largest and most reputed non-governmental organizations (NGOs) – the Aga Khan Rural Support Programme, India (AKRSP (I)) and the Navinchandra Mafatlal Sadguru Water and Development Foundation (Sadguru). The EC funds, to be disbursed over the course of eight years, signaled a precedent for development aid: it was the European Community's largest and first bilateral allocation of funds directly to the non-governmental sector in India.[1]

The proposal which was the basis for the EC grant, began by outlining the social and physical conditions of rural western India:

Social development is failing in large areas of rural India because of environmental degradation. Population pressure, poverty and competition are undermining the natural resource base on which rural communities depend. Most rural families still rely on rainfed cultivation of unimproved crops, livestock grazing on degraded commons, and foraging for fuelwood in un-managed forests. As a direct consequence, large numbers of people continue to live below the official poverty line. Much of rural Gujarat and the neighbouring states of Rajasthan, Madhya Pradesh and Maharastra fit this pattern. (Aga Khan Foundation 1993: 1)

This early passage in the proposal points to a central assumption of the EC's "Community Management of Natural Resources" (CMNR) project. In examining "social development" in rural India, the proposal writers assumed that problems in development were a result of natural and local constraints: a limited physical environment that was being depleted by human activity. The proposal's stark visual imagery painted a bleak picture of rural India as an overpopulated wasteland. It was a landscape inhabited by families that have been left behind by material progress for they "*still* rely on...*unimproved* crops,...*degraded* commons, and...*un-managed* forests" (emphasis added). These statements attributed a "backwardness" to these communities; indeed, under official government classification, many of the communities inhabiting regions of extreme poverty are categorized as "backward classes." The problems associated with development were described as being "natural," and were called "environmental degradation."

A few paragraphs into the proposal, a solution to the problem of environmental degradation was provided:

Fortunately, much of the degradation is reversible. Soil, water, forests, and pastures recover if they are protected, even in arid areas and even after years of abuse: rural resources, like rural people, are resilient. The key to resource recovery is active management. But conventional approaches to managing natural resources in India have not succeeded, and new management systems have to be developed to produce results quickly, equitably and sustainably. (Aga Khan Foundation 1993: 1)

The proposed solution was one of better "management" of existing resources, more precisely, of "Community Management of Natural Resources." The authors of the grant proposal assumed that if environmental degradation could be reversed and natural resources harnessed, then the problems of poverty would be eliminated. In the proposal there was little reference to local history – a critical examination of past events that might provide clues as to why or how the current state of degradation has come to be (and thus how it might be reversed). Rural change was to be brought about through the introduction of new forms of expertise and assistance at the local level. The forms of management necessary for a rural transformation were, according to the proposal, embodied in the experience and expertise of the two NGOs (AKRSP (I) and Sadguru). The overall workplan for the project offered the following scenario for the years 1994–2001:

The project will enable [AKRSP (I) and Sadguru] . . . to expand and consolidate their experience in the 182 villages in which they already operate, and to extend their approaches to an additional 278 new villages. In a total of 460 poor villages with an estimated population of 350,000 people, a critical mass of transformed communities will be created. These communities will be able to conserve water and soils, re-stock forests, raise farm productivity, increase income earning opportunities, and save and invest in their own futures. (Aga Khan Foundation 1994a: 1)

The transformation of these villages was to occur through the introduction of technological expertise and managerial techniques by the two NGOs. Locally adapted technology combined with innovative and participatory management were seen as a key to solving the linked problems of environmental degradation and rural poverty. This approach to development, which emphasized *technological* as well as *managerial* expertise, and its application to land and water resources, is what I henceforth refer to in this book as "natural resource management" (NRM). NRM activities consist of discrete village-level projects, such as irrigation systems or erosion control structures, which combine specific technologies or scientific techniques with community involvement in implementation and management.

However, in examining the CMNR project, a number of questions come to mind regarding the conceptualization of the problem and its proposed solution. Why are issues of development and poverty described here mainly as problems of *natural* resources? Why is the introduction of technical and managerial expertise the logical solution? What other ways of analyzing poverty are masked by the emphasis on natural and physical constraints?

In the chapters which follow, I outline the emergence and evolution of this very specific approach to development called natural resource management. I demonstrate that this NRM approach has been shaped not only through the experiences of AKRSP (I) and Sadguru, but also through their interactions with a network of other organizations – especially international funding organizations. A key actor in this regard has been a Geneva-based organization known as the Aga Khan Foundation, which has played an intermediary role between the two Indian NGOs and the European Commission. AKF, as we shall see, has been instrumental to the articulation of an NRM approach, and shares considerable responsibility with AKRSP (I) and Sadguru in formulating their present activities in Gujarat. The proposal quoted above was written by AKF staff in close consultation with the two NGOs.

This book tells a story about the "making" of these two NGOs as a basis for theorizing about broader processes of organizational change. It is a story about events, ideas, and ways of thinking that shape NGO activities and their approaches to development and natural resource management. Some of these influences are of a global nature, coming from international funding organizations such as the EC and AKF and are informed by widely accepted ideas about what "development" is and how it should be carried out. As a key event, the 1994 EC grant provides a good point of departure for studying the influences of organizational relationships on behavioral change in NGOs. The years following the commencement of the grant, as well as those spent in preparing for it, have been accompanied by various changes in the activities, learning processes and outlooks of both AKRSP (I) and Sadguru. But local factors are just as crucial to shaping NGO behavior as global ones. NGOs respond, sometimes in unexpected ways, to the ideas and demands of funders. And, perhaps more importantly, they engage in complex learning processes that eventually lead to modifications in their activities and ideas about development. Sometimes these changes and learning even shape the ideas and behavior of funders.

Over the past decade, the development approach employed by AKRSP (I) and Sadguru – that of NRM – has become increasingly powerful and dominating to the extent of masking other approaches to addressing poverty in rural Gujarat. Other approaches to development may involve, for example, an emphasis on altering *policies* of natural resource use and agriculture (e.g. policies which encourage excessive extraction of groundwater and abuse of forest resources, or agricultural prices and subsidies which encourage the intensive production of high risk crops), or increasing the *access* of rural communities to state-level decision makers and services. While the NRM approach may at times affect resource policies and citizen access to political processes, its primary emphasis is on the production of discrete projects at a local level.

If the increasing dominance of NRM is seen as problematic (due to its over-shadowing of other interpretations of development problems and solutions), then the problem lies at a systemic level, and not simply at the level of single organizations or individuals. The NRM approach is a dynamic product of multiple actors, interactions, and events. Moreover, AKRSP (I), Sadguru, AKF and the members of their organizational networks are not always in agreement on their understandings of NRM or of development problems and strategies. Although there is significant collaboration between network members, their relations are also rife with tensions, inconsistencies, and struggles for decision-making influence.

This book can be broadly divided into three types of enquiry. The first is an historical enquiry into the work of AKRSP (I) and Sadguru, focusing partic-ularly on the concepts of "development" and "natural resource management," and the technologies and forms of expert knowledge essential to the natural resource management approach to development. The second is an enquiry into resource flows, collaborations, tensions, and relations of power among organi-zations. The final enquiry, which is about learning processes in organizations, examines adaptation of organizations to changes in their institutional surround-ings, as well as forms of learning by NGOs from grassroots experience which then facilitate wider institutional change. While there is significant overlap among these three types of enquiry, the first two (i.e. the historical analysis and the examination of relationships among organizations) draw inspiration from the work and ideas of two French social theorists, Michel Foucault and Pierre Bourdieu. The third form of enquiry builds on ideas about organizational learning developed by the American organization theorists James March and Chris Argyris. Below, I summarize a few key ideas from the work of Foucault and Bourdieu and attempt to integrate these ideas into a conceptual framework for the book. Linkages between this literature and organizational learning are discussed at greater length in chapter 6.

Discourse on development

A key idea employed in my analysis of natural resource management in Gujarat is that of "discourse." In a general sense, discourse refers to language and communication. Dictionary definitions include "conversation; talk; a connected series of utterances; a text" (*Concise Oxford*, 1995). An analysis of discourse, then, often involves a study of spoken as well as written language. In this book, however, *development discourse* refers not only to how development is described and talked about, but also how it is thought about (i.e. its underlying assumptions) and practiced. These assumptions are reflected in text, conversation and in actual development projects and standard operating procedures. They are also reflected in development policies at national and international levels. As such, one can differentiate development discourse in terms of development thought, development practice, and development policy. An analysis of development discourse involves investigating the formation of that discourse (and its differentiated parts) in order to identify the assumptions and rules peculiar to it, how it operates, as well as how it changes over time (Foucault 1984c; Rabinow 1984: 12).

Foucault looked at writings in specific areas of scientific knowledge. For example, he examined discourses on "madness" as produced by "experts" such as state administrators, psychiatrists, and doctors, and he showed how these ways of conceptualizing madness have undergone radical, and sometimes abrupt, transformations over time (Foucault 1984a). He also examined how knowledge of a particular field of expertise can serve as a tool for domination. For example, the discourse on madness (and hence on "normality") created by experts silences the "mad"; they are, by definition, deprived of any knowledge of their own condition except through the assistance of experts, and thus the "mad" are rendered powerless. The knowledge embodied in a discourse is seen by Foucault not as some representation of a universal truth but rather as an exercise of power, which he denotes as "power/knowledge" (Foucault 1980: 93; Foucault 1984b: 170–78). For example, in referring to the introduction of doctors in asylums established by Samuel Tuke and Phillipe Pinel in the seventeenth century, Foucault asserts:

It is thought that Tuke and Pinel opened the asylum to medical knowledge. They did not introduce science, but a personality, whose powers borrowed from science only their disguise, or at most their justification. These powers, by their nature, were of a moral and social order... (Foucault 1984a: 160)

The functioning of a discourse has important consequences for power relationships within a society. A study of discourse thus also involves an examination of power exercised through the discourse. In other words, discourse analysis involves an investigation of the experts that produce and maintain the assumptions and core "truths" of the discourse. The use of knowledge to exercise power is accomplished through what Foucault calls "disciplinary technologies" or "technologies and techniques of power" (Foucault 1980: 93). These technologies may be physical, such as an architecture of prisons that enables constant surveillance, as well as social, such as use of "normalizing judgments" in which one's behavior is molded through comparison and ranking with others who are considered normal or superior, as occurs in schools and asylums (Foucault 1984b: 193–97; Shumway 1989: 128–30). Foucault's approach to history thus involves an analysis of the events and accidents that lead to the formation of a discourse, and of the functioning of power and knowledge within it (Foucault 1984b; Rabinow 1984: 9; Shumway 1989: 112).[2]

Examining the various underpinnings of a discourse can be elusive since the underlying assumptions of a discourse are frequently taken-for-granted or appear as common sense. James Ferguson, an anthropologist, eloquently expresses this dilemma in the opening paragraph to his study of the development industry in Lesotho:

What is "development"? It is perhaps worth remembering just how recent a question this is. This question, which today is apt to strike us as so natural, so self-evidently necessary, would have made no sense even a century ago. It is a peculiarity of our historical era that the idea of "development" is central to so much of our thinking about so much of the world. It seems to us today almost non-sensical to deny that there is such a thing as "development," or to dismiss it as a meaningless concept, just as it must have been virtually impossible to reject the concept of "civilization" in the nineteenth-century, or the concept of "God" in the twelfth. Such central organizing concepts are not readily discarded or rejected, for they form the very framework within which argumentation takes place. (Ferguson 1990: xiii)

Development as we think of it today – the struggle of Third and Second World countries to "catch up," in economic terms, to the First World – is a post World War II variant of a nineteenth-century theory of linear progress, often referred to as "modernization" theory (Gardner and Lewis 1996: 12; Watts 1993: 259). The nomenclature used to describe countries, regions, and even populations in terms of their degree of modernization is itself molded by the evolutionary and normative principles of development: "developed" and "less developed" or "developing". As in the case of the discourse on madness, a relationship between knowledge and power is implicit in development discourse. Nederveen Pieterse (1991: 6) argues this point:

The central thesis of developmentalism is that social change occurs according to a pre-established pattern, the logic and direction of which are known. Privileged knowledge of the direction of change is claimed by those who declare themselves furthest advanced along its course. Developmentalism is the truth from the point of view of the centre of power; it is the theorization (or rather, idealization) of its own path of development...

Beginning in the late 1960s, but especially in the 1970s and 1980s, however, modernization perspectives were heavily criticized by neo-Marxist theorists who argued that underdevelopment was a result of unequal relationships between the powerful nations of the "North" and the exploited (and often colonized) nations of the "South." (e.g. Frank 1967 and Wallerstein 1974). From this perspective, the key to development was not a simple modernization of industry and infrastructure but radical change in the political and economic structures of the state. Despite these critiques, however, modernization perspectives remain strong in development thought and practice today. Contemporary development discourse continues to assign a central position to economic development (and the measurement of it) and is formally institutionalized in international bodies such as the World Bank, the International Monetary Fund (IMF), some organizations within the United Nations (UN), various bilateral agencies, and in departments or ministries within each nation-state. These organizations are the repositories of development "expertise," and they operate as centers of knowledge (and thus power) that define and influence what "development" is and isn't.[3]

The dominance of a discourse, however, does not mean that alternatives to that discourse do not exist. For example, economic reforms, structural adjustment programs, and various development projects promoted by the World Bank in the South are being challenged and rejected by an increasingly coherent "anti-development" discourse (Manzo 1991; Nederveen Pieterse 1991; Watts 1993). These resistances not only include alternative forms of economic development and challenges from within the economic paradigm (e.g. limits to growth, or the neo-Marxist critique above) but in some cases, a rejection of the very premises of economic development. As such, a development discourse is not monolithic, but is comprised of multiple and competing discourses in a continuous state of flux.[4] In our present age, non-governmental organizations and citizen's movements have become important agents in presenting alternative perspectives on development.

In summarizing, I present two complementary definitions of discourse that can be used in an analysis of development. One of these definitions is from a study of the relationship between computers and Cold War discourse:

A discourse, then, is a way of knowledge, a background of assumptions and agreements about how reality is to be interpreted and expressed, supported by paradigmatic metaphors, techniques, and technologies and potentially embodied in social institutions. (Edwards 1996: 34)

The second definition is from an analysis of the role of anthropologists in development practice:

[D]iscourse theory refers to the idea that the terms in which we speak, write and think about the world are a reflection of wider relations of power and, since they are also linked to practice, are themselves important in maintaining that power structure. (Gardner and Lewis 1996: xiv)

As such, a discourse is a specific and historically produced way of looking at the world and is embedded within wider relations of power – power that is manifest, for example, in the scientific "expertise" of development economists, professionals, and expatriates that serve as advisers, funders, and consultants to Southern governments and NGOs. One can imagine numerous interconnected discourses in which these development experts and organizations might be located: natural resource management discourse, sustainable development discourse, human rights discourse, and so on. In studying the effects of development discourse on organizational behavior, one might ask: What are the core assumptions of development? Who are the experts that produce knowledge about development, and how is this knowledge (and the power it confers) exercised in relations between NGOs and their funders? What are some of the ways in which NGOs or funders have altered or challenged development discourses?

These questions about the operation of dominant discourses, their effects on human action, and the possibilities for challenging or resisting them, point to a central set of problems in social theory: problems concerning structure and agency.

Structure, agency, and reproduction

A key debate within western schools of social science concerns "structure" vs. "agency", or in other terms, the debate between "objectivism" and "subjectivism". Structuralist thought has focused on language, and the rules that languages follow. Language is seen as a very ordered, rule-bound system which creates the conditions through which we express ourselves and communicate; we follow these rules even though we may not be conscious of them. The structuralist anthropologist Claude Lévi-Strauss attempted to show that our actions and even our thoughts are constrained by the limits and rules of language. Because these rules are seen as being external to individuals, they are described as being "objective" (rather than "subjective"). Lévi-Strauss (1976) argued that, like language, all human relations are governed by a system of overarching rules – a "structure."

This structuralist perspective was opposed by those from subjectivist schools of thought, who held that human experience is the key element of social life, and that we, as individuals, have very different experiences and a range of choices through which we can change our lives and society. This emphasis on human ability to affect change, is the force behind the term "agency" – the capacity to act as agents of change. For the subjectivists, agency rather than structure is the central issue in understanding behavior. A key proponent of this view was Jean-Paul Sartre whose writings emphasized that, although we as individuals or groups may be oppressed in certain ways, we still have some choices for which we are fully responsible (Matthews 1996). The oppositions between these two perspectives, with one favoring the influence of certain objective rules as determining human behavior and the other placing importance on individual action and freedom, is known as the structure-agent debate.

How does this structure-agent debate figure into an analysis of NGO-funder relations? A considerable literature on North–South relations has noted how the demands of funders constrain NGO action (e.g. Clayton 1994; Drabek 1987; Hudock 1999; Society for Participatory Research in Asia 1991). These demands can be conceptualized as being located within an institutional context, that is, as being part of a structure within which NGOs are embedded. But, while NGOs are constrained by funders in certain ways, they also resist and occasionally challenge the demands and viewpoints of funders, sometimes overtly, and at other times in subtle ways. To see how this happens, it is necessary to link the effects of structure on NGO behavior with the forms of agency exercised by NGOs. Using a combination of the ideas of Foucault and Bourdieu is helpful in examining this link.

The work of Foucault, while defying neat categorization, was strongly influenced by structuralist perspectives. As discussed above, he looked at ways in which human thought and behavior are constrained by discourses. But as a historian, Foucault also examined changes in discourse over time, and in this sense he departed from the structuralist convention of freezing time in order to isolate the rules (i.e. the structural features) operating at a particular point in time. In adopting a historical perspective, Foucault was able to identify moments in the formation and change of a discourse. These formative instances constitute the "events" of his histories. Although these events were sometimes moments of political crisis in society, often the rise of a discourse or the emergence of a new form of knowledge was based on a long history of accidental events (Foucault 1984c: 81). So while Foucault may be considered a structuralist because of the importance he ascribed to discourses in constraining behavior and thought, he was also a subjectivist in that he demonstrated how the workings of knowledge and power (and thus the formation of a discourse) are sometimes a result of a series of chance events, rather than only a product of some grand structure. Foucault believed that, despite the controlling effects of discourses, there are alternative ways of perceiving the world. Changes in the rules of society were thus possible (though limitedly so) through resistance to accepted norms and through the promotion of alternative viewpoints. Foucault was able to link this notion of resistance to political action, for example, by using his influence to attract television reporters to a prison, and then allowing the prisoners to speak for themselves – to express their perspectives on conditions and functions of imprisonment, and thus challenge common understandings of the role and effects of prisons in France (Fillingham 1993: 109; Foucault 1984b: 178). For a study of organizational change, Foucault's work implies the adoption of a broad view of organizational history, where "events" are not only changes in organizational activities or in leadership, but also changes in the ways in which organizational members perceive, talk about, and justify their work; that is, events are also changes in discourse.

While Foucault looked at change over time, and at the mechanisms through which power is exercised, he did not theorize extensively about how human action, at the level of everyday practice, recreates or gradually transforms a discourse. The work of Pierre Bourdieu addresses this problem directly. Bourdieu sought to transcend the agent-structure debate by developing a theory with an explicit focus on the relationship between structure and agency. He set up a dialectical relationship between structure and agency – a relation in which a cyclical pattern of influence exists, with structure guiding human behavior, and human behavior constantly modifying structure, albeit largely at the margins. According to Bourdieu, the relationship between structure and agency is dynamic and recursive, with neither structure nor agent independent of the other (Bourdieu 1977: 3). Bourdieu calls this result a "double structuration" (Bourdieu 1987: 158 as cited in Harker, Mahar, and Wilkes 1990: 202).

A key feature of Bourdieu's research is his emphasis on empirical work (ethnography in particular) as the basis for theorizing about the structure–agent relationship. Because of his emphasis on empiricism, he contends that his theoretical position is as much a method as a theory: a method for the analysis of a dynamic and context-based process that he calls "practice." For Bourdieu, the properties of social structure are embedded in everyday events, and thus structure and action can only be investigated by observing actors engaged in everyday events. He calls his method a "theory of practice" (Bourdieu 1977; Mahar, Harker, and Wilkes 1990: 8).[5] In addition, it is through everyday action and thought (practice) that the structures which guide human behavior are, in Bourdieu's words, "re-produced." Bourdieu's work on the idea of "reproduction" dates back to the 1960s when he analyzed the field of education. He outlined the practices through which the French schooling system reproduces class distinctions amongst its students, and how this is concealed under the veil of a seemingly class-neutral system (Harker 1990). He was able further to refine this notion of reproduction in the 1970s through the development of his theory of practice which devotes attention not only to the *re-production* (or perpetuation) of existing structures, but also to the *production* (or creation) of new ones.

To aid in his analysis of structure, action, and reproduction Bourdieu introduces a number of conceptual tools, of which I introduce only two here: *habitus* and *capital*. Habitus, which is the most central of Bourdieu's conceptual tools, is defined as "a system of durable, transposable dispositions which functions as the generative basis of structured, objectively unified practices" (Bourdieu 1979: vii). This definition needs some unpacking. At its most basic level, habitus refers to the orientation of individuals – each one of us possesses an habitus, an orientation or disposition, that guides our behavior, and which is a product of structure and specific historical circumstances. Social interactions are informed by habitus. For example, the relationship between a professor and student is governed by certain norms of behavior. The student is predisposed to treat the professor with deference, while the professor is expected to provide guidance to the student. The interaction between a professor and student is thus structured, and is often consistent (durable) over time. It is also transposable in the sense that both individuals carry their dispositions into other contexts; the student carries his identity as a student into interactions with other students, professionals, and family, much as the professor does with hers. But the relationship is also subject to improvisation, to change, and thus to modifications in structures over time. This notion of habitus is also extendable to social class, in the form of a class habitus, which informs the behavior of entire social groups.

Bourdieu's analysis of social groups is aided by another conceptual tool – capital – which refers to the "capacity to exercise control over one's own future and that of others. As such, it is a form of power" (Postone, LiPuma, and Calhoun 1993: 4). Capital can take a variety of forms and can include material things or money (economic capital), non-material attributes such as prestige, status and authority (symbolic capital), and culturally valued tastes and preferences including art, education, and language (cultural capital) (Bourdieu 1977: 178–79; Mahar, Harker, and Wilkes 1990: 13). In social relationships, capital is exchanged between individuals, groups, or social classes. These different kinds of capital are convertible, with each providing opportunities for domination. The relation of capital to power is most obvious in the case of economic capital which determines relations of economic dependency (and is thus closest to a Marxist perspective on domination). But for Bourdieu the most powerful form of capital is the symbolic form – authority which comes with prestige and status (Bourdieu 1977: 179). This is where the "expert" enters, as an individual or group that is socially sanctioned (e.g. doctors, lawmakers, teachers, development consultants), to determine what is right and what is wrong – to create "the official version of the social world" (Mahar, Harker, and Wilkes 1990: 13). The relevance of this insight to a study of development is eloquently expressed by Michael Edwards, who is both a development practitioner and researcher. I quote him here at length (Edwards 1989: 118):

The natural consequence of a concern for technical interpretations of reality is that knowledge, and the power to control it, become concentrated in the hands of those with the technical skills necessary to understand the language and methods being used. The idea that development consists of a transfer of skills or information creates a role for the expert as the only person capable of mediating the transfer of these skills from one person or society to another. Herein lies the justification, if justification it is, for the 80,000 expatriate 'experts' at work south of the Sahara today. They are there to promote 'development', defined implicitly as a transfer of knowledge from 'developed' to 'underdeveloped' societies. Yet this 'expert' status is usually quite spurious. As Adrian Adams has pointed out, 'In Britain a doctor is a doctor; he'll be a medical expert if he goes to help halve the birthrate in Bangladesh . . . what matters is the halo of impartial prestige his skills lend him, allowing him to . . . disguise political issues, for a time, as technical ones.'[6]

This passage from Edwards provides a link between Bourdieu's notion of symbolic capital ("the halo of impartial prestige") and Foucault's ideas about the centrality of the "expert" (and expert knowledge) to the workings of power.

It is helpful to conceptualize relations between NGOs and their funders in terms of habitus and capital. Each funder or NGO can be conceived as having its own habitus – an orientation based on, but not determined by, the organization's historical circumstances, its present institutional environment, and the dispositions of its members. Using habitus to characterize a funder or an NGO provides three hypotheses about organizational behavior:

- The history of an organization (its past patterns of behavior) plays a crucial role in guiding present behavior;
- The present institutional environment (conceptualized as discourses) is also important in structuring behavior; and,
- Improvisation, creativity, and change are possible as a result of the unique combinations of past and present circumstances, and the dispositions of various individuals within the organization.

Bourdieu's notion of capital is also helpful for it widens attention from only economic forms of struggle to those that include exchanges of other types of resources that are based on information and knowledge. The flow of financial resources from funders to NGOs is a pivotal part of their relationships, but reputation, prestige, and flows of information are equally crucial elements of their exchanges. The generation and use of information is particularly important, given the centrality of reporting and monitoring systems to NGO-funder relations. A good deal of NGO literature has examined struggles over funding (e.g. Clayton 1994; Drabek 1987; Fowler 1997; Hudock 1999; Perera 1997), but research on the role of other resources such as information, reputation, and prestige, has been spare. Struggles between organizations occur over these different forms of economic, cultural, and symbolic capital, with organizational members engaging in strategies to secure more capital and thus more influence over the actions of others. These strategic behaviors are not always deliberate or conscious. As Bourdieu explains (in the context of habitus), some behaviors "function below the level of consciousness and language, beyond the reach of introspective scrutiny or control by the will" (Bourdieu 1984: 466 as cited in Mahar, Harker, and Wilkes 1990: 11).

Using the above lens, it is possible to view relations between NGOs and funders as following a pattern or a set of general rules. In other words, the relationships are structured. These structures are established through practice – routines of communication, routines of capital exchange, and even routines of resistance and antagonism. Through these practices, the structures which guide these relationships are, in Bourdieu's words, "re-produced." For this theoretical perspective to find empirical support, however, it would be necessary to uncover some of the mechanisms through which relations of NGOs with key funders are reproduced, and how some of the tensions in these relations continue to be reproduced.

In short, the work of Bourdieu is relevant to a study of development organizations for it enables a conceptualization of development as occurring in a context where:

- organizational behavior and relations are highly structured, although they are also open to incremental improvisation and change (i.e. reproduction and production); and,
- there are struggles between organizations over various kinds of resources (capital), of which symbolic capital is an important form of power because of its association with expertise and thus with knowledge production.

The ideas introduced above are relevant to studies of organizational behavior and change. Drawing from Foucault, one can view the histories of development NGOs, and the evolution of their activities, within the context of a discourse on development. In linking this perspective to the work of Bourdieu, it becomes possible to see the actions of NGOs as being structured by development discourse, but also as being capable of innovation, of transformation over time. These actions are enmeshed in struggles for power, where what an organization does is subject to various influences from its organizational and social environment.

Summary

The work of Foucault and Bourdieu, as discussed above, provides several potentially useful insights to the study of organizational behavior, and particularly on NGO-funder relations in an international context. First, organizational activities and interactions can be viewed as taking place within the broad confines of a discourse or set of discourses (e.g. on sustainable development, economic development, etc.). Understanding how this set of discourses has altered over time can shed light on organizational change. As such, an historical analysis of organizational change and its embeddedness in wider social norms and discourses becomes essential to making sense of current practices, relations, and tensions. This task is undertaken in chapter 3 of this book, which details global discourses on development and resource management from the early 1970s onwards, and documents their effects on AKRSP (I) and Sadguru.

Second, Foucault points us to the pivotal role played by "experts" in producing discourses. In international development, these experts might include development consultants, economists, and scientists at organizations such as the World Bank and bilateral aid agencies, students of development studies, and NGO staff. For purposes of research, this insight directs us to the examination of documents generated by these experts and a critical analysis of the problems and solutions to development identified by them. It also points to the importance of questioning the conventional expert wisdom, by considering alternative and subjugated viewpoints in an effort to step outside of dominating perspectives. This insight links Foucault's work to that of Bourdieu by pointing to the dialectical relationship between structure and agency. Bourdieu provides us with conceptual and methodological tools for examining human agency and how it changes and challenges the structuring effects of discourses. His insights are especially important for examining NGO-funder relations which are commonly described as being funder-controlled. While it might be true that funders often "call the tune," it is equally useful and interesting to examine the complex strategies used by NGOs to resist funder influence or to buffer themselves from unwanted interference. In particular, Bourdieu's notion of "capital" forces us to look beyond organizational interactions based on funds, and to include other resources such as information, reputation, status, and prestige in our calculus of organizational exchange and interdependence. Chapters 4 and 5 examine NGO-funder relations through this lens, with special attention to the role and functioning of symbolic capital.

In addition, the concept of habitus or "structured improvisation" suggests that social and organizational change is likely to be slow and incremental. As such, it becomes possible to think about organizational learning as normally being a process that is highly circumscribed by organizational histories, discourses, and relations of power. The broader challenge lies in identifying these structuring factors, and then developing informed strategies for learning and change. Chapter 6 adopts this perspective in detailing processes of learning in NGOs and the influence of funders.

Finally, Bourdieu shows us the importance of ethnographic analysis in interpreting social behavior, demonstrating that it is through a detailed examination of "practice" (e.g. social and organizational routines) that one can gain insight into the structured and yet improvised nature of human and organizational behavior. Demonstrating the relevance of such analysis to the study of organizational change is a broader aim of this book.

In short, both Foucault and Bourdieu provide a series of conceptual tools that can be applied to the study of organizations and the discourses in which they are embedded. Their insights, coupled with my analysis of the cases in this book, demonstrate both the boundaries of and avenues for human and organizational action. Perhaps by identifying the limiting effects of discourses and structure, and the relations of power embedded therein, it may become possible to rethink, challenge, and rework those very constraints.

2   The NGOs and their global networks

This chapter provides essential background information to the key organizations discussed in this book: AKRSP (I), Sadguru, the European Commission, the Aga Khan Foundation, the Ford Foundation, and the Norwegian Agency for Development Cooperation. It first provides an introduction to the genesis of Sadguru and AKRSP (I) and a summary of their primary activities. This material is followed by details on key international funders. The descriptions below are kept brief, with additional information being provided as necessary in subsequent chapters.

The Southern NGOs

Sadguru

A primary objective of the Navinchandra Mafatlal Sadguru Water and Development Foundation is "to improve the living conditions of rural and tribal people, chiefly by developing environmentally sound land and water resources programmes" (Sadguru 2001: n.p.). The organization prioritizes efforts to increase long-term economic productivity of land and water resources and also to reduce rural–urban migration. Since its founding in 1974, the NGO has worked primarily with the "tribal" populations of Dahod District in north-eastern Gujarat state (see figure 2.1), and it has also expanded its activities over the past decade into the neighboring states of Madhya Pradesh and Rajastan.

The work of Sadguru developed out of the activities of an organization known as Shri Sadguru Seva Sangh Trust (SSST) in the early 1970s. SSST was initially involved in natural disaster relief and was financed by a major Indian industrialist, who had been inspired by a "free kitchen" set up by a humanitarian figure during droughts in eastern India in 1967.[1] Among many other activities, an eye-care camp was set up in the Dahod region of eastern Gujarat by SSST in 1974, with considerable support from volunteers. Two of these volunteers, a husband and wife team, formed a special rural development wing called "Sadguru" which eventually became an independent organization under their dual directorship.[2]

Figure 2.1 Districts in Gujarat, India with AKRSP (I) and Sadguru programs

In 1976, Sadguru began irrigation projects in the region, which have since become its primary activity. These irrigation activities are frequently combined with a range of complementary programs in watershed development, forestry, agriculture, rural energy systems, and income generation (as detailed in a subsequent section below). In its nearly three decades of operation, Sadguru reports to have set up over 476 village organizations with a membership base exceeding 38,000 individuals and serving almost half a million people (Sadguru 2001: 58). In addition, over the past decade, the organization has become increasingly involved in providing professional training in natural resource management to local communities, to NGOs across the country, and to state and federal government officials. As of the year 2001, all of these activities were supported by approximately eighty staff members.

While Sadguru has long attracted government funding, much of its growth was fueled by a snowballing of international funds since 1987, beginning with support from the Ford Foundation and followed by the Aga Khan Foundation, the Norwegian Agency for Development Cooperation, the European Commission, and the International Labour Organisation (ILO). Sadguru's major funders in 2000 included various government agencies and programs (45 percent), the EC (29 percent), and NORAD (14 percent), with total expenditures amounting to Rs. 91 million (US$ 2.3 million). In recent years, the NGO has also begun to establish an endowment, with support from its founding industrial sponsor and two other corporate trusts based in Bombay.

AKRSP (I)

The Aga Khan Rural Support Programme, India was set up in 1983 as a rural development organization in the state of Gujarat in western India. Its current mission statement places emphasis on the "empowerment of rural communities and groups, particularly the underprivileged and women, to take control over their lives and manage their environment, to create a better and more equitable society." In practical terms, the NGO follows a "watershed approach" in which it provides a range of programs to regions within specific hydro-geological and ecological (rather than political) boundaries. These programs, as detailed below, include agricultural extension, water resource management, soil and water conservation, savings and credit, alternative energy, and forestry. Central to the watershed approach is the formation and training of local-level village organizations for managing natural resources. As such, the watershed approach enables AKRSP (I) to integrate both the natural and human resource components of its development activities.

At its founding, AKRSP (I) was endowed with a substantial corpus fund (or endowment) of Rs. 25.9 million (US $ 650,000) through the Geneva-based Aga Khan Foundation.[3] AKF has continued to play a key role in providing the NGO with logistical, programmatic, and financial assistance, and it also retains a permanent seat on AKRSP (I)'s board. The corpus fund provided an unusual advantage to AKRSP (I) in establishing itself, since most non-profit organizations rely solely on yearly grants and donations. In addition, AKRSP (I) was set up as a non-profit company with a Board of Directors comprised of prominent figures from Indian industry, government, and NGOs, thereby giving it immediate visibility.[4] This board was able to recruit, as its first Chief Executive Officer, an influential government official who had recently retired from the top rural development post in the state.

Under the guidance of the new CEO, three rural field offices or "spearhead teams" were set up in 1985, with a central office in the major urban center of Ahmedabad. Each of the three field regions was noted to face distinct natural resource challenges, ranging from salinity ingression and groundwater depletion in Junagadh District, to drought in Surendranagar and undulating terrain and soil erosion in Bharuch (see figure 2.1). Starting with a handful of staff, the organization grew to 150 staff in its four offices by the end of the year 2000, and reported having established 507 village organizations with nearly 28,000 members (AKRSP (I) 2001: 4). Moreover, AKRSP (I) has sought to work in collaboration, rather than in confrontation, with government in order to access natural resources and eventually to influence policymaking. In particular, it has been a pioneer in establishing protocols for "Joint Forest Management" and "Participatory Irrigation Management" in India, thus enabling government-controlled natural resources to be jointly managed by communities and public agencies.

AKRSP (I) has, since its inception, been a recipient of international funds from donors such as the Canadian International Development Agency, the British Department for International Development, the European Commission and the Ford Foundation. AKRSP (I)'s primary funds in 2000 were an EC grant (70 percent), which is administered through AKF, and various state and federal government funds (19 percent), with total expenditures amounting to Rs. 53.1 million (US\$ 1.33 million) (AKRSP (I) 2001: 91).

Activities of AKRSP (I) and Sadguru

Both organizations implement a range of similar activities that are broadly circumscribed by the term "natural resource management" and which are described in table 2.1. Although most of these activities are offered by both Sadguru and AKRSP (I), a number of features distinguish their implementation. In AKRSP (I), these resource management activities are combined with two "human resource management" programs. The first is a "gender in development" program directed towards increasing the involvement of women in natural resource activities and in local village organizations, developing new activities or approaches which reflect women's priorities, and conducting gender-sensitization workshops for NGO staff, communities, and other organizations. Women-only groups, particularly in the form of savings and credit groups, have also been formed. While Sadguru also works extensively with women, especially in its forestry, biogas, and income generation programs, it does not conduct explicit gender-sensitization activities.

The second human resource program in AKRSP (I) concerns the building of "village institutions" or local organizations. The formation of village-level organizations is in many ways the cornerstone of AKRSP (I)'s approach, and is based upon the creation of community-based organizations for managing local

Table 2.1 *Activities of Sadguru and AKRSP (I)*

Activity	Description
Water resource development	Two primary activities under this program are the construction of checkdams and lift irrigation (LI) systems. Checkdams are small concrete and masonry structures that check the flow of rivers and soil loss during monsoons, resulting in reservoirs that retain water. Lift irrigation involves the "lifting" of water via large pumphouses (often from checkdam reservoirs) to a high point in the topography, from which it is distributed by gravity to farms. Local users groups are established to distribute water, collect user's fees, and maintain and manage the systems. Lift irrigation forms the backbone of Sadguru's work. AKRSP (I) has also engaged in Participatory Irrigation Management (PIM) which involves the transfer of government irrigation canals to farmer groups which manage the systems.
Soil and water conservation (SWC)	A variety of structures and techniques are used to reduce soil erosion and water loss from farmland, particularly on unirrigated land. Stone or earthen "bunds" are built along land contours and boundaries to reduce soil loss during monsoons, and also to slow water drainage from sloping fields. Small stone dams known as "nullah plugs" are built across gullies or ravines to reduce erosion damage. In some cases, land is leveled or terraced. Farmers are encouraged to plow their fields along the contours of the land to reduce moisture loss. In AKRSP (I), SWC has become part of a larger "micro-watershed" approach used to treat of large tracts of private and public land.
Farm forestry and wasteland development	Farm forestry refers to tree-planting programs that occur on private farmland. A few members of a village, usually women, are hired to run nurseries to raise seedlings until they are fit to be sold to local farmers. Upon the requests of local women farmers, Sadguru increasingly has emphasized the farming of fruit-bearing trees. Wasteland development refers to afforestation of "wasteland" or unused government land, either with hardy species or those that have some commercial or household value. AKRSP (I) was among the first organizations in Gujarat to establish a Joint Forest Management (JFM) program in which rural communities work with the state Forest Department to manage and protect publicly controlled land.
Biogas development	Biogas plants are small domed or cylindrical structures that use cow manure or other organic materials to generate methane gas for cooking. AKRSP (I) constructs the "Deenbandhu" model, which is built underground and ranges from 1–3 cubic meters in size. Cow dung, once it has been processed by a biogas plant, serves as a crop fertilizer. Plants are generally built for individual households rather than for communities. Sadguru's program is similar to that of AKRSP (I) except that it is smaller in scale and is managed largely by women.
Agriculture extension, input supply and marketing	Agricultural activities involve the supply and promotion of agricultural inputs such as seeds and fertilizers at low cost, especially in newly irrigated villages. Technical advice is provided through a cadre of extension workers. Farmers are linked with local banks to secure credit

(cont.)

Table 2.1 (*cont.*)

Activity	Description
	for purchasing inputs. In AKRSP (I), agricultural services have changed over the past decade to include the promotion of integrated pest management, use of bio-pesticides, and organic manures. Local extension workers are involved in encouraging farmers to try new practices, to share local knowledge and to aid in distributing inputs.
Women's income generation	Women's groups are formed to produce bead ornaments, bamboo works and garments in their spare time, in order to supplement their income. Products are sold in Gujarat and are also exported to the United Kingdom. This program is implemented solely by Sadguru.
Training and human resources development	Training is provided to communities, government officials, and other NGOs on various aspects of natural resource management. Sadguru has constructed a large "training institute" for training local village groups on the implementation and management of projects such as lift irrigation. Governmental and non-governmental organizations, domestically and internationally (particularly from Africa), have also made use of Sadguru's training services. AKRSP (I) has also established a training wing which provides workshops in gender sensitization, participatory rural appraisal, and natural resource management.

resources. These village institutions are separate from local political bodies (the *panchayats*) and are responsible for particular projects such as a lift irrigation system, or for overall natural resource management in the village. Over the years, the village organizations have evolved into different forms in each of the three districts. For example, users groups such as lift irrigation societies have become common in Junagadh district where it has proved difficult to mobilize entire villages, differentiated by caste and class, into a single group responsible for a variety of activities. More homogeneous communities of Bharuch have formed more comprehensive village organizations as well as users groups, and are now beginning to federate with groups in other villages. Surendranagar district has faced numerous difficulties in group formation due to caste conflicts, and is now looking at group formation on a watershed basis.

By comparison, Sadguru's village-level organizations consist largely of Lift Irrigation Cooperative Societies. These are users groups responsible for managing their irrigation projects. A unit in Sadguru known as the "LI Coop Cell" provides managerial training to executives of each cooperative society, and secures electricity hook-ups and water-lifting permits from the government. In 1997, a lift irrigation federation of forty cooperative societies was formed with the purpose of taking over routine maintenance activities and government communications normally conducted by Sadguru staff. The mainstay of Sadguru's work is lift irrigation, and the NGO is reputed throughout western India to have rapid and efficient execution of projects, excellent construction quality, and well-managed lift irrigation cooperatives.

In short, both NGOs have somewhat different approaches to setting up village organizations. AKRSP (I) emphasizes the *process* of engaging community members in extensive dialogue on their needs, in building rapport, and in building community members' capacities to articulate and plan their own development interventions. The actual technological intervention is seen as being a means to community organization. For Sadguru, however, this emphasis is reversed: the technological intervention is paramount, as it is the technology that is seen as resulting in an increase in rural incomes (e.g. increases in agricultural income through lift irrigation technology), whereas the village organization is necessary for implementing and managing that technology.[5] Despite this general difference in emphasis, however, both AKRSP (I) and Sadguru see village organizations as essential to natural resource management.

AKRSP (I) might be described as both a *product* and *process* oriented organization. On the product side are technical projects such as checkdams and tree nurseries. On the process side are less tangible components such as community mobilization, and the establishment of multiple kinds of village organizations. This "process" dimension of AKRSP (I) has often been linked to its extensive use of Participatory Rural Appraisal (PRA) – a set of interactive methods that employ group discussion, mapping, and walks through villages and fields with community members to learn about the community and its resources. They employ both "general" PRAs that serve as introductory tools to generating dialogue with communities, and "topical" PRAs aimed at learning about specific issues such as local forest resources. While very few rural development organizations systematically use PRA as a tool for collecting information and generating dialogue, AKRSP (I) has been a pioneer in adapting and systematizing this tool.

Sadguru, in contrast, has often been characterized by its funders as well as by other NGOs as a *product* oriented organization, where tangible outputs take precedence over *process* inputs such as community mobilization and the building of democratic organizations. The NGO's establishment of 187 Lift Irrigation Cooperative Societies by the end of 2000, however, suggests that Sadguru has also developed considerable skills in the building of village-level organizations.

Links with Northern organizations

Sadguru and AKRSP (I) maintain links with a global network of organizations. These relationships are crucial not only for purposes of funding, but also are instrumental to the formation of global discourses and knowledge on development and natural resource management. Both NGOs have a number of international connections in common: the European Commission, the Aga Khan

Foundation (especially its headquarters in Geneva and country offices in New Delhi, London, and Ottawa), and the Ford Foundation. In addition, Sadguru is well connected to the Norwegian Agency for Development Cooperation. Each link is described in brief below.[6]

European Commission

The EC has dominated AKRSP (I)'s funding since 1994 providing an average of 72 percent of the NGO's total annual expenditure, and has been a major funder for Sadguru, covering 38 percent of its yearly spending. The EC grant for the "Community Management of Natural Resources" is administered by the Aga Khan Foundation through its office in New Delhi. The EC is headquartered in Brussels, but maintains a delegation in New Delhi.

The European Commission is a large bureaucratic agency accustomed to dealing with governments rather than NGOs, with the CMNR grant being its first allocation of bilateral funds directly to NGOs. Given its bilateral focus, the EC has neither the time nor the human resources to cultivate more than a contractual relationship with the NGOs. Its Delhi office supports a Project Officer responsible for the CMNR grant as well as for a multitude of smaller grants to other NGOs. Despite considerable interest in the work of AKRSP (I) and Sadguru, the Project Officer based in New Delhi rarely has time to visit them or even to review all reports submitted by them. There has also tended to be considerable turnover in the post of Project Officer, with the years 1993–97 seeing three different officers.

As a result of limitations on the EC's attention to NGOs, the actual contract for the CMNR project is between the EC and AKF, with the two Indian NGOs serving as "implementors." Thus, direct communication with the EC is handled by AKF's offices in India, the United Kingdom, and Switzerland, while the two NGOs generally communicate indirectly with the EC through AKF India. Reporting requirements consist of quarterly reports on "physical and financial progress" (e.g. on numbers of checkdams constructed, acres of land treated, expenditure in comparison to budget, etc.) and a "narrative report" every six months. The NGOs turn in their reports to AKF India, where they are consolidated, edited, and eventually forwarded to the EC. Details of funding and reporting are discussed in chapters 4 and 5 of this book.

Aga Khan Foundation

The Aga Khan Foundation has played a central role in supporting both AKRSP (I) and Sadguru. AKF forms one node in a very large network of development organizations founded by the Aga Khan. The Aga Khan is the spiritual leader (or *Imam*) of a diasporic Muslim community known as the Ismailis, and is also a philanthropist and businessman. He heads a large network of development organizations and activities, collectively known as the Aga Khan Development Network (AKDN). The three main activity areas of the AKDN are: *social development*, which includes health, education, rural development, and housing activities; *economic development*, which includes financial services, and industrial and tourism promotion, and; *culture*, which includes architecture programs and awards, as well as community development through historic city restoration and reuse (Aga Khan Development Network undated: 2).

The Aga Khan Foundation is one of several non-denominational organizations within the social development area of the AKDN.[7] Founded in 1967 in Switzerland, AKF was initially involved in managing the "social development properties it owns" such as hospitals, health centers, schools, and social and cultural centers (Aga Khan Foundation 1992: 15), many of which were located in regions of South Asia and East Africa with significant Ismaili populations. In 1981, however, AKF began to shift its focus away from property management towards the funding of development activities. This shift was accomplished through the appointment, by AKF's Board of Directors, of a General Manager and Program Officer in the early 1980s (both of whom had previously worked with the Ford Foundation) who then drafted a "Programme Strategy" for AKF which laid out key areas of interest in primary health care, education, rural development, and the management of renewable natural resources (Aga Khan Foundation 1983; 1992: 15).

By 1996, AKF had expanded into a network of branches and independent affiliates in eleven countries in addition to its headquarters in Geneva. The "developed country" offices in Canada, the United States, and the United Kingdom were focused on fundraising and development education, while "developing country" offices in East Africa, South Asia, and Central Asia were concentrated on supporting and monitoring the activities of grantees. The Geneva office was responsible for coordinating all of these activities and funds, and for setting overall strategies.[8]

AKF's overall funding for development activities has grown considerably since 1982 from a program expenditure of US $3.3 million to approximately US $50 million in 1997 (Aga Khan Foundation 1992: 15; 1998a: 54). AKF does not directly fund Southern NGOs like AKRSP (I) and Sadguru; it obtains these funds primarily through grants from bilateral agencies as well as through donations from other organizations and individuals. AKF, as an intermediary, thus occupies the precarious position of being simultaneously a donor and a recipient, or a funder and an NGO. In fact, official descriptions of AKF portray it as both a "major non-governmental organization" and as a "funding agency" (Aga Khan Development Network undated: 6).[9]

The rural development experience of AKF has centered around the work of four key South Asian NGOs: AKRSP (I), AKRSP Pakistan, Sadguru, and

BRAC (formerly the Bangladesh Rural Advancement Committee). Of these four organizations, AKF was instrumental in establishing the former two NGOs, and has been an important funder of the latter two NGOs. More recently, AKF has also set up relief and rural development programs in Tajikistan and in Kenya, and is central to a major AKDN development and relief effort in post-war Afghanistan. The AKF network, and particularly AKF Geneva, have played significant roles in the histories of both AKRSP (I) and Sadguru. AKRSP (I) was initially set up through an endowment provided by the Aga Khan, and AKF Geneva holds a permanent place on the board of AKRSP (I). The early years of AKRSP (I), in the 1980s, witnessed several annual visits from Geneva staff for the purposes of providing management and programming inputs. AKF Geneva has also played an important hand in the history of Sadguru. It has been responsible not only for organizing the present European Commission funding, but also facilitated contact between Sadguru and NORAD in the late 1980s, and arranged funding from various bilateral sources from 1988 to 1993. A major effect of AKF Geneva's support (in financial and networking terms), was a rapid expansion of Sadguru's activities after 1988.

AKF has also been active in "NGO enhancement" activities which include the provision of managerial and financial training to NGOs, as well as setting up and supporting a series of NGO-support organizations in Southern countries. These support organizations offer technical expertise, managerial training, and applied research skills to other NGOs in their home countries. For instance, AKF has been involved in establishing an NGO Resource Center in Pakistan and in Zanzibar, as well as the Kenya Community Development Foundation (Aga Khan Foundation 1997: 15, 47).

As discussed above, AKF's activities extend considerably beyond simple fund provision. In the organization's own words, "The Aga Khan Foundation is a funding agency, but it also involves itself actively in the intellectual genesis and evolution of its projects" (Aga Khan Foundation 1992: 16). As will become evident in later chapters, however, AKF's extensive involvement in the work of AKRSP (I) and Sadguru has resulted in relations that are marked by collaboration and collegiality on one hand, but also by tension, resistance, and misunderstanding on another.

Ford Foundation

The Ford Foundation provides very little financial support to AKRSP (I) and Sadguru, but has been a key promoter of two activities: Joint Forest Management and Participatory Irrigation Management. Both activities involve interaction between government officials and village members, either over the use and management of forest resources or of government irrigation canals. As facilitators of state–citizen interaction, both AKRSP (I) and Sadguru have set up citizen's groups that work with Gujarat's Forest Department to reforest and protect government forest land from illegal felling. In exchange, citizens are granted usufruct rights to various non-timber forest products (such as grass and fruit), as well as a share in final timber harvests (Campbell, Palit, and Roy 1994). In PIM, AKRSP (I) has arranged for the transfer of defunct government-owned irrigation canals to farmer groups. These groups are responsible for canal repair, maintenance, collection of users' fees, and coordination with Irrigation Department officials for timely water releases.

The Ford Foundation has promoted JFM and PIM in India not only through the provision of small grants, but more importantly, by bringing together government agencies and NGOs in Gujarat as well as in other states. The Foundation was instrumental in setting up a State Level Working Group on JFM in Gujarat, thus enabling dialogue between NGOs and the Forest Department.[10] The Foundation was also the first organization to lend financial support and legitimacy to AKRSP (I)'s endeavors at PIM. Overall, the financial support provided by the Ford Foundation to AKRSP (I) and Sadguru is relatively insignificant but has had the effect of encouraging NGO involvement in multi-stakeholder dialogue and in policy issues concerning land and water. In addition, Sadguru's first foreign funds were obtained from the Ford Foundation in 1987. This initial grant encouraged AKF India and AKF Geneva to extend their support to Sadguru the following year, marking the beginning of what were to become very large foreign investments in Sadguru's work.

Norwegian Agency for Development Cooperation

Sadguru also receives funds from the Norwegian Agency for Development Cooperation. Sadguru's contact with NORAD was initially facilitated by AKF's staff in India and Geneva who helped the NGO obtain an initial grant from NORAD in 1991, and which has since led to continuous Norwegian support. NORAD is significant not only as a funder, covering an average of 14 percent of Sadguru's expenditure over the past several years, but also as the first supporter of Sadguru's "training institute" and offices, as well as of the NGO's expansion of activities into the neighboring state of Rajastan.[11] In the early years of NORAD funding, staff from the Norwegian Embassy in New Delhi paid occasional visits to the field, and, in cooperation with the AKF network, organized reviews of Sadguru's work in 1990 and in 1993. The evaluation teams submitted very positive reports on both occasions (Khanna and Hiremath 1990; Nyborg et al. 1993), after which NORAD has continued to provide support with minimal reporting requirements and intervention. In the mid-1990s, NORAD's assistance in linking Sadguru with universities and funders in Norway led to Sadguru's involvement in a collaboration between six development organizations and universities in Norway, India, and Ethiopia, on issues of natural resource management and training (Sadguru 1997: 58).

Links with government agencies

Sadguru and AKRSP (I) also maintain important relationships with government agencies within their home country. Although interactions between NGOs and government agencies do not form a central part of this book, they are significant linkages since government departments (at both federal and state levels) legally control much of the India's forest and water resources. The government is also the country's largest development actor both in terms of budget and in terms of the geographic scope of its activities. AKRSP (I) and Sadguru interact with various government units primarily in order to obtain legal access to natural resources such as rivers and protected forest lands, to secure financial resources, and to acquire technical certification for water resource projects such as check-dams and irrigation systems. Both NGOs interact with a number of government organizations, and in particular with the District Rural Development Agencies (DRDAs), state Irrigation Departments, and state Forest Departments. Relationships with the former two agencies have been generally positive, while interactions with the Forest Departments have been difficult at best. Additional details on these relationships are elaborated as needed in subsequent chapters.

Summary: NGO-funder relationships

The primary function of this chapter has been to provide a descriptive backdrop for the more analytical chapters which follow. It does, however, bring to the foreground three significant observations about the organizational context of NGO activity. First, NGOs are situated among a range of diverse organizational actors, many of which must be mobilized in order to put a project into effect. Putting up a lift irrigation facility, for example, involves multiple steps which include not only design and construction, but also obtaining domestic and international funding, securing government permission and certification, developing relationships with rural communities and establishing village organizations.

Second, flows of funds and information concerning NGO activities often pass through multiple organizational tiers. For example, in the case of the CMNR project funded by the European Commission, funds flow through four tiers: from the EC to the Aga Khan Foundation (which involves flows from AKF UK to AKF Geneva to AKF India) to AKRSP (I) and Sadguru, and finally to villages in the form of actual physical activity or infrastructure. Information on activities also traverses these multiple tiers, but in reverse order, flowing from the village level through NGOs or consultants to funders.

Third, international support for NGO activities requires a global discourse that legitimates community-based natural resource management. NGOs like AKRSP (I) and Sadguru face considerable pressure from various members of their global funding networks to emphasize some activities while downplaying others. As such, assessments of NGO activities which view them as unitary or isolated actors, miss key features of NGO environments and thus of NGO behavior.

It is these complex inter-organizational dynamics that form the focus of the chapters which follow. Understanding the impacts of NGO-funder relationships on development discourse as well as on organizational reporting, monitoring, and learning, are central to making sense of NGO behavior and change.

3   NGO behavior and development discourse

The history of international development can be periodized in terms of shifts in development thought, policy, and practice over time. Beginning with the establishment of the Bretton Woods institutions after World War II, development programs of governments in the South and of international organizations and aid agencies in the North have navigated a constantly changing course – from an emphasis on large-scale infrastructure, industry, and agriculture in the 1950s and 1960s, to a "basic needs" focus on individuals and families in the 1970s, followed by attention to participation, sustainable development, and gender equity in the 1980s and, more recently, to issues of economic liberalization and civil society (Edwards 1994; Escobar 1995; Fisher 1998; Guhan 1988; Ruttan 1989; Sukhatme 1989). This chapter details these shifts in development "discourse" over time and demonstrates their effects on AKRSP (I) and Sadguru. It concludes with some thoughts on the broader relevance of a discourse approach to understanding NGO behavior.

As detailed in chapter 1, a discourse is a specific and historically produced way of looking at the world and is embedded within wider relations of power – power that is manifest in the scientific "expertise" of development economists, professionals, and expatriates that serve as advisors, funders, and consultants to Southern governments and NGOs. One can imagine numerous interconnected discourses in which these development experts and organizations might be located: development discourse, environmental discourse, human rights discourse, and so on. In examining the effects of development discourse on NGOs, I ask the following questions: How is NGO behavior influenced by prevailing development discourses? How do NGOs respond to or challenge these dominant perspectives on development? What are the processes through which global discourses are transmitted to local levels, and how do local actions affect global discourses?

The above questions are examined through historical analyses of Sadguru and AKRSP (I). Founded in 1974 and 1983, respectively, both NGOs have been pioneers in natural resource management in India and are ranked amongst the older and more established NGOs in this field. And given that the entire international development industry is itself barely fifty years old, Sadguru's twenty-five-year history spans half of what might be termed the history of modern development.[1] At the same time, however, the NGO community in India is extremely varied in terms of size, activity, and philosophy (see for example Alliband 1983; Robinson, Farrington, and Satish 1993; Sen 1993; Sen 1999). Thus, many of the details in this chapter are specific to the two case study organizations only and cannot be generalized beyond them. Nonetheless, the broader development context which I describe and the changes in that environment over time are part of a larger series of transformations in development thought, activity, and policy over the last three decades. As such, many changes in development context experienced by AKRSP (I) and Sadguru have been shared by NGOs and development organizations elsewhere.

The "basic needs – integrated rural development" era, 1974–80

The establishment of Sadguru in 1974 was preceded by a series of events, both nationally and internationally, that were to have a profound effect on the organization's role in rural development. The post-World War II era was, for India and many other countries, also a post-colonial era. The governments of newly forming "underdeveloped" states saw modernization, particularly in terms of industrialization, as a means to economic growth. The Indian government, under the leadership of Nehru, embarked upon a massive "planned development" strategy with considerable support from both within India as well as from international donors including the United States Agency for International Development (USAID) and the World Bank (Sukhatme 1989). Development, as understood at the time, was built upon an ideal of economic progress – progress as greater production, economic growth, and industrialization.

The mid-1960s witnessed drought and famine in eastern India and a global food crisis. These events led to a shift in the attention of governments and aid agencies from a focus on industry towards issues of agricultural production. From the mid-1960s to the mid-1970s, the proportion of total official aid to India allocated for agriculture rose from a mere 2 percent to 30 percent, while aid allocated for industrial development fell from 60 percent to 30 percent (Lipton and Toye 1990). Green Revolution technologies played an increasingly important role in development strategies from the mid-1960s onward, as India's planners sought to achieve self-sufficiency in foodgrains (Bernstein 1992: 57). This period marked a concurrent shift in perspective amongst development planners away from macro-level industrial growth strategies to efforts focused on meeting the "basic needs" of the poor. The Indian government launched programs in the early and mid-seventies to improve food supply, nutrition, elementary education, rural health facilities, and basic infrastructure including water supply, roads, electrification, and housing (Guhan 1988: 190).

This period might also be seen as a refocusing by development planners and practitioners on the conditions of individuals rather than on the national economy at large, and was fueled by a pledge in 1973 by Robert McNamara, then President of the World Bank, to allocate resources to improving productivity and welfare of the rural poor. In June of 1976, the International Labour Organisation organized a conference where it proposed a "Basic Needs Approach" to development "aiming at the achievement of a certain specific minimum standard of living before the end of the century." The increased attention to issues of "basic needs" was not, however, at odds with the perceived ideal of linear and ever-increasing economic growth. Advocates of a "basic needs" approach justified it in terms of relatively low-cost investments that would eventually lead to increased human and economic productivity (Ruttan 1989: 176). Radical structural change, however, such as land or income redistribution which had played a significant role in the early 1950s, was not only de-emphasized in policy-making in the 1970s, but was eventually erased from the range practicable possibilities (Bernstein 1992: 56; Government of India 1951).

Sadguru emerged within this context. The organization was formed as a response to the famines of the mid-sixties, and in a national and international institutional environment that had turned its attention from developing large-scale industry and infrastructure to need-focused issues of rural poverty and agricultural production. But it was also formed in response to highly localized needs. Between 1974 and 1976, the two founding directors of Sadguru conducted a survey in villages of Panchmahals district of Gujarat, in order to develop a sense for local conditions and demands. Finding a strong local demand for irrigation, extensive seasonal migration in search of wage employment, and the availability of water in government water tanks and rivers, Sadguru's directors decided to take up lift-irrigation as an experimental activity in villages in eastern Gujarat. These early irrigation projects quickly evolved to become the backbone of the NGO's work.[2] Sadguru secured funds for irrigation systems from existing state and federal government programs, while operating costs of the NGO were borne by a corporate donor, the Mafatlal Group.

The fit between Sadguru's activities and existing federal and state government programs, made it possible for the NGO to secure government support for its work. For example, both India's Five Year Plan for 1978–83 and Sadguru's development program in 1978 set forth a series of rural development goals that emphasized employment generation, increasing productivity in agriculture, and a "comprehensive" or "integrated" development approach that combined agriculture and irrigation with the provision of basic needs in healthcare and education. Even the name of Sadguru's program was Integrated Rural Development (IRD), the same name used in the Government's Five Year Plan (Government of India 1978; Shri Sadguru Seva Sangh Trust 1978). Indeed, throughout the late seventies and early eighties, IRD programs emerged in virtually all parts of the developing world, promoted by bilateral and multilateral organizations as well as by governments.

At the root of this "integrated" or "comprehensive" development approach was the goal of growth in agricultural productivity and rural income, which was to be achieved through rural employment programs, agricultural (green revolution) technology, and coordination of agriculture with other activities. The approach was largely technocratic, and dismissed (or at least did not directly address) the role of social relations and the larger political economy in rural change.[3] Within this discourse, poverty was understood as being a result of poor resource use and coordination. The solution to poverty, according to this view, was to coordinate resources better, either by coordinating labor power through employment programs, or by coordinating natural resources through irrigation and agricultural technologies.

What distinguished the government and Sadguru approaches to development was that the NGO, as a result of its more localized efforts, was closer to the field and was thus able to speak more concretely about specific local issues such as rural–urban migration caused by economic distress. More importantly, Sadguru's perception of rural needs had emerged from direct contact with village communities, and this was reflected in its decision to attempt lift-irrigation as an intervention. Despite these differences, both Sadguru and India's Planning Commission shared a "basic needs" or "integrated rural development" perspective. The development objectives of both Sadguru and the government were informed by this shared fundamental framework which assumed that poverty could be eliminated by supplying basic needs; it was in implementing the basic needs approach that they differed.

The apolitical nature of this approach made it possible for Sadguru to work with government agencies and to secure state support for its "service delivery" or "welfare" activities. This orientation was not adopted by all NGOs of the time. The late 1960s and 1970s in India witnessed a rise in NGO activities that were critical of state development approaches and which, in some cases, were violently anti-state (Sen 1999: 337–8). During this period, state agencies continued to support welfare-oriented NGOs, especially those providing services and relief in flood- and drought-prone regions and those working with refugees from the Bangladesh war in 1971, but increased their control and monitoring of groups involved in political activities and those linked to foreign funders.[4] This dualistic approach to NGOs by the Indian government might be described in terms of a "shadow state" – support for the creation of a parastatal apparatus of voluntary organizations that provide welfare services and over which some degree of control can be retained, and opposition to organizations that challenge this order (Sen 1999; Wolch 1990).

It would be unjustified, however, to portray Sadguru merely as a product of state-sponsored development discourses. Sadguru's early activities, particularly in irrigation and migration reduction, were embedded in local conditions and in the outlook of its founding directors who sought to change state behavior by working in collaboration with government. While the Rural Development administration in Gujarat state was highly skeptical of NGOs in the 1970s, this changed with the appointment of a new Secretary of Rural Development in 1980, who was very supportive of NGO activity and was particularly impressed with Sadguru. This public official later went on to become the first Chief Executive Officer of AKRSP (I). As we shall see, Sadguru's development model was to have an impact on the formation of AKRSP (I), and both organizations were to have wider policy impacts, particularly in evolving participatory development interventions within Gujarat state and elsewhere.

The rise of "participation"

Just as the "basic needs" and "integrated rural development" approaches dominated development discourse in the 1960s and 1970s, the idea of "participatory development" rose to popularity amongst development practitioners and planners in the 1970s and 1980s. The ascent of "participation" to prominence in development discourse – both in terms of practice and policy – came about for two reasons. The first was that the benefits of centrally planned development strategies had failed to reach the poor. The emphasis of development programs on large-scale and heavy industry in the 1950s and early 1960s had little impact on the predominantly agricultural population, while green revolution technologies favored regions with irrigation and infrastructure (Bernstein 1992: 56–57; Ghosh and Bharadwaj 1992: 155–56). This bias towards big projects contributed to the emergence of a class of rich modernized farmers, a growth in income disparities between regions, and an increased marginalization of the rural poor. Thus, when Indira Gandhi returned to power in 1971 it was with the campaign slogan *garibi hatao* (abolish poverty) that promised increased spending on programs intended to help the poor more directly. A second reason for the increased attention to "participation" was that alternatives to top-down planning, particularly as demonstrated by social activists and NGOs, had emerged by the late 1970s and early 1980s. For example, social and political change were emphasized in the work and writings of Paulo Freire in South America on "conscientization" (published in the early 1970s), and in other works on a set of methodologies known as Participatory Action Research (e.g. Fals-Borda and Rahman 1991; Freire 1973). At the same time, however, more moderate social workers and organizations were promoting citizen involvement as leading to more cost-effective economic change and service delivery (Rahnema 1997).

Sadguru was one among many organizations that began promoting citizen involvement in development activity in the 1970s and 1980s. By the early 1980s, Sadguru's efforts had focused on the activities of lift-irrigation and agro-forestry. In lift-irrigation, the NGO's attention had initially been focused on technical expertise and on construction quality – the irrigation systems were operated and maintained by Sadguru staff, while farmers were responsible for paying water users' fees. As NGO staff gained experience in working with farmers, however, responsibilities for operation, maintenance, construction, collection of users' fees, and overall management of the irrigation systems were transferred from NGO staff to the farmer-run Lift Irrigation Cooperative Societies (LICS). In setting up these relatively autonomous LICSs, the NGO was able to demonstrate a participatory alternative to traditional government programs in which a government agency delivered services to farmers without any community involvement. While the form of participation which Sadguru encouraged was limited to the confines of a specific project, it was a powerful and tangible alternative to government irrigation activity in Gujarat. This work was also to have an effect on the formation of AKRSP (I).

Participation and professionalism, 1980–86

In the same way that Sadguru can be considered a product of the "basic needs" era, AKRSP (I) was also profoundly influenced by the development climate surrounding its emergence – in particular by two trends in development practice that had become evident by the early 1980s – and also by the experiences of other rural development organizations. The first of these two trends, as I have noted, was "participation," while the second was the "professionalization" of NGOs.

AKRSP (I)'s activities and participatory approach were partly modeled on the experiences of two organizations. One of these organizations was Sadguru, whose assistance was secured in establishing a participatory irrigation program in the new NGO. AKRSP (I)'s formation was also influenced by a sister NGO in Pakistan which had developed the idea of routing all its development interventions through local-level organizations which it called "village institutions." The kind of village-level organization used by AKRSP (I) was not the same as Sadguru's irrigation cooperative. From Sadguru's "basic needs" perspective, the physical intervention and its economic impacts mattered most, and user's groups (e.g. irrigation cooperatives) were viewed as necessary for managing the interventions. AKRSP (I)'s "participation" perspective reversed this relationship: the village organization, as a unit of social and economic change, was seen as mattering most, but a physical activity resulting in economic benefits was needed to bring organizational members together. As such, the village organization was not only a user's group for a particular resource, but a focal point for a range of resource activities.[5]

It should be noted that AKRSP (I) emerged in a local political climate that was considerably more welcoming of NGOs than that faced by Sadguru about a decade earlier. AKRSP (I)'s first CEO, who had previously been the Secretary of Rural Development in Gujarat state, had played an important role in nurturing a positive relationship between governmental and non-governmental organizations. Having been both a senior public official and now an NGO leader, he was uniquely positioned to facilitate collaboration between the two sectors. In addition, a number of political leaders in Gujarat at this time had previously been key figures in the state's agricultural cooperatives, and were thus generally supportive of "people's institutions" such as NGOs.

As such, in the late 1980s and early 1990s, AKRSP (I) was able to take the notion of participation one step further, by linking state agencies with local communities to jointly manage state-owned irrigation canals and forest lands. Under a scheme known as Participatory Irrigation Management (PIM), the NGO was able to facilitate the turnover of defunct state canals to farmers groups which then repaired and managed the canals with assistance from Gujarat's Irrigation Department. AKRSP (I) is now widely credited for reviving abandoned canal irrigation projects and in facilitating an important transformation in the Government of Gujarat's approaches to citizen involvement in irrigation activity. In a similar program, known nation-wide as Joint Forest Management (JFM), AKRSP (I) organized community groups to protect, from illegal felling, state forest lands adjacent to their villages. In return for this voluntary protection, Gujarat's Forest Department agreed to permit village members periodic harvests of minor forest products such as grass (for fodder), and sometimes even wood. In addition, both AKRSP (I) and Sadguru have begun, since the mid-1990s, to experiment with the formation of district-wide federations of irrigation societies. Once firmly established, these federations could become important local political forces, and capable of increasing the bargaining power of village-based organizations in their interactions with state agencies and NGOs.

Participation was one of two trends prevailing among international development organizations that influenced AKRSP (I)'s formation. The second trend was the increasing "professionalization" of the NGO sector. Throughout the 1970s and 1980s, India as well as many other countries of the South witnessed an unprecedented growth in NGOs, particularly in the form of young, educated, and professional individuals joining and creating development organizations (Alliband 1983: 48; Fisher 1998: 7; Society for Participatory Research in Asia 1991: 31). Many of these professionals were dissatisfied with state development practices, and sought to develop more participatory alternatives of their own. A number of these newly formed organizations sought financial support from foreign funding organizations and Northern NGOs. This was common not only in India, but throughout the developing world (Crow 1992: 268; Fisher 1998: 7).

The "professionalization" of AKRSP (I) took place on three fronts. On one side, the organization offered attractive salaries to engineers, agricultural scientists, social workers and managers from reputed academic institutions. Second,

AKRSP (I) was formed at a time when many educated and socially committed youth were turning to rural development and were either founding their own organizations or were looking for NGOs in which to work. These two groups of professionals were to be the "experts" in the field. At a third level of professionalization, AKRSP (I) interacted closely with its key international promoter, the Aga Khan Foundation, to prepare reports and studies of high quality in order to secure funding from bilateral agencies. AKRSP (I) also had access to various levels of government through linkages afforded by its CEO and members of its Board of Directors. As a result, AKRSP (I) appeared from its very beginning, not as a small voluntary organization on a shoe-string budget, but as an organization with professional staff, government access, and substantial foreign funds.

The professionalization of NGOs within India, and elsewhere, was to be an increasing trend throughout the 1980s and into the 1990s, as new organizations emerged with support from Northern NGOs (Robinson, Farrington, and Satish 1993: 95; Society for Participatory Research in Asia 1991: 79). This professionalization was, in part, motivated by increasing interactions with foreign funders which made it necessary that NGO staff be sufficiently trained to manage substantial funding, reporting, and monitoring requirements.

This period of expanding interactions with foreign funders was, however, also a time of growing tension with state agencies. During the 1980s, the Government of India made concerted efforts to control NGO activity, particularly in the arena of political organization. During this decade, over 900 organizations were monitored for suspected subversive activities, all NGOs receiving foreign funds were required to set up special bank accounts to be monitored by the Home Ministry, and tax exemption laws governing contributions to NGOs were tightened (Sen 1999: 343). In short, while the state welcomed NGOs and foreign funding for purposes of advancing state objectives of welfare and service delivery (i.e. in creating a "shadow state"), it increased control over all other types of activity. Sadguru and AKRSP (I) were relatively sheltered from this period of turmoil, largely due to their established links with local government agencies and their emphasis on service delivery.

The era of foreign funds and consultants, 1986–93

The late 1980s and early 1990s were, for both AKRSP (I) and Sadguru, a period of change and experimentation, as well as of expansion. A number of changes at this time were a direct result of linkages between the two NGOs and international funding organizations and of the consequent integration of NGOs into global development discourses. In this section, I examine processes through which new development ideas have been transmitted from international levels downwards to the two NGOs, as well as upwards from local to global levels.

AKRSP (I) had always been a recipient of international funds, while Sadguru began receiving foreign funds in 1988, first from the Ford Foundation and later from the Geneva-based Aga Khan Foundation (AKF) and the Norwegian Agency for Development Cooperation (NORAD). The relationship of both NGOs with AKF was particularly important since AKF served as a key conduit for funds from bilateral agencies, provided various forms of expertise and training, and organized evaluation visits and consultancies. As a result of its frequent and varying interactions with NGOs, and its position amongst international organizations, AKF played a pivotal role in transmitting donor perspectives to AKRSP (I) and Sadguru and in packaging the actions and innovations of the same NGOs in terms acceptable to donors. A number of mechanisms have been employed in this transmission: consultants, reports and evaluations, reporting requirements, conditions of funding and terms of reference. Two of these mechanisms – consultants and funding conditions – are briefly discussed here.

Consultants

A handful of consultants and technical experts played a particularly critical role in the transmitting new technologies and development methodologies to AKRSP (I) and Sadguru. AKRSP (I)'s biogas energy program was begun in 1986 through the technical support of a British consultant hired by AKF. Soil and water conservation activities in both NGOs were introduced in 1989 by a watershed expert hired by AKF. In another case, a practitioner from the US and Honduras motivated AKRSP (I) to develop an agricultural training and experimentation approach in collaboration with farmers on their own fields rather than at separate research sites (i.e. farmer-to-farmer extension). At the request of AKRSP (I)'s Chief Executive, AKF also arranged for several visits by scholars and practitioners who specialized in participatory research methodologies, eventually leading to the establishment of Participatory Rural Appraisal (PRA) as a cornerstone of AKRSP (I)'s work and interactions with rural communities. PRA consists of a series of interactive tools and methods for gathering information about a community or its resources (e.g. about local forest or water resources, about community wealth and social rankings, about local priorities and concerns, etc.), while simultaneously facilitating the establishment of rapport between researchers and community members and also enabling community action. AKRSP (I)'s experimentation with and adoption of PRA techniques led to a transformation in the organization's terms of engagement with rural communities, as PRA partially reversed the conventional expert-trainee hierarchy: as a method of learning about a community and its resources from village members themselves, PRA demanded that villagers be seen as experts in their own right.

Funding conditions: environment and gender

Another mechanism through which development ideas and practices are transmitted from international to local realms is through conditionality over funds. During the late 1980s, international organizations began to promote activities related to "environment" and "gender." Two documents played critical roles in the globalization of these themes: The Bruntland Commission's report of 1987 (World Commission on Environment and Development 1987) which catapulted the phrase "sustainable development" into the popular imagination, and Ester Boserup's (1970) work which brought to attention the differential effects of development on men and women. International concern for the environment can be traced back to the early seventies to the UN Conference on the Human Environment in Stockholm in 1972 and the formation of the United Nations Environment Programme (UNEP), but this concern for the environment came to a climax with the Bruntland Commission's report. Sustainable development discourse had the effect of legitimizing the work of NGOs like AKRSP (I) and Sadguru, which were already working on environment and development issues. The work of AKRSP (I) and Sadguru did not change as a result of the effects of the Bruntland Commission's report, but the language used to describe and conceptualize their work did.

Two of the central words of this new discourse were "sustainability" and "environment." Organizations such as AKRSP (I) and Sadguru, whose primary goals had been of economic growth (achieved through the use of land and water resources) could now describe and legitimate their work in terms of environment and sustainability. AKRSP (I), for example, subdivided "sustainability" into three component parts to inform its own work: organizational sustainability, measured in terms of the ability of village organizations to function without managerial support from AKRSP (I); financial sustainability, measured in terms of the ability of projects and village organizations to function without financial support from AKRSP (I), apart from start-up costs; and environmental sustainability, measured in terms of the extent to which a project or activity maintains or enhances the local natural resource base.

At about the same time that AKRSP (I) was introducing the concept of sustainability into its work and reporting, Sadguru was undergoing a modification of its objectives. In 1989, one of the objectives of the NGO was to strengthen "the rural economy by undertaking measures for proper water and land use..." (Sadguru 1990), but by late 1992, this aim had been disaggregated into two new objectives that reflected the changed discourse, with special emphasis on "environment" as a key word – "To improve the living conditions of rural and tribal people...mainly by developing environmentally friendly land and water resources programmes" and "To improve the environment through various programmes which may in turn improve the natural resource base" (Sadguru 1993). While both AKRSP (I) and Sadguru had always seen the maintenance of land and water resources as crucial to their income-generating activities, they were able to appropriate sustainable development discourse in order to recast their work.

In contrast to sustainable development discourse, pressures arising from development discourses on women and gender have not been easily internalized by AKRSP (I) and Sadguru; in fact, the broad international discourse on gender and development has resulted in some significant changes in behavior in both organizations. The evolution of discourses on gender in development can be traced through an archaeology of terms: women in development (WID), women and development (WAD), and Gender and Development (GAD), which mark a general transition from an emphasis on including women in development activity, to a focus on relations of power in society and seeing women as agents of political and social change (Moser 1989; Rathgeber 1990).

According to Rathgeber (1990), the WID approach emerged around the early 1970s, followed by WAD in the second half of the 1970s, and GAD in the 1980s. International attention to WID/GAD issues began to rise in the 1970s. As one of the first international development organizations to form a WID policy, the United States Agency for International Development established an Office of Women in Development in 1973. In 1975, the United Nations organized a Conference on Women and Development in Mexico City, and launched the UN Decade for Women (Escobar 1995: 178). By 1980, many countries and international agencies had made efforts to include women's issues in development plans by setting up special bureaus, offices and in some cases ministries. It was not until 1987, however, that the World Bank established a Division for Women in Development (Escobar 1995: 178).

Changes in NGOs, as a result of pressures from funders (expressed as conditions on funding) to consider issues related to women and gender, have generally been focused on interventions based on WID rather than GAD. The former approach emphasizes improving program "efficiency" by using women as productive resources, while the latter stresses interventions to enhance opportunities for empowerment of local people (especially women) affected by development projects. The pressures on AKRSP (I) were felt early in its history. According to AKRSP (I)'s first Chief Executive, "In '84, gender was not on our agenda. And [I was told] you better include it, or CIDA money won't come to you. I was not opposed to it."[6] Such pressures exerted by funding organizations initially translated into the inclusion of women into existing activities such as agro-forestry, but did not reflect a change in organizational strategy. In the forestry programs of both AKRSP (I) and Sadguru, tree nurseries eventually came to be operated largely by women. Sadguru staff found that women were carrying out much of the tree-tending work anyway, and that they were more familiar with tree species and their uses. The forestry program thus came to be seen by Sadguru staff as a way of working with and generating dialogue with women (Grant 1989; Khorakiwala 1997a).

Additional pressure on AKRSP (I) from a visit by a pair of internationally reputed development scholars in 1991 resulted in the recruitment by AKRSP (I) of a senior staff member for a new WID portfolio. A strategic shift in the way the organization worked with women, however, did not occur until 1993 with the appointment of a new Chief Executive who was regarded as a "gender specialist." Within two years of his appointment, AKRSP (I) had altered its mission statement to reflect a new emphasis on the "empowerment of rural communities and groups, particularly the underprivileged and women" (AKRSP (I) 1994: n.p.) and had embarked upon gender sensitization training programs for its own staff as well as for members of other NGOs, state agencies, and village organizations.

In comparison to AKRSP (I), Sadguru's approach is largely WID-oriented even though the organization does not have a formal WID strategy or program. Women are included in existing activities, with some activities such as agro-forestry, biogas, and an income-generation project being exclusively operated by women. The NGO has resisted establishing a formal WID program, insisting that formalized steps are not necessary, given that one-third of its Board of Directors is comprised by women and half of its managerial staff are women. The entry of women into managerial positions, however, was facilitated by an international funder (the Aga Khan Foundation) which, in 1993, linked Sadguru with young graduates of a reputed social science institute in Bombay.

Reverse influence: from local to national and global

While both AKRSP (I) and Sadguru have been influenced by external forces advocating various principles and practices (through consultants and funding conditions), it would be inaccurate to suggest that NGO behavior has been determined by these external influences. Indeed, there is considerable evidence of *reverse influence*, in which NGO experiences have been transmitted to national or global levels.[7]

The experience with Participatory Rural Appraisal has shown that the relationship between NGOs and consultants hired by international funders can be a reciprocal one. The learnings from AKRSP (I)'s testing and development of PRA techniques have been spread to funders and other organizations, sometimes by the same consultants that initially introduced the idea to AKRSP (I). For example, Robert Chambers of the Institute of Development Studies at the University of Sussex, UK, has been a key proponent of PRA techniques and has frequently visited AKRSP (I). The experiences of AKRSP (I) and other organizations with PRA have been incorporated into his work (see Chambers 1994b). In this way, consultants sometimes serve as mechanisms not only for the transmission of international ideas to local arenas, but also as carriers of field-level experience to global levels.

Such "upward" or "reverse" transmissions of NGO experience to national and international levels also occur as NGO staff themselves become consultants to other organizations or move on to new jobs. A former AKRSP (I) manager, for example, served as a key consultant to the World Bank in implementing a Participatory Irrigation Management program in Nigeria in the years 1999 and 2000. Two other former AKRSP (I) managers now work for the World Bank in New Delhi and Washington. And Sadguru has formed a consortium with organizations in Ethiopia and Norway to which it has provided training on natural resource management.

At a national level, both AKRSP (I) and Sadguru have played central roles in influencing the development approaches of other organizations. With funding from the European Commission and the Norwegian government, Sadguru has established a large "training institute" where it provides government agencies, other NGOs, and rural communities with workshops and training programs on natural resource management. According to Sadguru's annual report for the 1997 fiscal year (Sadguru 1998a: 46), a total of 166 NGOs and 116 government organizations participated in programs or workshops held at its training institute during that year. AKRSP (I) also hires out its expertise to others. In 1996, its staff offered about two dozen training programs to government departments, NGOs, and academic institutes (AKRSP (I)1997: 113–14), and in 1998, the NGO formally began marketing these offerings as "AKRSP (I) Services."

AKRSP (I) and Sadguru have also facilitated the spread of their work through involvement in a watershed development program supported by the Government of India. This federal program has made available substantial funds to NGOs and government agencies for the implementation of natural resource management programs in rural areas. The guidelines for this program were developed with considerable input from AKRSP (I)'s former Chief Executive Officer. Both AKRSP (I) and Sadguru are "Program Implementing Agencies" for this effort, with Sadguru being specially designated as a key training resource for other Program Implementing Agencies in Gujarat. In addition, the NGOs are members of district-level government advisory committees for this federal watershed development program.

Finally, AKRSP (I) and Sadguru are indirectly involved in transmitting their work through a program funded by the India–Canada Environment Facility which aims specifically to spread the experiences of both NGOs in natural resource management to other organizations in western India. This objective is accomplished by providing less experienced NGOs with funding and training in the design and implementation of natural resource management activities, by funding a small number of "support NGOs" which serve as key nodes for the provision of managerial and technical training in natural resource management to other organizations, and by supporting research, networking, and policy advocacy on related matters.

As such, while the activities of both AKRSP (I) and Sadguru have clearly been influenced by their linkages to international organizations, the NGOs have also succeeded in spreading their own experiences to national and international levels. Consultants and funders have been particularly important in carrying NGO experiences to other organizations.

Liberalization, civil society, and recent changes

Changes in AKRSP (I) and Sadguru have also been informed by more recent shifts in the international development environment. Following the end of the Cold War in 1989, a distinctly new policy approach has emerged amongst international aid organizations. This "new policy agenda" is characterized by a combination of two key elements – macroeconomic reform and "good governance" (Edwards and Hulme 1996: 961; Robinson 1994: 36). Economic reform, based on an assumption that markets and private sector initiatives are the most efficient mechanisms for achieving economic growth, is not new. What is new, however, is a policy agenda that combines economic liberalization with elements of "good governance" and democratization. A World Bank study in 1989 on recent economic crises in Sub-Saharan Africa attributed the region's difficulties to a "crisis of governance" that can be corrected by "a systematic effort to build a pluralistic institutional structure, a determination to respect the rule of law, and vigorous protection of the freedom of the press and human rights" (World Bank 1989: 61 as cited in Robinson 1994: 36). Good governance has been described as consisting of "transparency, accountability, freedom of speech and association, greater participation in political decision-making, and due process" (Lateef 1992 as cited in Clark 1995: 594). The new aid agenda, which marks an important departure from a primarily neoliberal (market reform and state retrenchment) approach, has for several years been a key feature of development funding policy in the World Bank, the International Monetary Fund, the European Community, and Japan (Archer 1994: 7; Edwards 1994: 67).

Associated with the new policy agenda has been an increase in attention amongst the international aid community to civil society organizations and institutions. While civil society organizations are not limited to development oriented NGOs, it is important to recognize that there has been increasing international attention to the work of development NGOs like AKRSP (I) and Sadguru for two reasons: NGOs are viewed by many official aid agencies and the public as being more efficient than governments in providing development services and in reaching the poor, and, they are also perceived as being important players in democratization processes (Edwards and Hulme 1996: 961).

This convergence of liberalization and democratization approaches into a new policy agenda, have contributed to substantial change in the NGO sector. Not only is development aid being increasingly channeled through NGOs rather than through governments, but there has also been pressure on NGOs to expand and scale-up their work, sometimes to the extent of replacing state services. The proportion of total bilateral aid channeled through NGOs from Organisation for Economic Cooperation and Development (OECD) countries has increased from 0.7 percent in 1975 to 3.6 percent in 1985 and to at least 5 percent in 1993–94, totaling US$ 2.3 billion (Edwards and Hulme 1996: 962). Fund transfers from NGOs in the North to the South increased four-fold from US$ 0.9 billion in 1970 to $ 4 billion in 1985, accounting for 10 percent of total aid from OECD countries (Cernea 1988: 6; Crow 1992: 268). This growth in NGO numbers and funding has occurred despite a lack of sufficient empirical evidence to support the assumptions that NGOs are more efficient service-providers or significant players in democratization processes (Edwards and Hulme 1996: 963; Mackintosh 1992: 80).

In India, the effects of these changes have also been widely felt. For the first time in 1985, the Government of India officially acknowledged the role of voluntary organizations as development actors in its Five-Year Plan and earmarked funds for rural voluntary agencies (Government of India 1985: 68). In 1986, the government created the Council for Advancement of People's Action and Rural Technology (CAPART), an agency which now funds various NGO activities throughout the country. It was also decided that all new recruits for the Indian Administrative Service (the most elite cadre of Indian civil servants, who operate state and federal agencies) would be required to spend ten days with a rural voluntary organization as part of their training. In the subsequent Plan, the government announced its intentions to create a country-wide network of NGOs (Government of India 1992: 39–40). In terms of foreign funding, India's annual NGO revenue from abroad (from bilateral, multilateral, and Northern NGO sources) in the early 1990s was estimated at about US$ 0.52 billion, which was equivalent to about 25 percent of official aid flows (Robinson, Farrington, and Satish 1993: 93). The number of NGOs registered with India's Ministry of Home Affairs under the Foreign Contribution and Regulation Act increased from 5,099 in 1985 to approximately 16,000 in 1992 (Mohanty and Singh 1996: 15; Tripathi et al. 1991).

In the cases of AKRSP (I) and Sadguru, recent grants have emphasized a scaling up and replication of the NGOs' activities. In 1994, the European Commission (EC) awarded a grant of nearly US$ 2 million per year, for eight years, to the Aga Khan Foundation for the work of AKRSP (I) and Sadguru. It was one of the largest grants ever provided by the EC directly to NGOs.

The funds are intended to enable AKRSP (I) and Sadguru "to expand and consolidate their experience, to extend their approaches to more than 350 poor villages, and to create a critical mass of transformed communities..." (Aga Khan Foundation 1993: summary). Another large grant to AKF, funded through the India–Canada Environment Facility, seeks to spread the experiences of AKRSP (I) and Sadguru through other organizations and by developing "the capacity of selected NGOs to operate at scale" (Aga Khan Foundation 1995). The Government of India's national watershed program, as noted above, is an effort to nationally replicate the approaches of NGOs like AKRSP (I) and Sadguru in small-scale watershed development.

At the same time that AKRSP (I) and Sadguru are being encouraged to scale up their activities and to develop the managerial capacity to do so, however, concerns have arisen among the NGOs and their funders over the abilities of the NGOs to remain sensitive to local conditions and needs. If NGOs are to scale up, does this not imply a compromise on the extent of community mobilization and participation? If NGOs spend too much time on participatory processes, can they ever scale up?

The above questions, arising from the new policy agenda, underlie the predicaments faced by AKRSP (I) and Sadguru – the double burden of scaling up efficiently and in a manner that does not compromise their efforts to encourage local participation. As a result of the EC grant of 1994, AKRSP (I) has been under pressure to improve its planning procedures in order to better set and meet its financial targets. A look at the NGO's recent past shows that its financial target-achievement record (i.e. expenditure as a percentage of budget) oscillated from 53 percent in 1993, to 87 percent in 1994, and 76 percent in 1995 (AKRSP (I) 1994; 1995; 1996). These years were characterized by a struggle in AKRSP (I) to develop planning procedures to enable the rapid replication of projects and also to forecast its budgets more accurately. The year 1996 marked a turnaround in this effort, with annual spending reaching 98 percent of the budget (AKRSP (I) 1997).

Sadguru's financial target achievement record, over the years 1994, 1995, and 1996 was 155 percent, 168 percent, and 152 percent respectively (Sadguru 1997b: v)! In contrast to AKRSP (I), achievement of targets has long been a key feature of Sadguru, where success has largely been interpreted in terms of target achievement. Sadguru's dilemma, while different from that of AKRSP (I), represents the flipside of the policy coin. Sadguru's burden lies in justifying its interventions in terms of enhanced citizen participation and equity within the villages it serves. In particular, Sadguru has faced queries from funders about how "sustainable" or "participatory" are its Lift Irrigation Cooperative Societies, and about the efforts it is making to reach rural families which do not have access to these irrigation projects. The extent to which the NGO has actually needed to change its activities or standard operating procedures in order to respond to these enquiries is unclear, but Sadguru has begun to represent itself as being attentive to process issues of participation and equity, especially in its annual reports and in other public documents.

While these changes in AKRSP (I) and Sadguru seem unrelated at first, both have been influenced by concurrent shifts in development discourse. As official aid organizations increase the flow of their funds to NGOs, they are doing so under a policy which assumes that NGOs are efficient service providers as well as participatory members of civil society. In this context, AKRSP (I) has been subject to the scaling-up pressures arising from expectations of efficiency, while Sadguru has come under scrutiny to demonstrate its attention to social issues of citizen involvement and equity.

Conclusions

While the specific details of the above case histories cannot be extended beyond AKRSP (I) and Sadguru, they give rise to a series of observations of more general interest to the study of NGO behavior. First, NGOs can be profoundly influenced by conditions surrounding their founding. They are, at least in part, products of the discourses prevailing during their initial, formative stages. Sadguru, for example, can still be characterized as a "basic needs" organization that views poverty as being an outcome of material constraints such as a lack of access to resources – financial, technological, physical, and managerial. The task of the NGO, then, is to provide or facilitate access to these resources through, for example, the creation and coordination of irrigation societies. Similarly, AKRSP (I)'s emergence in an era of "participation" continues to guide its emphasis on village organizations as the fulcrum of its work. What both NGOs share, however, is their embeddedness in a wider discourse that prioritizes economic improvement, which is to be achieved through a combination of both community mobilization and technological intervention. In short, the initial conditions surrounding an organization's founding are persistent: they are not unalterable, but they do inform future behavior and change.

This argument, about the importance of founding conditions, is not without precedent since Stinchcombe (1965: 164) and Hannan and Freeman (1977: 931–2) have made related arguments about constraints on organizational change. What is new, however, is the conceptualization of discourse as an organizational founding condition or, more specifically, the embeddedness of NGO behavior in development discourses. While there may be no unified development discourse at any period of time (given the existence of competing discourses), it is still possible to articulate general trends in discourse that affect NGO attitudes and practices. For the cases presented here, I have focused on trends of a global nature from the mid-1970s onwards.

A second observation concerns changes in global development discourses over time. While founding conditions appear to be very important in affecting organizational behavior, they are not necessarily *more* important than subsequent events or crises. As certain development approaches and strategies fall in and out of favor, they are transmitted to NGOs through a range of mechanisms including consultants, reporting requirements and conditions of funding. For example, Sadguru is increasingly paying closer attention to its irrigation societies as it comes under pressure to demonstrate that they are "participatory" or "equitable" or "sustainable." AKRSP (I)'s increasing attention to issues of gender was precipitated by pressures from funders and recommendations by international consultants. Both NGOs have adopted new technologies and methodologies as a result of visits from consultants, some of which, such as biogas, soil and water conservation, and participatory rural appraisal have become standard activities and methods. More generally, these cases point to the importance of consultants and funding conditions in transmitting global ideas to local levels. They also underscore the necessity of examining organizational histories and past practices for purposes of understanding present organizational behavior.

Perhaps more significant, however, is the observation of a two-way relationship between NGOs and funders over time, or more generally between the global and the local. Despite the influence of global discourses in shaping organizational behavior, NGOs are sometimes able to challenge and adapt certain influences to suit their own needs and circumstances. Sustainable development discourse, for example, has provided a vocabulary for both AKRSP (I) and Sadguru to articulate and legitimize their own work, without necessitating changes in their activities. Moreover, local experiences can occasionally spark wider structural change. The field level experiences of the case NGOs have been transmitted to national and international levels, sometimes through foreign consultants, sometimes through NGO staff who later serve as consultants to other organizations or move on to new jobs, and at other times through the efforts of governments and international funders to spread and replicate NGO experiences. In this way, through everyday practices and innovation, NGOs can be seen as capable of modifying the conditions in which they operate. More generally, then, this chapter presents a view of NGOs as being constrained by discourses and yet as capable, albeit at the margins, of challenging and changing established practices and policies of development. The chapters which follow are a closer look at these dual processes of constraint and creativity, particularly as they are played out in relationships between NGOs and funders.

4 Interdependence and power: tensions over money and reputation

Money talks. Funds, control over funds, and conditionalities associated with funds are common themes in debates over relations between NGOs and their international funders (e.g. Drabek 1987; Hudock 1999; Hulme and Edwards 1997; Society for Participatory Research in Asia 1991). But while financial interactions are central to NGO-funder relations, an analysis of organizational interactions based primarily on funds misses other crucial forms of resource exchange, particularly of symbolic types of resources such as reputation and status.

A key point to be made in this chapter is that while NGOs depend on funds to maintain and expand their operations, funders also rely on NGOs for information, and to maintain or enhance their own reputations. In other words, NGOs and funders have strongly *inter*-dependent relations – and they are constantly engaged in struggles for control over and access to financial and symbolic kinds of resources. These interdependencies are examined not only by tracing resource flows and exchanges, but also through an analysis of *perceptions* of relationships. I investigate how members of NGOs and funding organizations perceive and talk about their relations with one another, and what sorts of exchanges they view as being important to their relations. I also explore tensions in relationships arising from differences in perceptions and asymmetries in resources.

In the discussion which follows, I use the term "capital" synonymously with "resource." Drawing from the work of French social theorist and anthropologist, Pierre Bourdieu, I distinguish between two forms of capital: (1) economic capital which includes material resources such as money and property, and (2) symbolic capital which includes non-material resources such as prestige, status, authority and reputation (see chapter 1 for details).[1] From this perspective, funds are important but they are one element in a wider array of exchanges. For Bourdieu, the most powerful form of capital is the symbolic form – authority which comes with prestige and status, and which is invested in the "experts" of our society such as doctors, lawmakers, teachers, and even development professionals. From this perspective, international development activity may be conceptualized as occurring in a context where there are struggles between organizations over various kinds of resources, and in which symbolic capital is an important form of power because of its association with expertise and thus with knowledge production.

I begin my investigation by presenting financial resource flows from funders to AKRSP (I) and Sadguru, followed by an examination of resource dependence based on these flows of economic capital. I then enrich this analysis by presenting some statements of funders and NGOs about how they view their relationships with one another. Drawing from these perceptions, I provide an analysis of resource interdependence based on an exchange of both economic and symbolic forms of capital. The data show that, in order better to understand organizational relationships and interdependence, it is necessary to consider not only flows of economic capital, but also flows of symbolic capital and the mechanisms through which these resources are exchanged.

Financial resources

The financial data presented below represent yearly expenditures by AKRSP (I) and Sadguru. For AKRSP (I), data are provided from 1985 onwards, the year in which the NGO commenced operations. While Sadguru began operations in 1974, the financial information available from 1974 to 1985 is not disaggregated by source and is thus of little use for the present analysis. I thus begin with the year 1986 for the case of Sadguru. Since Sadguru was not a recipient of foreign funds until 1987, this truncation does not affect my analysis of foreign funding.[2]

AKRSP (I)

Figure 4.1 shows AKRSP (I)'s expenditure from 1985 to 2000 disaggregated by source. The bands at the base of the bars represent contributions to annual expenses from AKRSP (I)'s endowment, also referred to as its "corpus fund." This corpus fund was originally provided in 1983 by the Aga Khan, the chairman of AKF, and interest earnings and investments from the corpus have provided a steady source of funds. Funds from the endowment are used primarily for operational rather than program expenses, but they are particularly important as backup funds in years of lean external support. Use of the corpus expanded notably during 1991 and 1992, but then returned to pre-1990 levels. The NGO dipped into its endowment during these years in order to offset delays in disbursements by funders. The delays were partly a result of AKRSP (I)'s own doing, as the NGO had been tardy in turning in reports requested by funders. For our present discussion, it is sufficient to note that the corpus fund was able to provide AKRSP (I) with a safety net under conditions of uncertainty, and the availability of the corpus may have contributed to risk-taking behavior. Most NGOs in India do not have endowments.

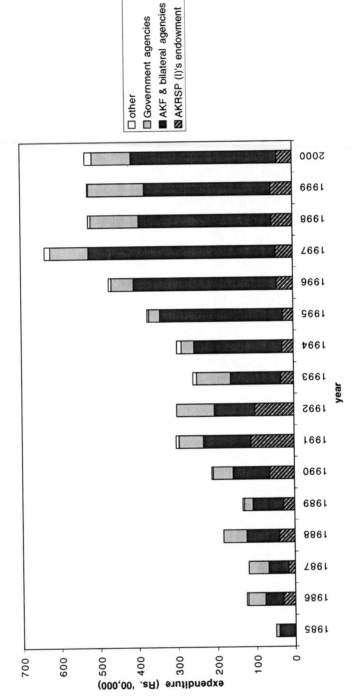

Figure 4.1 AKRSP (I)'s expenditure by funding source, 1985–2000

Sadguru's lack of an endowment, for example, has been a source of considerable anxiety in the NGO, especially given that Sadguru's annual expenditure exceeds that of AKRSP (I) by nearly 50 percent. Sadguru began, in 1996, to create an endowment for itself, seeking support from international and domestic sources.

The largest set of bands in figure 4.1 represent contributions routed through the Geneva-based Aga Khan Foundation. By and large, these funds were secured by the Aga Khan Foundation from bilateral agencies and were then transmitted to AKRSP (I). As such, AKF occupies an intermediary position between donor agencies and AKRSP (I). Most of the funds routed through AKF were provided by the Canadian International Development Agency from 1985 to 1987, the United Kingdom's Department for International Development from 1988 to 1992, an "NGO grant" from the European Commission from 1989 to 1993, and a "bilateral" EC grant from 1994 to 2001 entitled the Community Management of Natural Resources project.

AKRSP (I)'s records until 1994 lumped all of the above grants into the general category "AKF." This categorization is important for it shows that the NGO has had very little direct interaction with bilateral donors, and has depended almost entirely on AKF to secure foreign funds for it and to negotiate with donor agencies. AKF's network of offices around the world enable it to secure and distribute funds. The "developed country" offices of AKF in Canada, the United Kingdom, and the United States secure funds from agencies such as CIDA, the DFID, and the EC, while the "developing country" offices in South Asia, Central Asia, and East Africa distribute these funds to local organizations (such as AKRSP (I)) and provide managerial and technical support (Aga Khan Foundation 1998a). The Geneva office coordinates all of these activities and sets overall strategies. Since 1994, however, there has been increased direct interaction between AKRSP (I) and the EC, which maintains a delegation in New Delhi, and which periodically sends visitors, monitoring missions, and review teams to project sites. Formally, the EC grant is to AKF and not to AKRSP (I) directly; staff of AKF India thus attempt to mediate all communication and reporting between AKRSP (I) and the EC.[3]

Contributions from government sources (federal as well as Gujarat state) are marked by the third set of bands in the graph. These figures are often not disaggregated by government source in AKRSP (I)'s reports, and they can vary considerably on a yearly basis depending on agency disbursement procedures. The years 1994 to 1996 show a decline in the amount of support received by AKRSP (I) from government sources, followed by an increase in subsequent years. While in 1993 government sources accounted for 43 percent of expenditure, this figure had dropped to an average of 10 percent between 1994 to 1996, recovering somewhat to a mean of 22 percent from 1997 to 2000. The downturn coincided with two events in late 1993: the commencement of the bilateral EC grant and a change in the Chief Executive Officer of AKRSP (I). The EC grant alone provided more funds than AKRSP (I) could handle at the time, thus reducing the NGO's need to seek alternate funds. In addition, the new CEO had made it clear to AKRSP (I)'s Board that government interaction, while important, was not one of his key strengths. Although he found it necessary to maintain and develop government relations, his mandate (as provided by AKRSP (I)'s Board) and skills emphasized improving the NGO's performance in project implementation, reducing personnel turnover, and strengthening the equity and gender aspects of the NGO's work.

Funds from government sources began to increase from 1996 onwards, however, as a result of a number of factors such as improved collaboration on water resource projects with Gujarat's Irrigation Department and the Gujarat Water Supply and Sewerage Board, continued support from a state enterprise known as the Gujarat Agro-Industries Corporation for biogas and agricultural projects, and the launching of a nation-wide watershed development program of the Ministry of Rural Development. AKRSP (I) was designated as a "Programme Implementing Agency" under this watershed program, which is an effort to scale-up the watershed development efforts of organizations like AKRSP (I) and Sadguru; AKRSP (I)'s former CEO contributed to the drafting of guidelines for the program. Despite the improved government support, public agencies are nonetheless known to be notoriously slow and inconsistent from year to year. For example, while a substantial increase in government support from 1996 to 1997 assisted AKRSP (I) in fully achieving its expenditure targets for both years, a failure of promised funds to materialize contributed to a shortfall in target achievement in the year 2000 (AKRSP (I) 2001: 6).

Finally, the top band in figure 4.1 represent the contributions of other organizations such as the Ford Foundation and the Canada-based Partners in Rural Development. In relation to overall expenditure, the contribution from these sources is very small. The Ford Foundation, for example, provided US $31,000 for Joint Forest Management activities from 1991–95 and US $115,000 for water resource development activities from 1992–96, equivalent to about 2 percent of AKRSP (I)'s total expenditure during that period.

Sadguru

Figure 4.2 depicts total expenditure by Sadguru from fiscal year (FY) 1986 until FY 2000, while figure 4.3 provides a breakdown of Sadguru's *foreign* funding sources for the same period. Sadguru's funding differs from that of AKRSP (I) in a number of important ways: (a) Sadguru has a substantially larger annual expenditure; (b) it has a more diverse foreign funding pool; (c) it receives much greater contributions from government sources; and, (d) it has only recently begun to form an endowment.

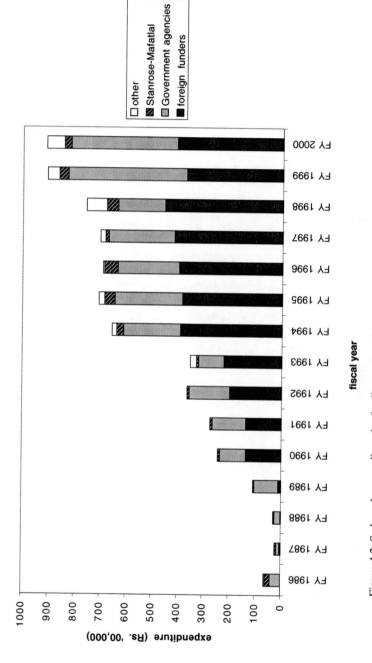

Figure 4.2 Sadguru's expenditure by funding source, fiscal years 1986–2000

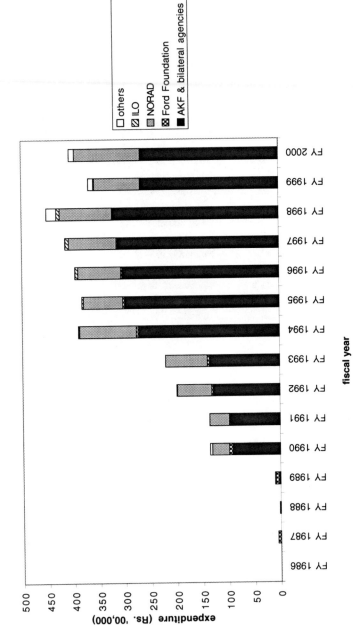

Figure 4.3 Sadguru's expenditure by foreign funding source, fiscal years 1986–2000

Sadguru was initially supported by funds from a corporate entity known as the Stanrose-Mafatlal Group of Companies. The NGO continues to receive annual allocations from Stanrose for its programs, and those allocations have increased from an average of Rs. 0.9 million per year in the early 1990s to a mean of Rs. 3.5 million (approximately US$ 88,000) from FY 1995 to FY 2000. In FY 1996 and 1997, Sadguru also received funds from Stanrose and other domestic sources for an endowment which, by March 1999, amounted to approximately Rs. 20 million (about US$ 500, 000) and is targeted to quintuple by 2006 (Sadguru 2001: 62).

In 1988, the Ford Foundation became Sadguru's first foreign funder, sparking off a period of rapid growth for the NGO. The Ford Foundation introduced Sadguru to AKF, which began funding Sadguru in 1988, and which helped link the NGO with NORAD. These linkages, established over a brief span of three years in the late 1980s, remain critical to Sadguru's present foreign funding network. As is the case with AKRSP (I), Sadguru's single largest supporter since 1994 has been the Aga Khan Foundation, which has served as Sadguru's intermediary in securing the large bilateral grant from the European Commission. This grant has amounted to 38 percent of Sadguru's total expenditure from 1994 to 2000, as compared to AKRSP (I)'s 72 percent. Sadguru's other key foreign supporter is the Norwegian Agency for Development Cooperation, which has consistently provided about 14 percent of the NGO's annual expenditure since 1990. Since the mid-1990s, the International Labour Organisation has been added to this network. While the financial contributions of the ILO have been small, ILO's high-profile international status makes it an important link to other potential funders.

One of the most striking features of Sadguru's annual expenditure is the very large contribution from government sources. The NGO's linkages with government agencies can be traced back to the late 1970s when it commenced building lift-irrigation systems and began a rural employment program. The capital costs for its first several irrigation schemes were borne by the Ministry of Rural Development. Throughout the 1990s, government funding to Sadguru kept pace with increases in foreign funds and accounted for over one-third of the NGO's annual spending over the decade. This figure amounted to Rs. 41 million (approximately US$ 1 million) in the fiscal year 2000 alone.

"Other" funds shown in figure 4.2 include revolving funds and donations from individuals or organizations. These funds are relatively small, with the exception of contributions from a series of Bombay-based trusts since 1997, which have supported Sadguru's projects as well as its efforts to build an endowment. As shown above, however, most of Sadguru's funds have been obtained from AKF, the EC, NORAD, and a mix of government sources. This chapter focuses primarily on foreign sources, especially given the importance of funds from AKF and the EC to both NGOs.

Resource dependence

A look at funds received by AKRSP (I) and Sadguru raises questions on the possible dependence of these NGOs on one or two key funders. This section examines the dependence of the case study NGOs on their funders for money, with dependence being characterized as a result of large asymmetries in resources. In a later section in this chapter, however, I examine how the NGOs attempt to manage resource asymmetries through the creation of *inter*-dependencies. Interdependence involves an exchange of resources rather than a flow that is predominantly in one direction:

> In social systems and social interactions, interdependence exists whenever one actor does not entirely control all of the conditions necessary for the achievement of an action or for obtaining the outcome desired from the action.
> ... [O]rganizations, to solve their problems of uncertainty regarding outcomes, are likely to be led to increase their interdependence with respect to behavior, that is, to interstructure their behavior in ways predictable for each. (Pfeffer and Salancik 1978: 40–43)

First, I discuss the relationship between the case NGOs and their key funders solely in terms of financial exchanges (or in other words, economic capital). I then move beyond this funding-dominated assessment to examine other types of resources and their importance in leveraging "power". I also provide examples of how organizations interstructure their behavior, where "interstructure" refers to strategies they use to increase coordination or mutual control over each others' activities.

Dependence on money

For AKRSP (I) and Sadguru, the most obvious crucial resource obtained from other organizations is money. Pfeffer and Salancik (1978: 45–51) outline three critical factors for determining the dependence of one organization on another, which I utilize here for examining financial resources: (1) Resource importance – the extent to which a resource is needed by an organization for survival and operation; (2) Discretion over resource allocation and use – the extent to which an organization can control how the resource received from another organization is allocated and used; and, (3) Concentration of resource control – the extent to which alternative sources of a resource are available and accessible.

While grants from funding organizations are essential to the daily operations of both AKRSP (I) and Sadguru, it is not clear from figures 4.1 to 4.3 the extent to which the NGOs must rely on a small number of funders, or how much discretion is permitted to the NGOs in using these funds. For the case of AKRSP (I), it is evident that the organization has relied on the AKF network for most of its past and present funding. Two key factors make it difficult for AKRSP (I) to reduce the role of AKF and to seek out alternatives. First, AKRSP (I)'s relationships with bilateral agencies in Canada, the United Kingdom, and Europe have been mediated by various members of the AKF network, which has corresponded with these donors, arranged visits, written grant proposals, publicized the NGO, and assisted in the preparation of reports. Thus, AKRSP (I) is not directly linked with bilateral donors, and does not have extensive experience in identifying and negotiating with international donors.

A second factor which makes it difficult for AKRSP (I) to reduce the role of AKF concerns the NGO's legal status as a non-profit "company." Under Indian law, a company's board of directors are appointed by the organization's members, which in most cases are shareholders or owners. As a non-profit company, AKRSP (I) has no shareholders, and thus its members are its original founders or promoters: the Aga Khan Foundation (Geneva), the Aga Khan Education Service (Bombay), the Aga Khan Health Service (Bombay), and Platinum Jubilee Investment Ltd. (Bombay). In other words, while AKRSP (I) is constituted as a legally distinct entity from the Aga Khan Foundation network and other members of the wider Aga Khan Development Network, its directorship is influenced by the AKDN.

On the other hand, AKRSP (I) does retain a large degree of autonomy in its use of funds. While AKF plays a very important role in grantwriting, actual proposals have been developed through extensive interactions among staff of AKF Geneva, AKF India, and AKRSP (I). For example, the Community Management of Natural Resources proposal funded by the EC was built upon goals and plans set by AKRSP (I) staff. AKF's primary role lay in packaging the proposal and in interacting with donor agencies. Once the proposal was accepted by the European Commission, however, no changes could be made without EC approval (Commission of the European Communities 1993a). While this condition is a constraint on fund discretion, the fact remains that the workplans were developed by the NGO.

Sadguru's funding context, as already noted above, differs considerably from that of AKRSP (I). It has a more diverse funding pool and is more experienced in dealing directly with foreign funders. Given the NGO's experiences with NORAD, the ILO, and the Ford Foundation, it is conceivable that upon the completion of the EC grant, Sadguru may be able to set up a direct relationship with the EC or another bilateral donor for continued funding without a need for AKF intervention. Unlike AKRSP (I), which has witnessed a decline in funding from other sources after the commencement of the EC grant in 1994, Sadguru has experienced an increase in funds from government sources, NORAD, and the Stanrose Group of Companies. In addition, Sadguru's directors have been exploring other funding options (e.g. with the ILO), and have become part of an international collaboration between six NGOs and academic institutes in India, Ethiopia, and Norway (Sadguru 1997a). Since 1997, Sadguru has also succeeded in acquiring additional domestic sources of funding, most notably from the Sir Dorabji Tata Trust, the Sir Ratan Tata Trust, and the Tulsi Trust.

Rather than being legally set up as a company, Sadguru, like many NGOs in India, is registered as a "society" and as a "public charitable trust." Both of Sadguru's directors are also two of its nine Trustees. Organizational policies are generally set by the two directors, with only formal approval granted by the Board of Trustees. Unlike the case of AKRSP (I), where the NGO's key funder has direct access to policy setting, Sadguru is more or less governed by its two top officers, the Director and Co-Director. In an effort to coordinate the demands of its funders, however, Sadguru has also set up an Advisory Council consisting of representatives from each of its major funders. This council, which had 35 members in 2001, was comprised largely of top development officials of the Government of India and the state Governments of Gujarat and Rajastan, key district level officials, as well as representatives from the EC Delegation in India, AKF India, NORAD, and the Sir Dorabji and Sir Ratan Tata Trusts. While the Advisory Council has no direct decision-making power, it serves to coordinate funder demands and to cement alliances with key funders, thereby reducing uncertainties in the behavior of important external actors. It also provides funders with an opportunity to review Sadguru's work and provide guidance, while also facilitating increased transparency in Sadguru's activities. Sadguru's establishment of an Advisory Council is an example of a way in which organizations can use councils or boards as vehicles for coopting or partially absorbing key external organizations with which they are interdependent. In this sense, councils and boards are important mechanisms through which organizations "interstructure" their behavior with other organizations which control needed resources (Pfeffer 1987: 42).

Another key interstructuring mechanism involves reporting requirements. Funders sometimes specify the types of information and reports they want from NGOs, which can then be fed directly into their own budgeting and reporting cycles. For example, the standard reporting format mandated by AKF and the EC lists the activities or "line items" for which funding is allocated to the NGO. These categories cannot be changed without approval of the EC. The reporting format also specifies how these activities are to be measured and requires details of "progress" both in terms of actual physical output (e.g. numbers of lift irrigation schemes under construction or recently completed, hectares of wasteland under treatment, etc.) and the financial resources spent on those activities. These reports of "financial and physical progress" are prepared on a quarterly basis by each NGO, thus enabling progress towards targets to be regularly monitored.

Based on the foregoing analysis, AKRSP (I) appears as being highly dependent on AKF for financial resources, while Sadguru is somewhat less dependent on AKF. Although both organizations have considerable influence over how funds are used, the availability of funds remains critical to their daily activities. And while Sadguru has significant alternatives to AKF funds, AKRSP (I) does not. Moreover, AKF does not appear dependent on disbursing money to Sadguru and AKRSP (I) since its allocation to these NGOs (approximately US $2 million per year) is a small figure relative to its total annual disbursement of about US $50 million (Aga Khan Foundation 1996b; 1997; 1998a).

This picture changes somewhat, however, if one focuses only on AKF's experience in what it calls "rural development." AKRSP (I) and Sadguru make up 3 of the AKF network's 10 rural development projects worldwide (with the others in Pakistan, Bangladesh, Tajikistan, and Kenya), and comprise 3 of 4 rural development projects in India. The other project in India is an effort to build the capacity of NGOs involved in watershed development, and draws directly from the experiences of AKRSP (I) and Sadguru. In other words, AKF's rural development experience and reputation in India is based almost entirely upon the work of these two NGOs. In addition, AKF's rural development projects in Kenya and Tajikistan are comparatively new and have been built upon the experiences of AKF supported projects in South Asia, especially AKRSP (I) and a similar organization in Pakistan.

The possibility that AKF may rely on AKRSP (I) and Sadguru for its reputation in India, and more broadly for rural development models and experiences to be employed elsewhere, points to the importance of expanding this analysis of resource dependence beyond those resources that are strictly financial or easily quantified. The following section explores interdependence over other, less measurable, kinds of resources.

Perceptions of relationships

In order to investigate non-financial forms of resource exchange between the case NGOs and their funders, I draw upon observations of organizational interactions and resource transfers, as well as organizational members' perceptions of interactions. In particular, I look at tensions resulting from demands and expectations of one organization on another. The focus of this analysis is on the relationships of the two NGOs with the AKF network. A discussion of relationships with the EC, NORAD and the Ford Foundation is also provided for comparative purposes.

At the most basic level, relations between NGOs and funders are characterized by NGO members as that of "funder" and "recipient," focusing on a one-way exchange of financial resources and the NGOs' dependence on funds. This funder–recipient relationship is not passively accepted by NGO leaders. For example, a former Program Executive with AKRSP (I) candidly asserted that "in a typical funder–fundee relation, the funder can threaten [the NGO]: 'I'll cut off the money'. Nine out of ten funders are like this. They point fingers when things go wrong."[4] Sadguru's Director was similarly critical of relationships with funders, contending that "Donors harp on 1 bad thing of 99 good" and that "You're on [the] receiving end – so you're more likely to be misunderstood than understood."[5]

Relations with funders are often described by NGO members in terms of financial dependence. Resistance to funders, at least verbally, is common among middle and upper management in both NGOs. Sadguru's Director is particularly vocal in criticizing funders for failing to understand the context and work of NGOs. Yet there is also a matter-of-fact air to this resistance, as though it is an expected and perhaps natural part of the relationship. This antagonism towards funders is, however, also contrasted by statements encouraging cooperation and implying interdependence, such as this one by AKRSP (I)'s former Chief Executive:

You always make some compromises for donors. It's not a totally different agenda [that donors have], but a different emphasis . . . But why resent it? They're giving the money! It's up to you to see where there is a common agenda. At the root of the problem is [an] assumption [by NGOs] that others shouldn't have an agenda. This is verging on arrogance.[6]

This statement suggests that the relationships between NGOs and funders do not simply consist of funding, but that there may be a common agenda, and that an antagonistic funder-recipient characterization is somehow deficient. A closer examination of NGO-funder relationships uncovers complex interdependencies characterized both by complementarity and tension. I begin below with a discussion on NGO relations with AKF, followed by an examination of relationships with the EC, and finally with NORAD and the Ford Foundation.

Relations between the NGOs and AKF

The relations of Sadguru and AKRSP (I) with AKF revolve around two key issues: (1) monitoring and reporting procedures and conditions, and (2) the nature of AKF's long-term involvement with each of the NGOs. AKF maintains very stringent monitoring procedures as a condition of funding. These reporting requirements include quarterly reports giving details on progress in terms of targets, as well as "monitoring missions" and reviews arranged by AKF and the EC. For AKF, its involvement in monitoring is linked to broader strategic goals that include getting AKRSP (I) and Sadguru to look at their visions for the future and to "force the agenda a bit" without which there is "a tendency to sit on one's laurels."[7]

Sadguru's Director, while very willing to satisfy AKF's information requests, prefers minimal monitoring requirements and minimal interference from funders. He describes relationships between his NGO and funders including

AKF as "excellent and very fruitful" and hesitates to characterize these relationships as also consisting of "tensions" concerning broader issues of strategy.[8] In doing so, he attempts to draw a clear boundary between Sadguru and AKF – for him the relationship should be centered on funds, and not on programmatic or strategy issues.

This boundary between funding and strategy issues is much less distinct in the case of AKRSP (I), where AKF has played a central role in founding AKRSP (I), and has since been instrumental to funding the NGO as well as in influencing organizational policy through its membership on AKRSP (I)'s board. This close relationship is not free of tension, causing AKRSP (I)'s CEO to note that "indirectly, pressures on how we should operate come from them. [They]...emphasize we're part of the AKDN and should network with them. Occasionally they indicate they're our real bosses...."[9] Yet, AKRSP (I) is far from being controlled by AKF, and its managers are cognizant of the crucial role that AKF has played as a middleman in securing international funding and in supporting and developing programs. Most importantly, AKF has served as a buffer between large bilateral agencies and NGOs, pushing NGOs to improve their monitoring and delivery systems on one hand, while at the same time defending them against donor criticism.

Ironically, while there is considerable tension between AKRSP (I) and AKF over issues of ownership, this is also a key source of security for AKRSP (I). The NGO is able partly to resist pressures from AKF because of an *interdependence* between the two organizations – the relative success of AKRSP (I) in rural Gujarat, combined with its position as AKF's primary rural development project in India, and AKF's history of investment in AKRSP (I) (in financial and programmatic terms), give AKRSP (I) a status that increases its power in relation to AKF. AKF's reputation is thus linked to that of AKRSP (I) because of the success of AKRSP (I)'s projects in Gujarat. This unique relationship between AKRSP (I) and AKF places the NGO in a financial situation that is very secure.[10]

It is noteworthy that there are conflicting views on the relationship between AKRSP (I) and AKF, which can be seen as both cooperative and antagonistic. On one side, there is a clear recognition of interdependence. As a Programs Manager at AKF's offices in London put it, "AKF is nothing without the programs it supports. Our credibility with donors is dependent on this. AKF India's reputation is based on Sadguru and AKRSP..."[11] Yet, as AKF's Program Officer at its headquarters in Geneva explained, this interdependence also involves tensions over autonomy:

AKRSP is always pushing for its own independent decision making. They think, "Why is AKF telling us what to do? They should give us the money and trust us." Whereas AKF has its own accountability. It has much intellectual input in AKRSP. The relative value of [those] intellectual inputs diminish over time, and so AKRSP's questioning of AKF increases over time.[12]

The interdependence between AKF and the NGOs is also directly influenced by AKF's reputation with donors. It is important for AKF to be able to portray AKRSP (I) and Sadguru as "successful" for this enhances AKF's own reputation. AKF is strongly interested in influencing the behavior and direction of both NGOs in order to prevent them, as one senior manager put it, from "becoming ossified."[13] AKF has been instrumental in introducing new activities and techniques to both AKRSP (I) and Sadguru through technical assistance and consultants (e.g. biogas energy systems, soil and water conservation practices, and participatory rural appraisal). AKF is accountable to donors such as the EC and is therefore interested in making certain that AKRSP (I) and Sadguru are changing in a direction that enables them to continue to be perceived and portrayed as successes. If either AKRSP (I) or Sadguru were to be perceived by donors as having become ossified, then AKF's own reputation for supporting innovative and successful projects would be at risk.

AKF's relation with AKRSP (I) is further complicated by their membership in the same "family." The tensions and dynamics between AKF Geneva, AKF India, and AKRSP (I) are akin to a family conflict in which different members attempt to find ways of influencing one another. AKF India in particular is caught between its duty to the family "patriarch" in Geneva and its empathy for the independence-seeking "teenager" in Gujarat. This metaphor was explained by AKF's Program Officer in Geneva:

There is a strong two-way dependency which we often forget... It's like a teenage child... now in adolescence. [AKRSP is] trying to break free but AKF won't let go. It could break free, but I suspect it wouldn't develop into what it could.[14]

The perspective of the teenager was highlighted by AKRSP (I)'s Chief Executive:

AKF's experience is so closely tied to AKRSP that they're unwilling to let go of us on new projects. They still hang on. The problem is attitudinal... I'm fine with being part of the family if there are structures for relating... [W]e'd like to be treated more as part of the family rather than as the renegade son.[15]

AKF's efforts to control AKRSP (I)'s behavior, and the interest of AKRSP (I)'s Chief Executive Officer in being treated as "part of the family" are both efforts (or wishes) to interstructure organizational behavior so as to reduce uncertainties in their interactions. While AKF staff may describe their efforts to chart AKRSP (I)'s future as being good for the NGO, these efforts are also a way of ensuring the continuation of their relationship with AKRSP (I) and hence their credibility with donors such as the EC.

The efforts of AKF and AKRSP (I) to influence each other give rise to inter-organizational tensions. As shown above, some of these tensions revolve around reporting requirements while others are related to long-term change and ownership. These tensions are an integral characteristic of organizational interdependence, since they arise from efforts of one organization to reduce the uncertainties associated with the behavior of another organization.

Relations with the European Commission

The relationships of AKRSP (I) and Sadguru with the EC differ significantly from their linkages with AKF. Interactions with the EC have been very contractual. The formal agreement for the Community Management of Natural Resources project was between the EC and AKF, with the two NGOs being regarded as implementors. The central concern for the EC, according to the head of its delegation in India, was to find "implementing agencies" that could "work efficiently and effectively" on EC-supported projects.[16] The positive implementation record of Sadguru and AKRSP (I) also represented an important publicity opportunity for the EC in terms of improving its visibility in the international development community. Pressures from the EC's headquarters in Brussels were felt directly by the EC's key project officer in New Delhi who remarked that "Brussels is very political: visibility in United Nations and internationally is key for them."[17]

The bottom line, as AKF's program officer in Geneva described it, came "down to spending the money" given that this "was the largest grant the EC had made to NGOs."[18] The outlook and impact of the EC was described by a senior member of AKF Geneva as follows:

They [the EC] want a program that looks good, is successful in the way it's predicted to be successful, is auditable. If you have a very successful program that's not auditable, it will be called a failure. [An auditable program is capable of] meeting targets that are quantifiable and can spend the budget.[19]

This observation is important, for it points to pressures faced by AKF Geneva, as well as by other members of AKF. As an intermediary organization, AKF is accountable to donors like the EC. Its own success is gauged by the success of the NGOs and it is thus in AKF's best interest to influence NGO behavior in terms acceptable to donors.

The EC's efforts to secure an international reputation had a downside with respect to relationships with NGOs. A key member of AKRSP (I) observed that it "became a typical grantor–grantee relation" in which AKRSP (I) could not initiate new activities or seek funds from other sources without EC approval. The EC's appraisal mission, he argued, wanted exclusive publicity rights to the AKRSP (I) program in order to avoid situations where "other funding for a different program could overshadow the EC's work!"[20]

At the same time, however, members of the EC delegation in New Delhi tried to be sensitive to the needs and concerns of AKF and the NGOs. Most of the

EC's projects with NGOs were overseen by two staff in New Delhi. One of these staff, a resident consultant, was particularly aware of NGO concerns about a "huge burden of procedures and formats" that the EC requires for monitoring and reporting purposes and the fact that "NGOs expect a little trust from us but don't see it."[21] But the EC's accountability to its member nations, he argued, necessitated a complex and unavoidable system of accounts. Yet this accountability, as his colleague project officer noted, was imbalanced: "We're asking for all these reports with all sorts of data on time, and yet... we're still disbursing funds late. So how can we expect [AKF and the NGOs] to respect us?"[22]

Despite these expressions of concern by members of the EC delegation in India, their interactions with the NGOs and with AKF were dominated by bureaucratic processes and demands (e.g. accounting systems, reporting and fund disbursement routines) which minimized the attention they could allocate to issues other than funding and reporting. In exchange for funds from the EC, the two NGOs were responsible for supplying rural services and infrastructure that could provide the EC with good visibility in the international development community. In brief, this is a highly contractual relationship that is monitored through a complex system of accounts which enables the work of NGOs to be interpreted by the EC in precise and predictable ways.

Relations with other international funders: NORAD and the Ford Foundation

Other international funders can be distinguished from AKF and the EC in a number of ways. For Sadguru, international funders are differentiated primarily by their monitoring and reporting requirements. For AKRSP (I), international funders are differentiated by the various kinds of non-financial support they provide to the NGO. These perspectives mark an important difference between Sadguru and AKRSP (I), for they point to differences in perceptions of what they consider appropriate or desirable in their relationships with funders. Sadguru's leadership desires minimal interaction with funders, preferring to be left alone to carry out its work undisturbed. AKRSP (I)'s leadership, on the other hand, expects greater interaction with funders in order to jointly resolve problems.

Sadguru's Director views his relationship with Norwegian Agency for Development Cooperation as nearly ideal, particularly in comparison with AKF and the EC. Most importantly, he notes that NORAD maintains a "very minimal, very simple relation" that requires the submission of only two short reports per year, measuring two to three pages each.[23] This reporting requirement stands in stark contrast to the quarterly reports on physical and financial progress required by AKF and the EC, in addition to an annual narrative report and multiple field visits. To be sure, NORAD did engage in an intensive review of Sadguru prior to first funding it in 1990, and again during a mid-project evaluation in 1993. But since then, the agency has adopted a relatively hands-off policy based on trust and an established historical record. NORAD's advisor on development projects in India noted that while his role includes "monitoring activities and giving suggestions for improvement" to Sadguru, he did not see it as his mandate to look at day-to-day work in the NGO.[24] As such, NORAD's relationship with Sadguru is similar to the EC's in that it centers on the delivery of particular services, but it differs in the sense that NORAD's reporting requirements are much less demanding than those of the EC. Benefits from the relationship are mutual, with NORAD publicizing Sadguru as one of its best projects, and Sadguru receiving funds with few conditions and requirements.

The Ford Foundation, which funds both Sadguru and AKRSP (I), is perceived quite differently by members of both NGOs. Sadguru's Director frames his relationship with Ford largely in terms of reporting requirements, noting that the Ford Foundation is the most liberal of his funders since it requires a report only once a year in any format. In comparing the Ford Foundation to AKF and NORAD, he observes that Ford doesn't "impose any monitoring system, whereas AKF has all sorts of formats and systems... NORAD has a half-yearly report and a simple format."[25]

Key managers in AKRSP (I), however, see the Ford Foundation from a very different perspective. Ford's interactions with both AKRSP (I) and Sadguru have largely centered on getting the NGOs to participate in state- and national-level dialogue concerning forest and irrigation policy. As a result, financial support to the NGOs has been minimal, directed primarily towards NGO state collaborations in Joint Forest Management and Participatory Irrigation Management. For AKRSP (I)'s Chief Executive, the Ford Foundation has been genuinely interested in and supportive of the NGO's work, especially in terms of forest policy dialogue in Gujarat state. He observed that the relationship is "not about funding so much" as it is about efforts to "try to influence government."[26] But the Ford Foundation's lack of direct involvement in NGO activities is not viewed positively by all members of the NGOs. In the eyes of one veteran manager in AKRSP (I), the Ford Foundation has demonstrated very little commitment to or interest in his organization. Providing an annual report to the Foundation and meeting with its program officer half-way through the year, he contends, is insufficient for making progress on difficult development and policy problems. In comparing Ford's approach to that of AKF, he explained that:

We gave them [Ford Foundation] a proposal and they gave us funds because our proposal fell into their purview. But with AKF, we sat with them and developed [a] proposal together and then looked for funds. Ford Foundation can remove funds if it has problems [with us] but AKF can't do this. And AKF looks for mutually agreeable arrangements.[27]

From the perspective of the Ford Foundation's program officers in New Delhi, however, their primary role is to get NGOs involved in policy dialogue with state agencies. As a result, they appear to be less interested in project implementation and funding than they are in networking. Ford's program officer for social forestry explained that funding to the NGOs was provided primarily to get them "involved in the JFM [Joint Forest Management] network and to maintain a relationship with them," especially since AKRSP (I)'s former chief executive had played a very important role in establishing a state level working group on JFM policy. Maintaining AKRSP (I)'s involvement was seen as being crucial for advancing Ford's own interest in policy change, thus leading the same program officer comment that "We probably need them more than they need us."[28] By the same token, the Ford Foundation has also provided minimal support to Sadguru to get it involved in JFM. Although Sadguru's experience has centered on irrigation rather than forest policy issues, Ford staff saw Sadguru's solid reputation in Gujarat as a potential asset if they could get the NGO more directly involved in JFM.

The Ford Foundation's work in irrigation has also been similarly focused on policy and capacity building issues rather than on physical infrastructure. The Foundation's program officer for water resources emphasized that the "Ford Foundation's total grants to irrigation have been less than the cost of building one minor irrigation scheme! From the very beginning, Ford's money in irrigation has been for capacity building and 'software' development."[29] This approach is markedly different from that of the EC which places greater emphasis on the building of tangible physical assets that can be more easily measured and reported upon.

While the Ford Foundation has very flexible reporting requirements and provides relatively small grants (in comparison to bilateral donors), it is nevertheless very particular about what it funds. As noted above, the Ford Foundation especially supports "capacity building" within NGOs and interaction between NGOs and government agencies (e.g. for Joint Forest Management and Participatory Irrigation Management). In contrast to NORAD which has chosen to provide overall organizational support to Sadguru, the Ford Foundation has extended funds to AKRSP (I) and Sadguru for specific activities only. This approach is also different from that of the EC, which is focused on efficient fund disbursement to NGOs and a desire for high international visibility. Interestingly, Ford is similar to AKF in that both organizations perceive their roles as extending beyond fund provision to include capacity building, strategic thinking, and networking with other organizations, although the former adopts a fairly "hands-off" approach while the latter is more directly involved in building and monitoring organizational capacity.

Analysis: interdependence and capital exchange

I now draw upon the above discussion – on relations of AKRSP (I) and Sadguru with AKF, with the EC, and with the Ford Foundation and NORAD – to provide a broad analysis of the interactions between AKRSP (I), Sadguru and their international funders. This chapter began with a look at financial dependence of NGOs on their funders. I suggested at that point that there are other, non-financial, resources being exchanged between NGOs and funders. Here I discuss this other form of capital exchange in greater detail.

In examining resource or capital flows I conceptualize resources, in simple terms, as organizational inputs and outputs (see figure 4.4). Funds are clearly an important *input* to the NGOs, particularly as both AKRSP (I) and Sadguru rely heavily upon external funding for their activities. Other less easily quantified inputs may include technical advice from AKF or the Ford Foundation (provided directly by funder staff or indirectly through consultants), information on the funding environment, and contacts with other members of the international development community or with various government officials.

The *outputs* generated by NGOs refer to the goods and services that they produce. There is some amount of measurable infrastructure and services that the case NGOs produce as outputs, which can be accounted for in terms of rupees spent, quantity of infrastructure provided, and numbers of cooperative societies or village organizations created. The consequences of these outputs – their *outcomes* – are harder to measure (Levy, Meltsner, and Wildavsky 1974: 4–8). For example, it is difficult to measure the social and environmental impacts of NGO activities, the level of community organization, and the "development" of a community as a whole. These outcomes (along with the outputs that generated them) are communicated to funders in the form of reports, impact studies, and evaluations. This information serves as an input to funders. Organizations like AKF seek funds from bilateral agencies such as the EC, DFID, or CIDA using the information provided by NGOs to validate and document their work (i.e. physical infrastructure projects and studies of various types). Bilateral agencies are responsible for justifying project selections to their governments, and thus they also rely on information from organizations they fund.

For the information provided by NGOs to be useful in generating funds, it must demonstrate that the funded activities have been "successful." But the measurement of success is often ambiguous and is complicated by the fact that individual decision makers "often seem to be able to reinterpret their objectives or the outcomes in such a way as to make themselves successful even when the shortfall seems quite large" (Levitt and March 1988: 325). One tool used by funders to reduce ambiguity in the measurement of success is the standardization of reporting formats. As discussed above, AKRSP (I) and Sadguru submit quarterly "physical and financial progress reports" to AKF India, which in turn consolidates the reports and forwards them to the EC. These reports provide details, based on pre-established line items, of the amounts of funds spent during the quarter and the amount of physical activity undertaken (e.g. numbers of checkdams built or under construction, numbers of hectares of land treated, etc.). The NGOs are not permitted to modify the line items on this form without

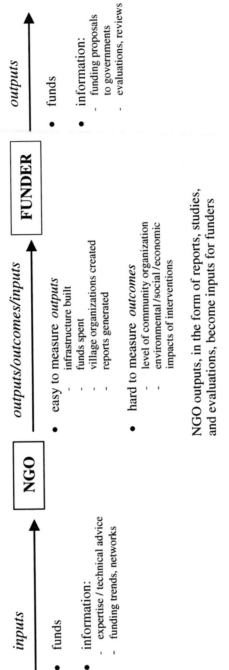

inputs

outputs/outcomes/inputs

outputs

NGO

FUNDER

- funds

- information:
  - expertise / technical advice
  - funding trends, networks

- easy to measure *outputs*
  - infrastructure built
  - funds spent
  - village organizations created
  - reports generated

- hard to measure *outcomes*
  - level of community organization
  - environmental / social / economic impacts of interventions

- funds

- information:
  - funding proposals to governments
  - evaluations, reviews

NGO outputs, in the form of reports, studies, and evaluations, become inputs for funders

Figure 4.4 Organizational inputs, outputs, and outcomes

the consent of the EC. The mid-year and end-year quarterly reports are supplemented with a "narrative report" which is essentially a narration, with some anecdotes, of the physical and financial reports. As such, these reports are little more than accounting documents which are designed to conform to the budget cycles of funders. Information is also collected in numerous other ways, but the physical and financial reports are the most closely examined and regularly collected type of information. For present purposes, I wish only to emphasize that information is an essential input to funders and is thus structured in a way so as to reduce uncertainty in its usefulness to them. This is not a new finding for, as Tendler (1975) has shown in her study of the United States Agency for International Development, donor agencies are capable not only of structuring information but also of "manufacturing" the project applications themselves. In doing so, the donor agency "lessens the high degree of uncertainty of the environment from which it must get its inputs, assuring a more reliable source of supply" (Tendler 1975: 103).

A central point to be made here is that the success of a grantee enables its funder to take credit for that success, and to build a reputation for finding and supporting projects that are good investments. Thus, a key resource which funders need for their continued operation is a good *reputation*, or more specifically, the *status* or *prestige* associated with that reputation. The information is valued for the reputation which it confers, but is not necessarily important in itself.

I use the term reputation not only to refer to general perceptions of an organization's standing and credibility, but also to the power derived from this standing. It is thus reputation, rather than information, that is a key resource needed by funders. The presentation of information in "successful" terms transforms that information into reputation and thus into a form of power. This link between information and reputation shall henceforth be denoted as "information/reputation".[30]

Sadguru and AKRSP (I) are among the largest and most visible organizations (in terms of budgets, government interaction, and international recognition) involved in rural development in Gujarat (and possibly in India), and are able to leverage their reputations for funds. Both NGOs are regarded by their bilateral funders (i.e. the EC and NORAD) as being among their best projects. Although funds to NGOs do not comprise a large part of bilateral disbursements, NGOs nonetheless play an important role in *legitimizing* the activities of bilateral funders by giving them greater visibility and a reputation for supporting innovative and grassroots activities. As such, NGOs have become important sources of symbolic capital for bilateral funders.

The relations between NGOs and funders in terms of flows of information/reputation and funds is diagramed in figure 4.5. In this diagram, I draw a distinction between two main types of funding organizations: (1) Primary

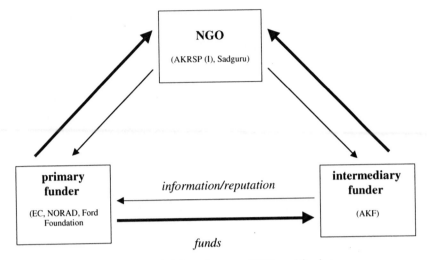

Figure 4.5 Basic capital flows between NGOs and funders

funders, which include bilateral "donors" such as the EC and NORAD as well as organizations with their own endowments such as the Ford Foundation, and (2) Intermediary organizations such as AKF which have limited funds of their own for development activities and turn to other organizations (usually bilateral donors) for funds to transfer to NGOs. As such, an intermediary organization is often directly accountable to a primary funder. In terms of international funding sources, AKRSP (I) is linked primarily to an intermediary funder (the AKF network), whereas Sadguru is linked directly to both an intermediary funder (AKF) and to a primary funder (NORAD). Both AKRSP (I) and Sadguru are also linked directly to the Ford Foundation, although funds play a relatively small role in this link.

Two flows of capital are central to figure 4.5: flows of funds (economic capital) from funders and flows of information/reputation (symbolic capital) from NGOs. Funds are not simply *transferred* to NGOs, but are *exchanged* for information/reputation. These forms of capital are thus inter-convertible: NGOs convert funds into information/reputation, and funders convert information/reputation into funds. As an intermediary, AKF plays a dual conversion role: it uses its own reputation (which is built upon the reputations of and information from NGOs) to secure funds from bilateral agencies, and it also uses the money which it obtains from donors to acquire information (and thus reputation) from NGOs. The survival of an intermediary organization depends on its ability to perform this dual conversion and on its ability to market its value-added to this conversion process. Thus, for example, AKF (especially its northern country units) markets itself to donors in terms of its track-record for managing large funds, securing timely reports from NGOs, and in identifying and supporting successful and innovative projects. At the same time, AKF (especially its southern country units) markets itself to NGOs in terms of its connections with funders, its knowledge of the jargon used by donors, and its awareness of changes in funding trends.

From my initial analysis of the relations of AKRSP (I) and Sadguru with the AKF network in connection with figures 4.1 to 4.3, it seemed that both NGOs (but AKRSP (I) in particular) were heavily dependent on AKF for funding. There is certainly a financial dependence, but as I have shown, the NGOs also possess symbolic capital. And it is this symbolic capital that enables them to negotiate with funders. Sadguru's Director is able to be very forthright in his dealings with funders because he has a reputation for delivering products on schedule, on budget, and with the predicted results. AKRSP (I), on the other hand, has historically performed less well in terms of targets, but is secure in its relationship with AKF; as part of the "family", AKRSP (I) is too large an investment to be dropped without damaging AKF's reputation in the international development community. AKRSP (I)'s position is arguably more secure than that of Sadguru, *because* nearly all of its funds are obtained through AKF. This difference in position between the two NGOs also helps to explain why AKRSP (I) has historically been less punctual than Sadguru in turning in reports to AKF India.

Conclusion

I have attempted to show above that a characterization of NGO-funder relations simply in terms of fund flows (with NGOs being dependent on their funders) is incomplete. Rather, there are exchanges of economic as well as symbolic types of resources between NGOs and funders. The possibilities for exchanging and converting between various kinds of capital enable organizations to develop *interdependencies*, thereby reducing the uncertainties associated with their respective behaviors and thus with the outcomes of their actions. The considerable interdependence between AKRSP (I), Sadguru, and members of the AKF network is evident in this exchange which forms a basic structure that guides their interactions (as depicted in figure 4.5).

While the interactions between the case NGOs and their funders cannot be reduced only to exchanges of money and information/reputation, especially since the NGOs and funders share a commitment to poverty alleviation, their relations are deeply structured by capital exchange. The implications of this patterning for the practice of international development and for organizational change are profound. The relations of Sadguru and AKRSP (I) with AKF and the EC are so embedded in capital exchange that it has become difficult to conceive of relationships outside of this mold. How might NGOs and international funders work towards their common goals of poverty alleviation without this constant struggle over the exchange of funds for reputation? I begin to address this question in the next chapter through a closer look at struggles between NGOs and funders over the use of information.

5 Information struggles: the role of information in the reproduction of NGO-funder relationships

Struggles over the shaping and use of information are central to relationships between non-governmental organizations and their funders. This chapter examines the effects of external funding on the structuring of information systems of NGOs, and the strategies used by NGOs to resist this external interference.

Research in the United States has suggested that the public funding of non-profits, especially for purposes of service delivery, has been accompanied by increased governmental oversight and regulation (Smith and Lipsky 1993; Young 1999). While monitoring and regulation are important for purposes of account-ability, government financing can significantly affect both the organizational culture of non-profits and the kinds of services they provide. And although governmental support, especially in the form of public service contracting, may enable non-profits to scale up and professionalize their activities, it can also divert non-profits from their original missions, effectively establishing a parastatal apparatus of service delivery organizations (Sen 1999; Wolch 1990). At the same time, however, it is important to note that NGO–government re-lations can take various forms, ranging from cooperation, supplementarity and complementarity, to co-optation and confrontation (Najam 2000; Young 1999).

The international development literature has similarly noted the expansion of NGOs, particularly in public service provision. This is a global phenomenon that has been fueled by the availability of funding, not only from domestic public sources but also from official bilateral and multilateral sources, as well as from Northern NGOs (Clark 1995; Dichter 1999; Edwards and Hulme 1996).

In order to monitor NGO activities, funds to NGOs have often been ac-companied by funder demands for specific outputs and the establishment of information systems. There is a significant literature that has described this tension between funders and NGOs as well as the processes through which ex-ternal funders shape NGO behavior (e.g. Clayton 1994; Hudock 1999; Fowler 1997). In these studies, however, there has been comparatively little analysis of the specific mechanisms through which this external influence is both exerted and resisted. Information flows and systems represent one such mechanism.

This chapter investigates the role of information in structuring the relation-ships between AKRSP (I), Sadguru and their two key international funders, the

77

Aga Khan Foundation and the European Commission. After providing details of information flows between the NGOs and their funders, I advance three key arguments. First, I show that the information requirements of funders impact NGOs not only by placing demands on their attention, but also by promoting positivist and easily quantifiable valuations of success and failure. This is not an intended effect, but a systemic one that emerges from reporting and budgeting protocols that favor "product" data over "process" data. Second, I demonstrate that NGOs resist funder attempts to structure their behavior through a series of strategies including the "symbolic" generation of information in order to satisfy funder needs, the selective sharing of information in order to protect their core activities from unwanted interference, and the strategic use of professionals to enhance legitimacy. Finally, I argue that this combination of funder demands for information and NGO resistance to external interference, serve to further entrench existing information systems. Ironically, it is through their very efforts to influence and resist one another that the NGOs and funders end up "reproducing" their relationships and tensions.

Information flows: product and process data

In examining information systems that link AKRSP (I) and Sadguru to their funders, two initial questions arise: What kinds of information exist in and on each NGO? What kind of information is shared between NGOs and funders? Information generated by NGOs and funders can take a variety of forms. Figure 5.1 provides a listing of information types, and it also depicts the flow of information between NGOs and funders (see Appendix 1 at the end of this chapter for descriptions of each of these information types).

The top left box of figure 5.1 includes only information generated by the NGOs and is divided into two kinds of data:

(i) "product" data – information that is generally about physical and financial details. Some data on social impacts of programs have been included under this label in figure 5.1, but with few exceptions product data are focused on easily measurable indicators and quantitative analysis.

(ii) "process" data – information that contains details of the qualitative and less easily measured dimensions of development work, for example, on the process and difficulties of mobilizing communities, on perceptual differences between NGO members and village members, on class and gender tensions within a community, etc. This material is difficult to generalize due to its context-specific and interpretive nature. Some types of process data are collected over short periods of time (e.g. through participatory rural appraisals), while others are gathered over long time spans (months to years) in order to capture gradual change in a community or context (e.g. through diaries and process documentation).[1]

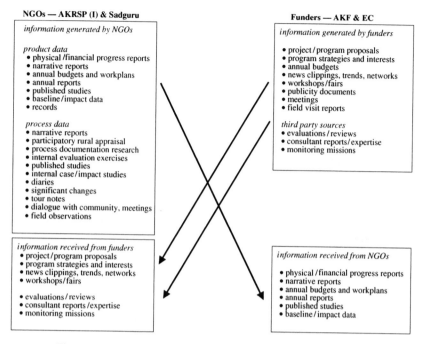

NGOs — AKRSP (I) & Sadguru

information generated by NGOs

product data
• physical /financial progress reports
• narrative reports
• annual budgets and workplans
• annual reports
• published studies
• baseline /impact data
• records

process data
• narrative reports
• participatory rural appraisal
• process documentation research
• internal evaluation exercises
• published studies
• internal case /impact studies
• diaries
• significant changes
• tour notes
• dialogue with community, meetings
• field observations

information received from funders
• project /program proposals
• program strategies and interests
• news clippings, trends, networks
• workshops/fairs

• evaluations /reviews
• consultant reports /expertise
• monitoring missions

Funders — AKF & EC

information generated by funders
• project /program proposals
• program strategies and interests
• annual budgets
• news clippings, trends, networks
• workshops/fairs
• publicity documents
• meetings
• field visit reports

third party sources
• evaluations /reviews
• consultant reports/expertise
• monitoring missions

information received from NGOs
• physical /financial progress reports
• narrative reports
• annual budgets and workplans
• annual reports
• published studies
• baseline /impact data

Figure 5.1 Information sources and flows

While each information source is categorized based on the primary insights it provides (i.e. in terms of products or processes), it should be noted that some of the information generated by NGOs crosses the boundaries of both product and process data types (e.g. published studies, baseline and impact data). The arrows show what kinds of information are passed on from NGOs (i.e. AKRSP (I) and Sadguru) to funders (i.e. AKF and the EC) and from funders to NGOs.

Drawing from the data flows depicted in figure 5.1, I make four general observations about information flows between NGOs and funders. First, it appears that very little process data are transferred from NGOs to funders. NGOs send funders standardized reports and studies that detail physical and financial information. But field level details which would require explanations of context and possibly also some degree of sociological or anthropological analysis are, for the most part, left out. This does not mean that such information is willfully omitted for, as I shall argue, the omissions result from a variety of factors that are linked to relationships of NGOs with funders.

To a very limited extent, process information is transferred to funders through narrative reports, baseline and impact data, and case studies. Narrative reports, however, are primarily a verbal elaboration of physical and financial data and reflect only a modest degree of critical analysis on the qualitative aspects of NGO interventions. Similarly, baseline data on villages (which is requested by the EC and the AKF network) also provide little process information. Baseline data are intended to be used for comparison with data collected after another five years in order to determine impacts of interventions. NGO staff have expressed concerns about the usefulness of some of the impact indicators, and are skeptical about the value of the baseline data. Baseline information can be valuable in helping to measure the impacts of an intervention, but it tells little about *how* or in *what stages* that impact was achieved, the difficulties faced in achieving it, or what unintended consequences (positive and negative) it may have led to. Because of an emphasis on end results, baseline and impact data fail to examine the political or social dimensions of NGO interventions except in very crude terms (e.g. numbers of village organizations formed, proportion of project costs borne by participants, number of government policies changed, etc.).

Finally, published case studies generated by the NGOs for public distribution are also poor sources of process information. These studies, with a few notable exceptions, tend to focus on "success stories" while overlooking less positive experiences of NGOs. Because process information is context-specific and frequently open to interpretation, a bias towards the portrayal of success can lead to simplistic and imbalanced analyses of the effects of NGO interventions.

My second observation about information flows is that the data transferred from NGOs to funders are suited to quick reading and analysis. Neither NGO nor funder staff have a great deal of time to spare in preparing or reading reports. Hence, information that lends itself to standard reporting formats and to relatively quick reading and analysis is favored. In addition, the information that is transferred deals with tasks that each NGO is already performing. Such data do not point out whether or not a program or activity is fundamentally flawed, but do point out where implementation is slow and needs closer attention.

Third, the collection and analysis of process data is much less systematized than the collection and analysis of product data. Both AKRSP (I) and Sadguru have now been able to routinize their collection and analyses of product data. While both organizations have made strides in collection and analyses of process data (partly through the employment of social scientists), they are far from making social and anthropological analyses a part of routine monitoring activity. While funders verbally encourage more attention to process data, little support is provided in terms of funds, expertise, or the relaxation of other data demands in order to make this possible.

My final observation about information flows is that very little information is routinely transferred from funders to NGOs. While third party reports such as evaluations and monitoring missions are initiated by funders, they are generally designed to generate information about the NGOs and not about funders, and that information is not often shared with the NGOs. Information about funders and the funding environment is relatively scarce, and little information about funders is actually forwarded to the NGOs. Consequently, much data exist on AKRSP (I), Sadguru and their activities, but there is only sparse information on funders and their circumstances. This observation makes sense when one views NGO-funder relations in terms of the types of resources sought by each kind of organization: funders seek information (on NGO activities and spending) while NGOs seek funds. Accessing key financial and strategy documents from funders proved very difficult (if not impossible) during field research, whereas it was relatively easy to obtain such information from NGOs.

These four observations point to the centrality of product data in analyses of NGO activity. While the gathering of product data is important to an assessment of NGO work, I argue below that a focus on product (rather than process) data has a depoliticizing effect. A product data analysis treats NGO interventions as a collection of simple, discrete, and socially undifferentiated projects amenable to quantitative analysis, while downplaying the embeddedness of those activities in complex social and political environments. An analysis of NGO interventions based on product data is depoliticizing because it disregards the effects of those interventions on social dynamics and political change. In developing this argument, I begin by showing *how* a focus on product data affects decision making in the case NGOs. Two key arguments are advanced below, one about the allocation of attention within NGOs as a result of information demands from funders, and another about the use of information by NGOs to resist funder intervention.

Paying attention

The information and issues to which NGOs allocate attention are influenced by their relations with funders. As shown in figure 5.1, product data are system-atically collected by the NGOs as a result of requests by funders and are thus available for decision making. For the case study NGOs, I argue that organiza-tional attention is focused on these product data. This is a significant claim for it implies that this product information, whether or not it is important with respect to the overall aims of the NGO, is influential in a decision process because of its availability.

Arguably, the regular collection of certain information in an organization results in a focusing of attention on that information. This necessarily restricts the time and attention devoted to other tasks or information sources thereby conveying the impression that this regularly collected information is important (Pfeffer and Salancik 1978: 74–75). In other words, information collected by an organization can become important to decision making simply because it is available. In cases where this information is dominated by the requirements of donors, it may "reorient accountability upward [i.e. to funders], away from the grassroots, supporters and staff" (Edwards and Hulme 1996: 968).

Since the commencement of the EC grant in 1994, a great deal of attention in AKRSP (I) and Sadguru has been focused on systematizing the collection and analysis of information for: (1) physical and financial progress reports, and (2) baseline and impact studies. While both of these types of information were being collected by the NGOs prior to 1994, there have since been marked changes in systematizing the collection and analysis of this information. Both of these types of data demands are examined below in terms of attention allocation in the NGOs.

Physical and financial progress

Both AKRSP (I) and Sadguru report on a quarterly basis to funders on their "physical and financial progress." Standard reporting formats mandated by AKF and the EC clearly identify the activities or "line items" for which funding is allocated to the NGO. These categories cannot be changed without approval of the EC. The reporting formats also require details of "progress" to be provided, both in terms of actual physical output (e.g. numbers of irrigation schemes under construction or recently completed, hectares of wasteland under treatment, etc.) and the financial resources spent on those activities. Once collected by the NGOs, these data are analyzed and consolidated by AKF India and then forwarded to the European Commission. In addition to enabling progress towards targets to be monitored, these reports fulfill another key function – that of maintaining accountability of the NGOs to their funders. The reports document that the EC funds are being spent according to their contract and on schedule, and in doing so they also enable the continued disbursement of funds to the NGOs.

In both Sadguru and AKRSP (I), there are procedures in place for a systematic collection of physical and financial data. Sadguru's reporting and planning procedures have always been highly centralized in the hands of its Director and Co-Director. These two individuals maintain constant contact with all departments in Sadguru and oversee all budgeting exercises. Overall targets are set by them as based upon negotiations with funders and consultations with individual departments within the NGO. To monitor progress, each department prepares a report which is presented at a monthly staff meeting. This assessment of progress or success is based largely on product information, that is, in terms of physical and financial target achievement. Sadguru has been able to adapt this well-established, flexible, and centralized system to the EC's quarterly reporting requirements with relative ease. The EC funds and the concurrent increase in targets have generally been welcomed by Sadguru's field staff, some of whom view limited funding as a key constraint to expanding their programs in irrigation and forestry.[2]

Sadguru's performance has far exceeded its targets for each year of the EC grant. Its quarterly reports are always submitted on time and according to funder specifications, and the reports invariably demonstrate overachievement. The NGO actually plans this overachievement by setting annual targets below capabilities. Because Sadguru has long been attentive to product information, the EC's requirements for product data have not posed a challenge to the NGO. As a result of this consistency between Sadguru and the EC (in terms of importance attached to product data), Sadguru has not been faced with the problem of redefining its understanding of success based on funder requirements for product information.

AKRSP (I), on the other hand, has struggled through the 1990s to routinize its collection of physical and financial data and to develop better planning procedures. Tensions between AKRSP (I) and AKF (particularly AKF India) have sometimes flared up as a result of the NGO's poor planning and because AKRSP (I) has submitted reports with inconsistent calculations of its physical and financial target achievements. Unlike Sadguru, which is highly centralized, AKRSP (I) maintains three distant and relatively autonomous field offices. These "Spearhead Teams" (SHTs) report to a central office in Ahmedabad, Gujarat. In the past, budgeting and planning was largely a responsibility of the central office which consulted with SHTs while drafting annual budgets. Although monitoring the implementation of budgets and plans was subject to protocols established by the central office (sometimes created on an ad hoc basis), strict adherence to these protocols was rare.

Since 1994, AKRSP (I) has been under considerable pressure from the EC, the AKF network, and its own board of directors to scale up its activities and to improve its performance with respect to targets. In order to meet this challenge, the NGO has had to improve its ability to plan, implement, and report upon physical and financial targets. AKRSP (I)'s response to these pressures has been to redesign and further decentralize its budgeting and planning systems. Since 1996, for example, each SHT has been made responsible for developing its own detailed annual budget and plan (rather than providing information to the central office to develop a plan). In this way, each SHT is now directly responsible for planning its activities and for monitoring them each quarter. In addition, considerable financial discretion has been decentralized to the SHTs (Haribhakti Consulting 1995). The responsibility of the central office has thus shifted from its previous role as overall planner to its new role as adviser and coordinator, while the SHTs have been made directly accountable for meeting targets.

This restructuring and decentralization of the planning and budgeting process to the field level in combination with the organization's efforts to expand its activities, have resulted in increased organization-wide attention to details of physical and financial progress. The importance of this attention is clearly articulated in a statement by a senior manager in AKRSP (I):

[In] the last 3 years, I've had only one mission – it was like a bloody cricket match – and that was to reach 100 percent target achievement... What you review determines very much what you do. If you review targets, you end up doing targets.[3]

This attention to targets has found its way to the field level. Referring to a meeting of the NGOs with their funders, AKRSP (I)'s Chief Executive explained:

At the PIC [i.e. Program Implementation Committee] meeting we're asked why we're not achieving [our predicted targets], and I have to listen to pressure saying [that] if you don't spend [your budget] then at the review there may not be funds forwarded... So I put pressure on staff [and] say we must be more accurate in forming targets and predictions. Once targets are set, yes, [there is] pressure on field [staff] to achieve them... We've landed a big grant and are expected to scale up. Everybody in the organization knows we must achieve more every year until we reach a plateau.[4]

It would be misleading, however, to suggest that target pressures emanate from funders alone since each Spearhead Team sets its own yearly budget targets. The failure to meet physical and financial targets can thus also be attributed, in part, to inadequate planning in the NGO.[5]

The increased attention to targets in AKRSP (I) has, however, had significant implications for how members of the NGO perceive success and failure. Since the organization's performance is reviewed every three months by the EC and AKF India in terms of its progress towards targets, meeting targets has become a proxy for success. For field staff, this view of success has resulted in a concern that "120 percent performance is okay, but not 80 percent"[6] and a fear that failure to meet targets will lead to a loss of funds.

Based on performance in meeting targets, AKRSP (I) had been failing in 1994 and 1995. So in 1996, when the organization was able to achieve 98 percent of its targets, it was seen by some of its own staff as crossing a hurdle. Changes to planning systems were a crucial part of this newfound "success." The attention to targets and the association of targets with failure or success triggered a search in AKRSP (I) for new and more efficient ways of planning and budgeting. This search did not occur in Sadguru since its information systems were already focused on targets and its interpretation of success and failure were coincident with the EC's emphasis on targets.

As suggested above, there are a number of reasons why information on targets has become important to decision making in the two NGOs. The idea that some information receives attention simply because it is regularly collected needs to be qualified, especially since organizations do collect information that they never use. For AKRSP (I) and Sadguru, the collection of data on physical and financial progress can be seen as focusing NGO activity on targets. But this focusing on targets has occurred because information on targets is regularly collected *and* because it is associated with assessments of success (or performance) by funders. Under conditions where product information is not associated with success (by funders or NGOs), one might not expect product data to influence NGO behavior as much. Thus, I hypothesize that information is more likely to influence NGO behavior if it is regularly collected *and* if it contributes to an assessment of success or failure.

As figure 5.1 shows, product data are more systematically collected and transmitted to funders than are process data. This difference can be attributed to a number of factors. First, reports about products are more *easily collected* and are also easier to present to funders. Second, funders find this information *easy to process* and are able to link it with their own budget cycles and plans. Although the NGOs collect considerable process data, it requires more complex analysis and is thus less likely to be transmitted to funders or to have a systematic influence on decision making. And finally, physical and financial information has become important to decision making in the NGOs because this information is gathered by virtually *all* subunits of the organizations. Nearly every subunit is linked to this data not only through its collection but also through its use in assessing organizational performance.

In sum, the information requirements of funders are capable of influencing NGO activities as well as NGO perceptions of success and failure. This influence is most evident in the case of AKRSP (I), where an increase in attention to product data and the regular use of this information by funders in assessing performance, has resulted in a recasting of success within AKRSP (I) in product terms. In Sadguru, however, there has not been a similar shift in perception because its interpretation of success and failure were already coincident with the EC's emphasis on physical and financial target achievement.

The baseline monitoring mission and logical framework analysis

In addition to the quarterly progress reports discussed above, the EC and AKF (particularly AKF Geneva and AKF India) have initiated systems in both NGOs for carrying out baseline and impact studies. These "monitoring systems" were established with the help of a Baseline Monitoring Mission (BMM) in 1994, and were further reviewed by a Joint Monitoring Mission in 1995. The task of collecting this data rests primarily with the monitoring department of each NGO. Most of the discussion below is devoted to tracing the formation of these monitoring systems, with special attention to the role of "logical framework analysis."

While the emergence of monitoring systems in each NGO can be traced back at least to the mid-1980s, foundations for the current systems were laid by two consultants hired by AKF Geneva in 1989 and in 1991. The first consultant's primary recommendations included a redesigning of quarterly progress reports to allow for a comparison of quantifiable achievements with planned objectives, and a further development of impact studies based upon regular collection of agricultural data, project baselines, and participatory rural appraisals (Poate 1989a; 1989b). The second consultant examined planning, budgeting, and monitoring in the two NGOs. Building upon the suggestions of his predecessor, he closely investigated procedures used by the NGOs to plan and budget their annual activities and suggested practical formats that could be standardized to help the NGOs schedule their work (Hampshire 1991a; 1991b). For monitoring and impact assessment purposes, he introduced a project management tool known as a "logical framework matrix" or "logical framework analysis" (LFA). The logical framework is a matrix in which a project's objectives and expected results are clearly identified, along with a list of indicators that are to be used in measuring and verifying progress towards achieving those objectives and results. LFA has turned out to be a center of considerable attention in both NGOs; although it was not immediately adopted by AKRSP (I) and Sadguru, LFA was reintroduced through the Baseline Monitoring Mission of 1994. The logical framework is now the primary organizing tool for monitoring activities in both NGOs.

An EC manual on project cycle management describes the logical framework as a method that can be useful for project preparation, implementation, and evaluation, but only within certain limits:

The method consists of an analytical process and a way of presenting the results of this process, which makes it possible to set out systematically and logically the project/programme's objectives and the causal relationships between them, to indicate how to check whether these objectives have been achieved and to establish what assumptions outside the scope of the project/program may influence its success...

The logical framework will be useful for those who prepare and implement projects to structure and formulate better their ideas and set them out in clear, standardized form. This is its only purpose. If the policy is misconceived or if the criteria are badly chosen, the logical framework will reveal the contradictions and oversights, but cannot of itself change or replace the policy or criteria. (Commission of the European Communities 1993b: 14–15)

LFA, as portrayed above, is a formal exercise to provide clarity in project management. In order to be an effective and useful tool, it requires a careful prior analysis of the relationships between a project's objectives, outputs, and outcomes and the ways in which these relations can be verified. It is seen as a flexible framework that should be updated and modified as the project progresses, and not as a rigid blueprint. But the real significance of the logical framework, as I detail below, lies not in its ability to provide clarity in project management but in the deceptive and seemingly neutral way in which this clarity is achieved. The LFA is a technocratic tool: it organizes and reduces complex social and political realities into simplified and discrete components of a "project."

The Baseline Monitoring Mission arranged by AKF Geneva and the EC in 1994 created a logical framework specifically for their project with AKRSP (I) and Sadguru (Weir and Shah 1994). This matrix listed a total of 89 different indicators which the NGOs are now using to monitor progress toward the objectives of the project – known as the Community Management of Natural Resources project. Approximately 72 of these indicators apply to Sadguru and 83 to AKRSP (I). A portion of this framework is attached as table 5.1. The second column, "intervention logic", lists the objectives, purpose and expected results of the CMNR project. The "overall objectives" are generally wider than those of the project itself and are to be achieved through a combination of projects or programs. The "project purpose" is the more specific objective of the CMNR project and is the expected product of a combination of "results" based on specific activities (e.g. building and strengthening village organizations, afforesting land, constructing checkdams, etc.). These results are programmatically organized in the sense that there is one main result for each of the NGO's primary programs such as watershed development, biogas, forestry, water resources, village institutions and so on. Table 5.1 lists only the first two, of a total of twelve, such "results." The third and fourth columns specify how progress towards these objectives, purpose, and results is to be measured and the information sources needed for this verification. The final column identifies assumptions that underlie the project's logic. It is necessary for these assumptions to be true in order for the project's activities to achieve its expected results, purpose, and objectives.

The logical framework is primarily geared towards collecting data that lend themselves to quantification (i.e. product data rather than process data). For example a large portion of the objectively verifiable indicators are numbers: numbers of new village institutions, numbers of water harvesting structures built, area of watersheds treated or wastelands afforested, and so on. The logical framework does allow for some data that are qualitative and which may be relevant to socioeconomic issues – e.g. data on increases in rural income, changes in cropping pattern, savings or changes in time collecting water or fuelwood, changes in incidence of health problems among women, changes in levels of indebtedness, etc., and to a lesser degree on the quality of village organizations (based on an index developed by the NGOs) and on the quality of training programs provided by the NGOs. But for the most part, these data are designed to be quantified and displayed on a spreadsheet.

Uncertainties related to process issues and politics are largely relegated to the "assumptions" section of the logical framework. It is assumed, for example, that vested interests opposed to village institutions or projects can be neutralized, that farmers agree to communal management, that government policies remain favorable to NGO activity, that NGOs are able to maintain influential contacts

Table 5.1 *Logical framework for community management of natural resources project*

	Intervention logic	Objectively verifiable Indicators	Sources of verification	Assumptions
Overall objectives	Household Incomes sustainably increased and environmental degradation reversed	• household incomes of participating villagers – including small farmers, landless and women – increased and sustained • productivity of natural resources improved and sustained • numbers of common property resources managed effectively by communities increased	• baseline and impact surveys reports, technical studies and NGO records • National Census (1999, 2001); Gujarat state statistics; National Sample Survey • baseline and impact surveys • technical studies • baseline and impact surveys and VI records	• Project purpose, results and activities relate directly to overall objective
Project Purpose	Improved income earning opportunities through improved and sustainable management of natural management by VIs in four districts of Gujarat	• increase in income earning opportunities and employment for participating villagers • increased income from individual and group savings • sustained increase in the productivity of natural resources, including crop yields • reduction in distress outmigration • increase in the number of mature VIs	• baseline and impact surveys • credit records, surveys • baseline and impact surveys, NGO and VI records, agricultural census data • baseline and impact surveys, case studies • VI maturity/performance index • case studies	• Improved management of natural resources is sufficient to increase income earning opportunities • natural resource base can support population • population growth rate will not increase significantly • there are no severe droughts or other natural disasters during the project period • Vested interests opposed to VIs can be neutralized
Results (1)	Existing Village Institutions (VIs) strengthened and new ones established	• Number of new VIs established as proportion of targets	• VI and NGO Records • VI and NGO Records	

	Narrative	Indicators	Means of verification	Assumptions
		• Number of existing VIs operating effectively as proportion of total • Number of VIs ceasing to operate [VI Maturity/performance Index] • Equity • Participation • Management • Finance • Sustainability	• VI and NGO Records • VI maturity/performance index • Annual analysis of VI records and 10 percent sample surveys of VI members • case studies	• government policies on formation and operation of VIs remain favorable
Results (2)	Micro-watersheds developed	• Area of watershed developed as proportion of targets • number of water harvesting structures constructed as proportion of targets (AKRSP only) • number of micro-watersheds completely treated as proportion of targets • number of micro-watersheds partially treated as proportion of targets • increase in cultivated area and changes in cropping patterns • increase in area under supplementary irrigation • rates of soil deposition • proportion of structures well maintained by farmers in the watersheds • increase in groundwater recharge • proportion of programme cost contributed by farmers	• VI and NGO Records • NGO Records • NGO Records • NGO Records • Baseline and impact surveys • Baseline and impact surveys • VI records/technical studies • Participatory Rural Appraisals • VI Records/technical studies • VI Records/PRAs	• Government policies on use of common property resources remain favorable • farmers in treated watersheds agree to communal management

Source: Weir and Shah (1994, Appendix 3.1, LFA Version 2.0, pp. 1–2).

with government, and so on (Weir and Shah 1994: Appendix 3.1: 1–14). The resulting logic emphasizes increases in rural incomes and in the natural resource base of a region, but it is silent about the process through which those increases are achieved and about the problems that are encountered along the way. For example, both AKRSP (I) and Sadguru had difficulty, in the late 1990s, in getting state government officials to cooperate with local communities in jointly managing public forest lands. As a result, their efforts in joint forest management crawled to a standstill in certain areas of Gujarat in the mid-1990s. LFA, as it is currently used, places government relationships in the "assumptions" column of the framework (e.g. assuming that government policies will "remain favorable") rather than addressing them directly as part of a more complex, and less easily measurable, "intervention logic." In this way, the monitoring system established through the logical framework makes little effort to monitor political and social variables such as relations with government, community conflicts, the extent or nature of gender, caste, or class-based inequities, and the cultural context within which these inequities are embedded.

In short, by forcing its user (the NGO in this case) to articulate its objectives within a positivist project management framework, LFA actually strips those aims of political, contentious, process-based, and ambiguous content. In other words, the logical framework achieves clarity in development planning by de-politicizing development interventions. By omitting possible negative results, the logical framework characterizes the project as if it will "succeed," leaving only the degree of success to be measured. This is not to say that LFA is without its proper uses. Indeed, it can be productively used as a tool for initially fram-ing a project, and it has been helpful in enabling the NGOs to better articulate their objectives and expected results. But its tendency towards simplification and quantification make the logical framework, in its current form, inadequate for monitoring complex development interventions. As noted by Edwards and Hulme (1996: 968), this critique of LFA also has broader implications for NGO accountability:

> The type of appraisal, monitoring and evaluation procedures insisted on by donors, especially their heavy reliance on "logical framework" approaches or their derivatives ... may also distort accountability by overemphasizing short-term quantitative targets and favoring hierarchical management structures – a tendency to "accountancy" rather than "accountability."

While there is little evidence to suggest that the case NGOs are opposed to this technocratic framework for describing and organizing their interventions, there have been some serious practical tensions with institutionalizing LFA and its attendant monitoring systems. These tensions concern the relevance of the monitoring systems to the needs of the NGOs.

Relevance of monitoring systems to AKRSP (I) and Sadguru

The problems associated with institutionalizing monitoring systems in AKRSP (I) and Sadguru are two-fold. First, there have been tensions between forming monitoring systems that meet the information needs of funders and those which are relevant to the practical needs of the NGOs. A second and related problem concerns feedback: the new monitoring systems have not contributed significantly to influencing decision making and behavior in the case NGOs.

To begin, the Baseline Monitoring Mission does not appear to have seriously questioned the suitability of LFA for AKRSP (I) and Sadguru, although it was clear that NGO staff were uncomfortable with it:

We suggest that the NGOs should ensure that copies of the logical framework – in English and Gujarati – are made available to project staff and that copies should also be displayed prominently... Staff are not yet really at home with the logical framework and we feel that it needs to be kept in view if it is to be used and demystified – a process which we recommend is supported by training. (Weir and Shah 1994: 7)

The logical framework is described by its proponents as a flexible tool for project planning, implementation, and monitoring. In the case of the Community Management of Natural Resources project, however, the logical framework is seen by the NGOs as a reporting structure or format to be followed. It has not been adopted as a tool that can be simplified and modified according to each organization's capacity and needs. As mentioned above, the BMM identified 89 "objectively verifiable indicators" for which data are being collected by AKRSP (I) and Sadguru. This is a very large amount of data to collect, sort, and analyze given that neither of the NGOs has ever before undertaken such formalized monitoring. According to the BMM, about one-third of these indicators were previously being reported by the NGOs and another third could be measured by analyzing existing information, thus leaving the remaining third to be verified through additional data collection.

The task of gathering data on these additional indicators and of sorting information from existing sources has fallen primarily upon the monitoring departments of the NGOs. While the BMM has succeeded in formalizing the task of monitoring within both organizations, members of the NGOs and especially the staff of monitoring departments see this recent attention to monitoring in a mixed light. On one hand, monitoring and research activities have become more focused and routinized and have received some recognition from the predominantly implementation-oriented staff of the NGOs:

They [the EC's consultants] have set up a whole outline for a strong monitoring system... [P]revious to this the Monitoring department was scattered and didn't know what to do...Only after the EC have we...become very clear about our own role, how to measure [the] success of a program, how to do an impact study.[7]

But on another hand, the utility of the new monitoring systems and especially of the logical framework have been questioned. A statement by AKRSP (I)'s Chief Executive summarized a frequently expressed perspective:

BMM was largely a requirement of AKF and the EU – that we should follow this internationally accepted [logical] framework. It should've been useful but [it] went overboard. Professionals were working with people who knew nothing of the log [i.e. logical] framework, [and] came up with 89 indicators. [This] is too much. It landed us with a task that was achievable in terms of requirements of donors, but not really usable for us.[8]

The frustration expressed by the Chief Executive is not so much about a monitoring system *per se*, but rather about developing routines that will actually be useful to the organization. A key resource which funders receive from NGOs is information that enables them (i.e. the funders) to justify the funds provided to the NGOs. By showing that these funds lead to "successful" activities, funders are able to justify this support, and are thus also able to establish a positive reputation for themselves. The BMM's emphasis on monitoring can thus be viewed as a strategy employed by funders to reduce uncertainty with respect to the types of information received from NGOs. The logical framework serves as means of organizing, prioritizing, and tracking the production of this information.

The monitoring system established by the BMM has overwhelmed staff at both NGOs and few have actually bought into it. In Sadguru, for example, the individuals responsible for baseline studies revealed that some of the studies were being conducted only to satisfy funders and that they were otherwise of little value to the NGO. In addition, some of the baseline data have been collected retrospectively and are rife with problems of recall, since farmers are asked to remember events and details from several years in the past. In fact, the collection of retrospective data is a requirement. The BMM's sampling guidelines specify that retrospective baseline data must be collected from ten percent of the villages in which Sadguru has worked, including villages in which the NGO commenced work as long as a decade ago (Weir and Shah 1994: 11). NGO staff do not foresee using this information for reasons other than justifying their work to funders.

While many senior staff and monitoring personnel in each of the NGOs feel that it is important to systematically monitor their NGO's activities, the monitoring systems linked to the LFA are not well adapted to their implementation needs, which require simpler and continuous feedback systems.[9]

On the other hand, the new systems are not simply a product of funder demands for specific kinds of information. As the report of the BMM points out, there is a surfeit of information collected by the NGOs which is not analyzed.

The BMM's guidelines were an effort to organize and make use of these data, and to establish a means through which research and monitoring could feed into implementation and planning. The BMM was made up of a pair of consultants who were very familiar with the two NGOs and their funders, had good relations with both, and sought to establish a monitoring system that would be useful to the NGOs and not just to their funders. In the report of the BMM, these two consultants note a problem in setting up a monitoring system in the NGOs:

> Not unreasonably, AKRSP (I) tends to respond to the requirements of the grant letter from AKF. If information is requested, then it is generally provided. Thus action on monitoring is often donor-driven. There has been a feeling in AKRSP (I) that there are monitoring requirements for the donor and [different] monitoring requirements for AKRSP (I), whereas in fact these largely coincide. The culture of both SWDF [i.e. Sadguru] and AKRSP (I) still tends towards seeing monitoring as the preparation of reports and as being separate from project management rather than being an integral part of it. (Weir and Shah 1994: 2)

In order to develop monitoring systems that would be useful to the NGOs, the consultants of the BMM devised a logical framework in collaboration with NGO staff. The great detail in the framework, along with its large number of objectively verifiable indicators, were thus developed together, with both NGOs inclined to increase the number of indicators rather than to reduce them (Weir and Shah 1994: 7). Thus it seems that the NGOs themselves are partially responsible for the overwhelming amount of data to be collected and analyzed, and have only acknowledged the data collection requirements as a burden in retrospect. A senior member of AKRSP (I) supported this view, noting that the "unrealistic number [of indicators] is more a reflection of the keen desire [by NGO staff] to acquire a lot of information . . . rather than any imposition by the BMM team."[10]

It also appears that the problems which the NGOs have with the logical framework are practical rather than fundamental: the NGOs are not opposed to collecting data based on the logical framework, but are concerned, in retrospect, about the volume of data and its suitability for meeting their practical needs. Despite the efforts and good intentions of the consultants of the BMM to develop systems useful to the NGOs, the monitoring efforts of AKRSP (I) and Sadguru remain donor driven (although, with NGO participation), and any reduction in the 89 indicators is subject to donor (i.e. European Commission) approval. Routines for the collection and analysis of baseline and impact data have been put into place, but the usefulness of these systems for the NGOs remains an open question. It is possible that AKRSP (I) and Sadguru may be able to modify these systems over time to better suit their needs, but for now they are focused on fulfilling funder requests for information.

Summary: comparing the influence of target and monitoring data

Earlier in this chapter I demonstrated how the focusing of attention on issues of physical and financial progress (i.e. targets) has influenced the behavior of the case study NGOs. This influence is most evident in the case of AKRSP (I), where an increase in attention to product data and the regular use of this information by funders in assessing performance, has resulted in a recasting of success within AKRSP (I) in product terms. In Sadguru, however, there has not been a similar shift in perception because its interpretation of success and failure were already coincident with the EC's emphasis on physical and financial target achievement.

I have now also shown how considerable attention has been devoted to the establishment of monitoring systems for conducting baseline and impact studies. But unlike the data on targets, the collection and availability of information on baselines and impacts has had very limited influence on decision making. The information collected is, for the most part, put aside until reports are required by funders. This difference between target data and baseline data can be explained partly by the fact that baseline and impact data have not yet been integrated into assessments of performance by funders. While baseline and impact data are being collected more systematically than in the past, this information does not regularly figure into assessments of success or failure. In reference to the BMM's report, the EC's Project Officer made its relative importance very clear by stating, "I admit I have not even read the report. I assume it will be useful at the end [of the CMNR project in 2001] when we wish to compare progress."[11] The information gathered through baseline and impact studies is, nonetheless, not viewed as being useless. Rather, it is just being put aside until a later date.

It is possible, however, that as the NGOs become more accustomed to the logical framework and are able to routinize the collection and processing of baseline and impact data, that these forms of information will become more readily available as inputs to decision making. Tensions between the needs of the NGOs and the systems set up by the BMM have arisen over practical issues: NGOs want information that can regularly be fed back into implementation whereas funders are interested in the impacts of interventions over the lifetime of a project (which is eight years in the case of CMNR). While these two perspectives are not mutually exclusive, it is difficult for implementers to see the value added in collecting large amounts of data which have no immediate use, and it is difficult for evaluators to see why implementers tend to be narrowly focused on short-term practical needs.

Finally, there is also the issue of involvement of key subunits in gathering or using information. As I have shown for the case of information on physical and financial progress, nearly every unit of the NGOs is involved either in gathering that data or in being evaluated based on it at regular intervals of three months.

As a result, there is a great deal of awareness about and attention on this information throughout the organizations. In contrast, most of the responsibility for collecting and analyzing baseline and impact data rests with the monitoring department of each NGO. Historically, these subunits have been marginalized by the implementation orientation of the NGOs. The importance allocated by the EC and the AKF network to monitoring activities has improved the relative status of the monitoring departments, but they still remain anomalies in the NGOs. It is possible, however, that the information generated by monitoring departments will receive greater attention over time, particularly as other organizational subunits become more involved in collecting data for monitoring purposes or participate in writing case studies, and particularly as monitoring departments take on the task of critically monitoring and assessing the work of their organization.

Strategies of resistance

In addition to the reasons proposed above, the impacts of the new monitoring systems on decision making and behavior in the NGOs have also been limited by NGO attempts to resist funder influence. This section explores some of these resistance strategies. More specifically, it examines ways in which NGOs protect their "core technologies" from the information demands of key funders, while also securing legitimacy and support from those funders. Below, I detail three strategies employed by AKRSP (I) and Sadguru, all of which involve the use of information: symbolism, selectivity, and professionalization.

The term "core technologies" refers to the activities and procedures that form the central task of an organization (Thompson 1967). For AKRSP (I) and Sadguru this central task can broadly be described as rural development or natural resource management. The core technologies of natural resource management include the planning and implementation of land and water resource projects and the establishment of managerial units such as cooperative societies and village organizations to operate and maintain those projects. The NGOs follow a sequential system in carrying out their central task; standard operating procedures guide project planning, village entry, implementation, and maintenance. Organizations seek to protect or seal off their core technologies from external influences in order to create stability in uncertain task environments. These efforts to insulate the technical core are known as "buffering" strategies (Thompson 1967). For example, organizations involved in technical processes such as irrigation system building may attempt to reduce uncertainties in material supply and quality by stockpiling raw materials or by carefully sorting inputs entering the technical core.

In addition to using buffering strategies for managing their *task* environments, organizations also develop responses to *institutional* aspects of their environments, that is, to the tacit "rules" that govern their interactions with other organizations such as funders (Scott 1995). For example, one such rule may be that, in exchange for funds, NGOs must provide funders with information which demonstrates that those funds are resulting in "successful" projects. In addition, funders expect NGOs to engage in some form of monitoring activity in order to be viewed as legitimate development actors. In particular, the NGOs are expected to use a widely accepted framework (i.e. the logical framework) for guiding their monitoring and planning systems. These expectations or tacit rules of behavior constitute, in part, the institutional environment of AKRSP (I) and Sadguru.

As demonstrated below, each of the three strategies used by AKRSP (I) and Sadguru act as buffers as well as bridges. They are buffers in the sense that they enable NGOs to insulate their key activities and decision processes from funder influence. And they are bridges in the sense that they enable NGOs to enhance their own legitimacy by conforming to funder demands for information.

Symbolism, selectivity, and professionalization

As shown above, the collection of information for baseline and impact studies has received considerable attention in Sadguru and AKRSP (I), but this information has not been feeding back into decision making. Evidence from the cases also leads to a complementary argument. Some information is collected only symbolically; it may never actually be used for decision making but is collected to lend legitimacy to an organization's activities.[12] In other words, the meaning or use of that information lies in the signals sent (to funders for example) by gathering it, and not necessarily in using it in decision processes.

Both AKRSP (I) and Sadguru are faced with the task of carrying out their primary activities (the core technology) while also seeking to maintain legitimacy amongst the wider development community (i.e. international funders and government agencies), and thus to continue receiving funds. The establishment of monitoring systems for the collection and analysis of information is necessary for legitimating the work of the case NGOs to the AKF network and the EC. Thus the NGOs incorporate baseline and impact surveys and logical framework analysis into standard practice even though these practices may not have a direct bearing on their primary activities or decisions. This is not an unusual finding, for in order to attain legitimacy without having to compromise on core technologies, organizations have been known to *decouple* formal structures and practices from key activities (Meyer and Rowan 1977: 357) or to decouple information from decisions (Feldman and March 1988: 417–19). This legitimacy derives from demonstrating that the organization is following expected, or institutionalized, practices and procedures. As such, decoupling can be seen as a buffering strategy that enables organizations to protect key activities or decision processes from external influence.

Decoupling is particularly evident in formal surveys and studies carried out by AKRSP (I) and Sadguru. In addition to the baseline and impact surveys already discussed, the Baseline Monitoring Mission recommended that the NGOs carry out case studies of particular projects or activities. It was intended by the Mission that these detailed studies be used to complement impact surveys by probing the qualitative and less tangible aspects of the NGOs' work, such as the operation of village organizations or issues of equity and gender (Weir and Shah 1994: 15). While increasing numbers of such studies are being carried out by the NGOs, they remain unintegrated with overall planning and implementation.

For example, case and impact studies carried out by Sadguru staff are, by and large, overwhelmingly positive and supportive of the NGO's work. Self-criticism, when present at all, is minor and there is a tendency to highlight success while downplaying negative events. This does not suggest, however, that NGO members are uncritical of their own work. Instead, they are highly self-critical but are reluctant to share their critiques with the outside world. As a senior member of Sadguru's monitoring department plainly noted, "I don't write anything negative about the organization because it may put it at a disadvantage with funders."[13] This comment was backed up by the organization's director, who explained that "Donors harp on one bad thing of 99 good" and that, as a result, the organization is very cautious in providing information to donors in order to avoid misunderstandings.[14]

The utility of formal studies (e.g. case studies, impact studies, and technical reports which are passed on to funders or are published) appears to lie in their justification of past decisions and strategies to funders, and not as an input to decision making. Many of the NGO's monitoring tasks are thus of symbolic value in the sense that they function primarily to legitimate the organizations' activities. What counts is that the studies are produced. As such, the use of information for symbolic purposes is an organizational survival strategy. In this light, Sadguru's use of impact and case studies is not an organizational dysfunctionality but points to its position within wider relations of power: Sadguru is concerned about sharing information with funders that might lead to unwanted funder interference in or misinterpretation of the NGO's activities. As a result, the symbolic information generated by Sadguru is also selective: it is chosen so as to portray the organization's work in a positive light.

AKRSP (I), on the other hand, has had a much longer and more entrenched relationship with its key funder, AKF, which played a central role in founding the NGO in 1983 and has since been instrumental to acquiring funds from various bilateral agencies. Due to this strong tie, AKRSP (I) might be less likely to produce studies for the purpose of legitimating its work. There is some evidence that this is the case. First, AKRSP (I) has been far slower than

Sadguru in responding to the suggestions of consultants to produce formal studies. While Sadguru generated over twenty case studies, impact studies, and technical reports in 1996 alone, AKRSP (I) produced only five such studies. Second, AKRSP (I)'s selection of case studies appears to be directed towards projects or programs that are likely to produce new and usable information. AKRSP (I) has a history of studying its own "failures" and has in the past conducted reviews of failing activities in order to inform decisions on whether or not to abandon those activities. While Sadguru may also conduct reviews of its "failures," these are not formally documented or disseminated beyond the organization. And third, AKRSP (I) has experimented with other forms of formal monitoring and research that have not been required by the EC or the AKF network but which might be more useful to the organization. For example, in 1996, the NGO initiated a very simple system of monitoring "significant changes" by field staff in order to keep track of important socioeconomic changes at the village level. Observations noted in the diaries of field staff from all three Spearhead Teams are aggregated by the central office and then shared across the organization on a monthly basis. This experimental exercise has the advantage that it involves all field staff (as opposed to just the members of the monitoring unit), encourages some degree of analysis and reflection amongst all staff, can be done rapidly, and does not overburden any single department or individual.

Although AKRSP (I) has not been very intent on producing studies for funders, the NGO is far from free of pressure to generate information. As already noted, both AKRSP (I) and Sadguru have devoted considerable effort to collecting data outlined in the logical framework, although the usefulness of a great deal of the indicators in the framework is not clear to members of either organization. As such, both AKRSP (I) and Sadguru are engaged in the generation of information for symbolic purposes, although to varying degrees. Moreover, it is difficult to determine whether this decoupling of information from decisions is part of a deliberate or passive strategy. On one hand, the symbolic generation of information may be part of a conscious effort in which NGO members intentionally separate information from decisions (as the quotes from Sadguru above suggest). On the other hand, this decoupling may be entirely passive: NGO members may conform to funder demands for information in order to enhance their own legitimacy, but may then be too busy with other tasks to actually use the information generated.

In addition to being symbolic, the information forwarded by the case NGOs to AKF India and the EC is also selective. As depicted in figure 5.1, the bulk of information transferred from the case NGOs to their funders consists of product data rather than process data. Process data are problematic to present for they are not easily subject to quantification using simple indicators, are more difficult to generalize than product data, and are not easily categorized in terms of success or failure. There are not many incentives to forward process data to funders since although both the EC and the AKF network have at times requested process data, the collection of product data remains a priority for them. In addition, the NGOs are already overburdened with information requests. By adhering to product data, AKRSP (I) and Sadguru are able to demonstrate success without having to reveal details of the processes through which those successes are achieved, or to reveal the potentially ambiguous nature of that success.

A third strategy employed by the case NGOs to minimize funder influence on their activities, while also enhancing their own legitimacy, is professionalization. During the 1970s and 1980s there was a trend towards professionalization in the NGO sector in India. At that time, organizations like AKRSP (I) hired well-educated experts such as engineers, agricultural scientists, social workers, and managers. As a more recent part of this trend, AKRSP (I) and Sadguru have begun to professionalize their information systems through computerization and staffing by research experts. Sadguru purchased computers for all of its senior management in 1996, while AKRSP (I) updated its computer systems at about the same time. Following the visit of the Baseline Monitoring Mission in 1994, both organizations expanded their monitoring departments and hired individuals with postgraduate degrees at the doctorate and masters levels. Since 1993 Sadguru has hired a host of well-educated young professionals to fill its managerial ranks.

At first glance these changes in personnel recruitment may be interpreted simply in terms of acquiescence to pressures from funders. But on closer examination, it becomes clear that these professionals have become instruments of resistance to funder intervention. By virtue of their roles as experts, and the fact that they were recruited in order to comply with funder recommendations, these individuals lend legitimacy to their organizations, and they act as spokespersons in defense of their organizations. Sadguru, for example, has often been criticized by funders and other NGOs for paying insufficient attention to community organization and other process issues. Now with a significant number of social scientists to back up its work, it has become more difficult to level this criticism against the NGO. The new expertise has also served to smooth communication between the case NGOs and funders. These professionals share with funders a common development language – terms such as participation, sustainability, cost-benefit analysis, impacts, indicators, and so on. Thus, the professionals are able to communicate their activities in terms acceptable to funders. By justifying their work in terms of a dominant currency, the NGOs are able to deter probes into their work.

It should be noted, however, that these three interrelated strategies – symbolism, selectivity, and professionalization – are not entirely successful in buffering NGOs from funder influence, are not used with all funders, are not always deliberately employed, and are not free of unintended effects. In fact, a great deal of the current activities and processes of the case NGOs are a result of funder intervention especially through the influence of consultants that have introduced new activities.[15] Moreover, the situation with funders other than AKF and the EC – such as the Ford Foundation and NORAD – is quite different because both of these funders request very little information and are not insistent on a rigid format for the presentation of information. As a result, there is less of a need for the NGOs to engage in the symbolic provision of information or to be particularly cautious in selecting information. For example, Program Officers at the Ford Foundation in Delhi generally expect that NGOs will face problems in implementing the programs which Ford supports (i.e. joint forest management and participatory irrigation management) since these are highly process-based activities aimed at increasing interaction between rural communities, NGOs, and government agencies. In this way, "failures" do not necessarily reflect poor performance on the part of NGOs, but may be indicative of more systemic problems. It is also noteworthy, however, that although the Ford Foundation and NORAD are less demanding of information from AKRSP (I) and Sadguru, they are also far less involved in supporting the NGOs with respect to enhancing their technical and managerial capacities.[16]

In addition, organizational leaders are not necessarily deliberate about using symbolism, selectivity and professionalization as strategies to reduce funder influence on their work and decision processes. In fact, it is sometimes difficult to distinguish between strategies that are deliberately or actively employed by NGO leaders and those which are unplanned or passive. The decoupling of certain kinds of information (e.g. baseline and impact studies) from decision making in an NGO may at times be a deliberate buffering strategy, but it may also be a reflection of the NGO's inability to integrate the new information into decision making (for example, if it is overwhelmed with other tasks, or simply does not have the resources to devote more attention to the new information). Similarly, selectivity with respect to information may be a deliberate effort by the case NGOs to limit what funders see, or it may reflect a general inclination in the NGOs towards implementation rather than reporting, and thus a tendency to do only as much reporting as is absolutely necessary (in order to maintain legitimacy). Professionalization can also be seen as both a passive and active strategy. As I have noted above, AKRSP (I) and Sadguru initially hired professional staff at the request of funders. The employment of water resource engineers, agricultural and social scientists, and trained researchers can thus be seen as a passive strategy through which NGOs conformed to funder requests and thereby enhanced their own legitimacy. Only over time, as these professionals became spokespersons for their NGOs, did they begin to actively defend their organizations against criticism from funders.

Finally, some of the strategies discussed above are also subject to unanticipated long-term dynamics of their own. For example, while the information generated by a monitoring unit may initially be largely symbolic, the professionals hired to collect and analyze that information may eventually find ways of making that information important to decision making. After all an individual who is a research expert is likely to believe that research is important, just as a social scientist is likely to devote attention to process issues, and a gender specialist is likely to care about issues of equity.[17] It is thus reasonable to expect that, over time, the information being collected by the monitoring departments of AKRSP (I) and Sadguru might feed back into decision making.

Conclusion: the reproduction of NGO-funder relations

The previous chapter examined the exchange of money, information, and reputation between NGOs and funders. That analysis was furthered in the present chapter with an investigation of how funders attempt to structure information produced by NGOs, and how NGOs in turn resist these efforts. I now bring these two themes together in order to provide a summary and more general analysis of the relationships between the case NGOs and their funders.

The first chapter of this book drew upon the work of Pierre Bourdieu to set up a framework for interpreting organizational change. From this perspective, power, or the ability to assert influence, is exerted through both structure and agency: how NGOs and funders interact may be constrained by structures or patterns of behavior, but these organizations are also capable of altering the terms of their engagement over time. Much of this chapter and the one preceding it have been devoted to describing the patterned or structured part of NGO-funder relations.

A central feature of NGO-funder relations for AKRSP (I), Sadguru, AKF and the EC, has been resource exchange – the exchange of information for funds, or of symbolic capital for economic capital. The information provided by NGOs to their funders is generally quantitative and easily measurable in nature (i.e. product data) and is designed to demonstrate that the supported projects have been "successful." Sometimes NGOs and funders interact directly, whereas at other times there are intermediary organizations such as the Aga Khan Foundation which facilitate this capital conversion process. In either case, the interactions between these highly interdependent organizations are structured by flows of resources.

Although patterns of capital exchange are a prominent part of NGO-funder relations, it should also be noted that these relationships are not only about an exchange of money for information. For example, interactions between NGOs and funders are often built upon a shared commitment to poverty alleviation and environmental improvement. There is little doubt that the projects of AKRSP (I) and Sadguru, as supported by AKF and the EC, have led to improvements in the living conditions of the communities in which they work. But these shared goals and positive results do not diminish the centrality of capital exchange to NGO-funder relations. The cases of AKRSP (I) and Sadguru suggest that as

NGOs grow and continue to seek funds, and as funders seek to maintain their reputations, it is this structure in which money is exchanged for information that becomes central to NGO-funder interactions, despite their common goals and visions.

Given the importance of resource exchange to NGO-funder relations, it is not surprising that funders and NGOs engage in strategies to increase their control over certain resources or at least to decrease the uncertainties associated with obtaining those resources. This chapter has focused on information as a resource, and it advances three key arguments regarding the role played by information in NGO-funder relationships. First, funders attempt to structure the flow of information from NGOs by providing special formats for physical and financial reports and by employing highly specific analytical tools such as the logical framework. These efforts by funders impact NGOs not only by placing demands on their attention and by affecting valuations of success and failure, but also by framing interventions in simplistic, quantitative, and depoliticized terms. In this way, the attempts of funders to secure very specific kinds of information also contribute to NGO perceptions of their own work. These efforts by funders to structure information should not, however, be seen as deliberate attempts to alter NGO values or activities. Rather, they are attempts to acquire information in a form suitable to measuring results and demonstrating success over short budget cycles. As such, the depoliticized nature of the information systems and interventions can be viewed as a *systemic* result rather than one arising from some systematic or intentional strategy.

Second, the case NGOs have resisted these attempts to structure their reporting and behavior. They have insulated their activities and decision processes from funder intervention while also finding ways of retaining their legitimacy (in order to continue receiving funds). The resistance of NGOs to funder demands for information is a crucial component of NGO-funder relations. Tensions arise not only from differences in perceptions between NGOs and funders (and within these organizations), but they also emerge through resistance. It is noteworthy that this resistance is not necessarily overt, deliberate, or easily identifiable. The generation of information for symbolic purposes, the selection of specific kinds of information, and the strategic use of professionals to achieve legitimacy may appear as compliance to funder requests rather than subtle forms of resistance which enable the NGOs to carry on as usual.

Third, there is another dimension to this resistance that is important to understanding the profoundly structured nature of the relations between the case NGOs and their funders. As figure 5.1 shows, most of the information transferred from NGOs to funders is in the form of *product* data. NGO resistance to information demands from funders has not changed the fact that product data dominates information flows. On the contrary, NGO attention is devoted to physical and financial reporting while *process* data, in the form of case studies and to a lesser extent as impact studies, remains largely symbolic. Thus most of the information which funders receive from NGOs emphasizes product data, not process information.

On one side, some members of the AKF network and the EC are also frustrated with the product emphasis – "we get tired of seeing reports with the first ten pages on targets"[18] – and they frequently ask about process issues during field visits. Yet, they persistently place pressure on meeting targets, thereby implicitly equating success with target achievement. At the same time, however, the NGOs do not provide process information (except symbolically) that might influence how funders think about development. In attempting to shield themselves from funder control, the NGOs provide only that information which is required by funders; they refrain from sharing the kind of information (i.e. process data) which might help shift the means of evaluating success away from the current reliance on targets.

NGO resistance to funder demands for information, which takes the form of symbolic, selective, and professional provision of information, thus serves to entrench further the existing emphases on product data. Rather than challenging this focus on product data, the case NGOs attend (either by active choice or by passive conformity) to improving their systems for the production of such information, while simultaneously decoupling formal structure from operations or information from decisions. Ironically – and this is the central point – it is precisely through these actions that existing patterns of information flow are reinforced and through which currently unshared process information remains excluded. As a result, the tensions between NGOs and funders (process–product tensions and insider–outsider tensions) are perpetuated or "reproduced." In other words, it is both through funder demands for information *and* through NGO resistance that tensions between NGOs and funders are produced and reproduced. Moreover, the relations of the case NGOs to their funders remain located squarely within this framework of capital exchange: neither the demands of funders nor the resistance exhibited by AKRSP (I) and Sadguru challenge this basic governing structure.

The above observations and arguments also contain normative implications. The long-term goals of organizations like AKRSP (I), Sadguru, AKF and the EC, include poverty alleviation, social equity, and environmental and economic sustainability. "Success" in reaching these worthy ends cannot be measured in terms of physical and financial target achievement, important as such measurements may be. Well developed information systems can assist NGOs and funders alike in improving planning and implementation procedures and also in identifying problem areas. Attention to product data can help NGOs better to set and meet annual targets. And there is little doubt that the emphasis of AKF and the EC on product-based reporting has helped the case NGOs to scale up their work. Yet the information systems that can assist NGOs and funders to understand the complex, ambiguous, social, and political nature of their interventions continue to receive comparatively scant attention and remain undersystematized. While both Sadguru and AKRSP (I) gather process data (e.g. through participatory rural appraisals, field visits, and case studies), its systematic collection and analysis continues to be overshadowed and displaced by the attention devoted to reporting on physical and financial targets.

The broader implications of this current situation are threefold. First, if NGOs are to develop systems that will help them to be attentive to the social and political impacts of their work, then funders will need to ease off on the physical and financial component of reporting, while supporting the development of simpler, qualitative, and less onerous information systems usable by field level workers. Second, if funders are to be expected to be responsive to NGO needs and constraints, then NGOs will themselves need to inform funders of those constraints and complexities. In other words, funders as well as NGOs share a responsibility in changing the relationship structure which is currently based on an exchange of funds for positivist demonstrations of success. And finally, revising the current structure of NGO-funder relations is likely to be a long-term and incremental process that, at its root, will require a rethinking of valuations of success and failure.

Appendix 1: Information types

The following types of information are generated by the case study NGOs (also see the top left-hand box of figure 5.1):

1 *Physical and financial progress reports* – provide target achievement figures in terms of funds spent and projects implemented (e.g. numbers of irrigation systems, hectares of watershed development, etc.); generated quarterly.

2 *Narrative reports* – provide qualitative details on NGO activities and accomplishments, with assessments of project performance; generated every six months.

3 *Annual reports* – highlight annual achievements in terms of quantitative targets and are supplemented with narration, anecdotes, and photographs.

4 *Annual budgets and workplans* – are forecasts of physical and financial targets for the year, and are used for planning purposes and as an accountability mechanism for funders.

5 *Published studies* – include case and impact studies of projects, villages, or target groups. They are made available for public distribution or sale.

6 *Internal studies* – include case and impact studies generated for internal use by the NGO.

7 *Baseline and impact data* – consist of information on a set of villages (prior to NGO intervention) that can later be used to determine impacts of interventions.

8 *Participatory rural appraisal (PRA)* – consists of a series of interactive tools and methods (e.g. mapping and ranking exercises) through which NGO staff learn about a community and its resources, while also building rapport with its members.

9 *Process documentation research* – involves step-by-step documentation of a process or activity; e.g. documenting the creation of irrigation cooperative societies.

10 *Internal evaluation exercises* – consist of peer evaluations of activities; e.g. an assessment of AKRSP (I)'s biogas energy program uncovered problems with repair and maintenance.

11 *Records* – are maintained by the NGOs on program implementation. Key village-level functionaries also maintain detailed records on projects, membership, and dues.

12 *Diaries* – consist of notes taken regularly by field staff. Supervisors may examine staff diaries to monitor staff work and to keep abreast of new developments in the field.

13 *"Significant changes"* – is a process recently instituted by AKRSP (I), in which each field-team member notes a few significant changes she has recently observed in villages (e.g. changes in cropping patterns). Selections of these changes are shared among field offices.

14 *Tour notes* – are the written observations of AKRSP (I) managers (in its central office) from "tours" to field offices. The notes help managers reflect upon field visits and connect policy decisions made at the central office to their effects in the field.

15 *Dialogue with community members and field observations* – includes information which emerges through informal interactions during field visits and meetings.

16 *Meetings* – include inter-and intra-departmental meetings in NGOs as well as meetings of village organizations (which are often minuted).

The following types of information are generated by two key funders – the AKF network and the EC (also see the top right-hand box in figure 5.1):

1 *Project and program proposals* – are grant applications to large donors written by the AKF network (e.g. AKF India, AKF UK, and AKF Geneva) in consultation with NGOs.

2 *Documents describing program strategies and interests* – include annual reports, public strategy documents, and policy papers prepared for the Board of AKF (which have restricted access).

3 *Annual budgets and "summary justifications"* – consist of annual budget papers for each AKF office, with summaries of current projects. These papers are confidential and are among the few documents that provide regularly generated information about the AKF network, since most AKF offices do not generate an annual report (or have begun to do so only recently).

4 *News clippings, trends, and networks* – include news clippings, journal articles and other information collected by AKF India for forwarding to grantees. Information on donor trends and government changes is informal and unwritten, and is occasionally verbally communicated to NGO management.

5 *Workshops and fairs* – are events arranged by funders on specific themes; e.g. AKF India organized a workshop on "Sustainability of NGOs and their Programmes" in 1995 and a "Developmental Learnings Fair" in 1996.

6 *Publicity documents* – include "Project Briefs" and other short documents prepared by AKF to publicize the development efforts that it supports.

7 *Meetings* – include meetings within and among funders. A key meeting is that of the Program Implementation Committee (PIC) which is comprised of the heads of AKRSP (I) and Sadguru, the CEO and Program Officer of AKF India, and representatives of AKF Geneva, the EC Delegation in Delhi, the Government of India, and the Commissioner for Rural Development of the Government of Gujarat. This committee meets to discuss key problems in implementing the EC grant to AKRSP (I) and Sadguru.

8 *Field visit reports* – are notes of impressions that funder staff obtain during visits to AKRSP (I) and Sadguru field sites.

9 *Evaluations and reviews* – are assessments generally conducted by third parties on: (1) the performance of NGOs; and (2) the work of AKF itself. Recent evaluations of AKF Canada are publicly available, while reviews of AKF Geneva have remained confidential.

10 *Consultant reports/expertise* – involve information and technical expertise obtained through consultants hired by AKF. In the past, consultants have provided inputs on biogas technology, soil and water conservation, baseline indicators, financial management, etc.

11 *Monitoring Missions* – are comprised of a team of consultants hired by the AKF network and the EC to advise NGOs on implementing and monitoring resource management activities. There were two missions between 1994 and 1996: a "Baseline" Monitoring Mission in 1994 and a "Joint" Monitoring Mission in 1995.

6   Learning in NGOs

This chapter examines organizational learning as a key process of change in NGOs. It shows that change through learning – even in very innovative NGOs – can be slow and constrained by a number of factors. For practitioners, policy-makers, and scholars who work with NGOs (and possibly try to facilitate change in them), it is important to recognize how learning occurs and what its limitations may be. The theoretical portion of this chapter draws heavily from the sociological literature on organizational behavior, and it may thus be of interest not only to those who work with NGOs, but also to those who work with organizations in the public and private sectors. In addition, this chapter may be useful to educators as it provides case studies for teaching how NGOs and funders learn. I draw primarily from the work of three organizational learning theorists: James March, Chris Argyris, and Donald Schön.

In investigating processes of organizational learning, my primary question is simply: How do NGOs learn? Beginning with a typology of learning, I then develop a general model of organizational learning. Those readers less interested in the theoretical material may wish to skip the sections entitled "A Basic Learning Cycle" and "A Stimulus-Response Model of Learning." Using the typology and model, I then examine learning processes in the case NGOs. I show not only how learning processes have led to behavioral change in these organizations, but how learning has been constrained. Finally, I discuss the role of funders in influencing learning in NGOs.

A typology of learning

Following Levitt and March (1988: 320), organizations can be seen as "learning by encoding inferences from history into routines that guide behavior." Learning, as such, involves generating knowledge by processing information or events, and then using that knowledge to cause behavioral change.[1] According to this usage of learning, simply generating knowledge is not enough; learning also involves the use of knowledge to influence organizational practices or procedures and may not always be an intentional process.[2]

I distinguish between three broad *types* of learning: learning by doing, learning by exploring, and learning by imitating.

Types of learning

Organizations learn from their own experiences through two primary mechanisms: learning by doing and learning by exploring. The first of these mechanisms, *learning by doing*, is a repetitive trial-and-error process. An organization is likely to repeat a routine that is associated with success in meeting a target, whereas it is less likely to repeat one that is associated with failure (Cyert and March 1963; Levitt and March 1988). Learning by doing is particularly evident in stable environments where organizations are rewarded for improving what they already do. For example, as an organization gains experience in manufacturing a particular product (e.g. computers or irrigation systems) it becomes more productively efficient, that is, it reduces the cost and time per unit produced (Huber 1996: 133). The use of a proven routine, and possibly improving on it, is also referred to as *exploitation* by March and colleagues (e.g. Levinthal and March 1993; March 1991).

A second form of learning from direct experience, learning by *exploration*, occurs when organizations search for new procedures and ideas "without knowing or anticipating the full consequence[s] of their work" (Sánchez Triana 1998: 167). March describes exploration as involving "search, variation, risk taking, experimentation, play, flexibility, discovery, innovation" (March 1991: 71). In this type of learning, an organization may sample various new procedures and adopt those it finds to be better than its current routines, sometimes employing unproven procedures or ideas or even developing new ones. The extent to which an organization engages in this form of learning partly depends on the organization's history of success or failure: failure to meet targets may trigger (or increase) a search for alternative routines, whereas success in meeting targets generally leads to decreased search and increased reliance on the past (March 1988: 3). Learning by exploration and learning by doing (exploitation) are both important:

> If the system [i.e. organization] engages in exploitation alone, it will find itself trapped in some sub-optimal state, failing to discover new directions or to develop competence in them. If the system engages in exploration alone, it never secures the advantages of its discoveries, never becomes good enough at them to make them worthwhile. (March 1992–93: 31)

In addition to learning from their own experiences, organizations also learn from one another by taking on the routines, strategies, hierarchies, or technologies of other organizations. *Imitation*, one of a number of mechanisms of "isomorphic" change in organizations, refers specifically to the copying of one organization's behavior by another (DiMaggio and Powell 1983). The diffusion of methodologies and procedures from one organization to another can occur, for example, through the movement of personnel and consultants or through contacts among organizations (Biggart 1977, as cited in Levitt and March 1988: 330). Mimicry is sometimes used as a survival strategy for organizations facing uncertain conditions, where they look to the activities or strategies of other similar organizations which they perceive to be more legitimate or successful (DiMaggio and Powell 1983: 152).

Learning by doing, by exploring, and by imitating constitute three main types of learning. Each of these types of learning can occur at different "levels" in an organization.

Levels of learning

Argyris and Schön (Argyris 1982; 1992; Argyris and Schön 1978; 1996) describe two different *levels* of learning in an organization.[3] One level of learning, which they call *single-loop learning*, leads to changes in organizational practices and strategies, whereas another level, called *double-loop learning*, leads to changes in the values (or "governing variables") underlying those practices and strategies.

To explain single-loop learning, Argyris (1992: 8) uses a feedback control system where learning occurs in the sense that errors are detected and corrected in a programmed way. For example, a thermostat is programmed to receive information about temperature and then to turn the heat on or off in order to maintain a particular temperature. In single-loop learning, the underlying values reflected in system operation (e.g. the temperature setting) are *not* questioned or changed. Double-loop learning is more fundamental in that learning leads to changes in underlying beliefs or values reflected in the operation of the system. Using the thermostat example, double-loop learning yields changes in the thermostat's temperature setting. Argyris and Schön (1996: 22) summarize the difference between these two levels of learning as follows:

Single-loop learning is ... concerned primarily with effectiveness: how best to achieve existing goals and objectives, keeping organizational performance within the range specified by existing values and norms. In some cases, however, the correction of error requires inquiry through which organizational values and norms themselves are modified, which is what we mean by double-loop learning.

The types of learning discussed earlier – learning by doing, by exploring, and by imitating – can occur at *both* single-loop and double-loop levels. Single-loop learning, which refers to improving organizational performance without questioning existing goals, can occur through repetitive trial and error processes (learning by doing), by experimenting with new approaches for meeting the same targets and objectives (learning by exploring), or by adopting concepts and technologies used by other organizations (learning by imitating). For example, an NGO that seeks to enhance rural living conditions through water resource projects may attempt to improve its performance in the following ways: building on past experience to improve procedures for project development; exploring new untested ways of managing irrigation systems (e.g. by turning over maintenance and fee collection to users groups); or, by imitating the procedures of more effective organizations.

Double-loop learning, on the other hand, occurs when an organization questions its values or the premises of its products, goals, and practices. Using the example above, the NGO could question whether building irrigation systems is the way to deal with the region's poverty problems, or whether alternative actions would be more appropriate. These issues concern the values underlying an organization's activities and goals, and the above-mentioned learning types (learning by doing, by imitating, and by exploring) can lead an organization to question its values. For example, an NGO might question and subsequently alter its focus on water resource technologies if it learns that its projects are leading to class differentiation and conflict in a community (learning by doing). A second NGO, by observing the experiences of the first NGO, might then begin to question and alter its own programs (learning by imitating). In each case, learning at a double-loop level is brought about by a different type of learning. I use the distinction between types and levels of learning to introduce a model of learning in NGOs.

A basic learning cycle

Figure 6.1 contains a basic cycle of learning steps that occur *within* an organization. The cycle involves four main steps: (1) acquiring information about the organization and its environment; (2) generating knowledge, either by analyzing and interpreting information or by reflecting on action; (3) acting, either by applying knowledge to organizational activity or by experimenting with new ideas; and (4) encoding knowledge and experience into routines or memory. As indicated by figure 6.1, knowledge and action can occur in tandem: knowledge can inform and guide action, and knowledge can be generated by reflecting on action. The cycle in figure 6.1 is iterative: in an ideal setting, knowledge is constantly being modified based on new information and feedback, and as a result, routines are constantly being refined.

The center of figure 6.1 includes "governing factors" that can constrain or enable learning: cognitive capacities, relationships of power, and perceptual frames. These factors impact every stage of the learning cycle.

The first of these factors, the cognitive capacities of individuals and organizations, generally constrain learning. Organizations and individuals are limited

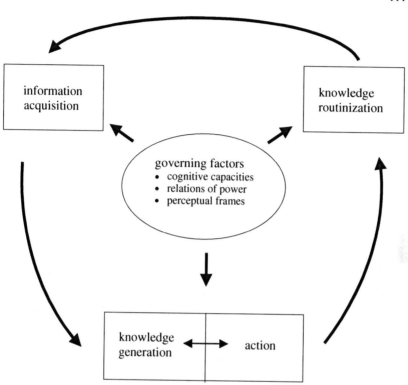

Figure 6.1 A cycle of learning steps

in terms of the information they can collect and their capacities for analyzing and interpreting what they collect. Limitations in cognitive capacity can lead to "superstitious" or "ambiguous" learning. Superstitious learning arises when organizational members incorrectly deduce that a specific action led to a particular outcome (March and Olsen 1988: 342). Ambiguous learning occurs when an outcome is so poorly understood that multiple explanations emerge for that response. This ambiguity can sometimes result in a leader or dominant coalition within the organization legitimating one interpretation (Hedberg 1981: 11). The learning which results is ambiguous because meaning is imputed – it is attached by individuals even though it may not be clear what exactly has happened, why it has happened, or whether what happened was good or bad (March and Olsen 1988: 348).

Attention to information is also an issue. The information to which organizations devote attention determines, to some degree, what they end up doing (March 1988; Pfeffer and Salancik 1978). External actors, particularly funders of NGOs, play an important role in determining what information is collected and therefore receives attention. For example, the monitoring department and part of the information systems in both Sadguru and AKRSP (I) have been set up with the assistance of funders in order to fulfill funder requests for information. As detailed in chapter 5, key funders such as the European Commission and the Aga Khan Foundation, have facilitated and guided the formation of these monitoring units through the use of consultants and monitoring missions sent to the NGOs. However, much of the information which is collected by the NGOs' monitoring departments is often designed to meet the needs of funders, and it is not always relevant to the needs of the NGOs.

A second important factor that shapes learning processes concerns power relationships both between and within an organization. For example, relationships between Sadguru, AKRSP (I) and one of their key funders, AKF, are based on an exchange of resources: AKF channels funds to the NGOs in exchange for information that enables AKF to establish a good reputation for itself in the international development community. These are relationships of power, in which there is an interdependence between Sadguru and AKF, with each organization trying to influence decision making in the other. Information acquisition within the NGOs is shaped by these dynamics of resource exchange and power, sometimes resulting in systems that facilitate learning (by generating knowledge that can be incorporated into action and routines), and at other times generating knowledge relevant only to funders.

Relationships *within* an organization are also important to learning processes. Individuals within an organization are sometimes constrained by their roles and have limited influence on organizational action (March and Olsen 1988). For example, a secretary's role within an organization may prevent him from suggesting changes in organizational procedures if those suggestions might be seen as an overstepping of boundaries. Learning and organizational change can also be affected by coalitions in organizations. For example, in a state agency responsible for water resources planning, technical professionals such as engineers may support the agency's emphasis on infrastructure building. Social scientists and environmentalists within the same organization, however, may be critical of its neglect of issues such as equity in water access or environmental sustainability. If there is some dialogue between coalitions, then organizational learning and change may occur across group boundaries, but if coalitions remain entrenched then change will be guided by the more dominant groups. Such intra-organizational differences, as well as other inter-organizational differences, can be characterized as relationships of power, with individuals, groups, or organizations vying for decision-making influence.

The third, and perhaps most important, factor affecting learning processes concerns the perceptual frames or worldviews that underlie individual and organizational action. Individuals filter information and stimuli from their environments and organize it into worldviews, or perceptual frames, that are meaningful to themselves. Individuals use these perceptual frames to make sense of their worlds. Citing the German philosopher Hegel, Hedberg (1981: 8) explains the importance of worldviews for learning:

Hegel's... term Weltanschauung – world view – recognizes that individuals, groups, and societies reorganize the world inside themselves. A Weltanschauung is a definition of the situation: it influences what problems are perceived, how these problems are interpreted, and what learning ultimately results.

Perceptual frames are not simply one of many variables affecting learning – they are the basic infrastructure through which situations are organized, defined and given meaning. These frames can constrain learning by structuring or guiding how (and what) problems are perceived, what sort of information is collected, and how that information is analyzed and interpreted.

Perceptual frames are partly a product of history. Sadguru, for example, was shaped by its emergence during the "basic needs" era of the 1970s, when poverty was viewed as being an outcome of material or physical constraints. The basic needs approach emphasized providing communities with basic services and infrastructure such as water, shelter, food, roads, health, educational facilities, and so forth. A "solution" which Sadguru developed – lift irrigation systems – was seen as a way of increasing the access of rural communities to water, thereby increasing their incomes. To this day, Sadguru remains a basic needs organization. Although it has expanded its range of activities to include forestry, biogas development, training, and so on, it has retained a focus on the physical (rather than, for example, the political or policy) dimensions of poverty.

Perceptual frames are also a product of an organization's institutional environment. As shown in chapter 3, for example, the activities of Sadguru and AKRSP (I) have been influenced by changes in global development discourse over time. As various development strategies emerged and faded (e.g. basic needs, participation, sustainable development, gender and development, economic liberalization, etc.), they were transmitted to the NGOs through various mechanisms such as consultants and conditions imposed by international funders. Over the past several years, AKRSP (I) and Sadguru have been under pressure from funders to scale up efficiently their activities on one hand, while also devoting attention to issues of equity and citizen participation. Information systems developed within the NGOs (and hence their learning processes) have been shaped by these external pressures, with the NGOs regularly generating reports on their progress in terms of physical output (e.g. numbers of irrigation systems built) and expenditure, as well as case studies that demonstrate the equitable and participatory nature of their work.

Although perceptual frames affect learning processes by influencing what information receives attention and how it is interpreted, learning processes also play a role in changing perceptual frames over time. For example, AKRSP (I) and Sadguru share a very similar institutional environment with many NGOs in western India (in the sense that the NGOs interact with the same funders and government agencies and are exposed to similar development trends over time), but each organization has a different history, and each is staffed and led by individuals with their own histories and biases. Perceptual frames may guide how individuals and organizations interpret stimuli from their environment, but individuals and organizations respond uniquely to those stimuli and change them over time. The relationship between a perceptual frame and a learning process is dialectical: the frame guides learning and behavior, but learning and behavior constantly modify that frame, although perhaps only at the margins. In other words, organizations do not simply respond to stimuli from their environment; they also create and change the stimuli which they perceive.[4]

The central location of perceptual frames in figure 6.1, along with the cognitive capacities of individuals and relationships of power, emphasizes their important, though often invisible, role in shaping learning cycles. This cycle can be placed within a larger stimulus–response model that accounts for an organization's environment more explicitly.

A stimulus–response model of learning

Figure 6.2 illustrates the "environment" of Sadguru and AKRSP (I). The NGOs are subject to changes in a wide range of components of this environment, including government policies concerning resource access and agricultural pricing, conditions imposed by funders, industrial development and pollution in rural areas, rural-urban labor migration, and physical factors, such as rainfall patterns and natural resource supply. Each component of the environment is in a state of flux and thus contributes over time to changing the conditions in which the NGOs operate. (These components also interact and overlap with one another.) For example, Gujarat state has attracted substantial economic investment and industrial growth since India began a program of economic reform in the early 1990s.[5] Rural industrialization is affecting the work of development organizations in Gujarat by causing changes in rural land prices, labor migration patterns, and water and air pollution. This is a diverse and constantly changing environment that presents uncertainties for NGOs as well as their funders.

The basic learning cycle depicted in figure 6.1 and the environment discussed in general terms above, are integrated into the stimulus–response (SR) model of learning shown in figure 6.3. This model places the organization within an environment that is constantly changing and providing stimuli to the organization. The organization responds to stimuli from its environment, but it is also involved in creating and selecting the stimuli to which it responds. In addition, the organization is sometimes able to affect change in that environment. The

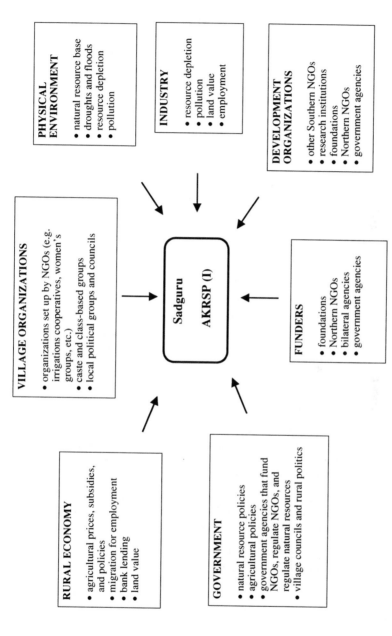

Figure 6.2 The environment of Sadguru and AKRSP (I)

PHYSICAL ENVIRONMENT
- natural resource base
- droughts and floods
- resource depletion
- pollution

INDUSTRY
- resource depletion
- pollution
- land value
- employment

DEVELOPMENT ORGANIZATIONS
- other Southern NGOs
- research institutions
- foundations
- Northern NGOs
- government agencies

VILLAGE ORGANIZATIONS
- organizations set up by NGOs (e.g. irrigations cooperatives, women's groups, etc.)
- caste and class-based groups
- local political groups and councils

Sadguru AKRSP (I)

FUNDERS
- foundations
- Northern NGOs
- bilateral agencies
- government agencies

RURAL ECONOMY
- agricultural prices, subsidies, and policies
- migration for employment
- bank lending
- land value

GOVERNMENT
- natural resource policies
- agricultural policies
- government agencies that fund NGOs, regulate NGOs, and regulate natural resources
- village councils and rural politics

THE "ENVIRONMENT"

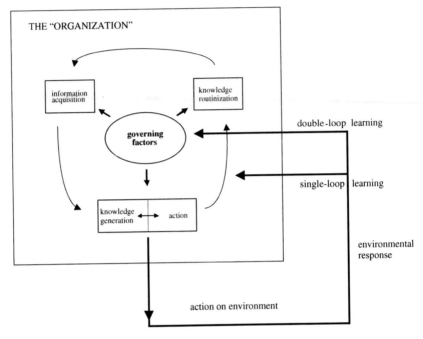

Figure 6.3 A stimulus–response model of learning

concept behind the type of stimulus–response model illustrated in figure 6.3 is explained by Hedberg (1981: 7):

SR learning models describe how organizations gather experience and knowledge as they respond to stimuli from encountered situations. Responses that match stimuli well become increasingly likely to to be evoked by the same – or similar – stimuli in the future, and searches for proper responses are gradually replaced by programmed SR chains (Cyert and March 1963; March and Simon 1958). To identify stimuli properly and to select adequate responses, organizations map their environments and infer what causal relationships operate in their environments. These maps constitute theories of action which organizations elaborate and refine as new situations are encountered.

Learning that occurs within this larger system can be divided into single-loop and double-loop learning. As noted above, single-loop learning focuses on finding better ways of achieving existing organizational goals, and objectives, and is frequently internal to an organization. Single-loop learning can yield refinements in information acquisition and interpretation in an organization. It can also lead to the introduction of new knowledge as an organization explores previously untested ways of achieving organizational objectives or as it imitates other organizations. But single-loop learning does not alter the basic governing factors of the system, that is, cognitive capacities, perceptual frames and relationships of power that underlie organizational action. The second level of learning, double-loop learning, modifies basic organizational values, goals, and practices, and this may come about as a result of changes in governing factors. Both single- and double-loop learning occur through the three *types* of learning noted above: learning by doing, by exploring, and by imitating.

The following two sections use the typology and model developed above to examine the types and levels of learning common in Sadguru and AKRSP (I).

Learning processes in Sadguru

I begin this section by showing that there has been a steady increase in Sadguru's production of natural resource projects over time. Drawing from details of the NGO's water resource development program, I then argue that this increase in projects over time has been partly a result of learning by exploring, by imitating, and by doing that has occurred at a single-loop level. I also present alternative explanations for this increase in production. I then discuss examples of learning in Sadguru's forestry and training programs that have led to changes in the NGO's basic approach to development (i.e. double-loop learning).

Sadguru's physical achievements

Table 6.1 lists the key physical outputs of Sadguru, broken down into four-year periods during the fiscal years (FY) 1976 to 1997.[6] One of the most striking features about Sadguru is its consistent growth in output over time. There has been a steady and substantial temporal increase in output for each listed activity, with two exceptions. First, production of lift irrigation systems declined during FY 1986–89. This drop can be explained by a temporary decrease in government funding to Sadguru during the 1987 and 1988 fiscal years, and a serious drought in Gujarat from 1986 to 1988 which made irrigation impossible in many communities at that time. Second, the number of saplings planted by Sadguru's forestry department fell significantly from 13.4 million during FY 1990–93 to 9.3 million during FY 1994–97. Staff of Sadguru's forestry department offered numerous explanations for this decline. First, Sadguru had already implemented afforestation programs in villages closest to its office by the early 1990s, and thus subsequent afforestation efforts took place in more distant and difficult-to-reach villages, thereby reducing the number of programs that staff could implement per year. In addition, the number of staff in Sadguru's forestry department dropped from fifteen in the early 1990s to ten in 1996. More importantly, since 1994, Sadguru's forestry program has relied less on federal and state funds (which are large in quantity, but unpredictable and thus unreliable for

Table 6.1 *Physical achievement in Sadguru, FY 1976–97*

	FY 1976–81	FY 1982–85	FY 1986–89	FY 1990–93	FY 1994–97	TOTAL
Lift irrigation (number of systems)	4	26	14	41	67	152
Checkdams (number of dams)	0	0	0	56	72	128
Forestry (millions of saplings)	0	1.5	9	13.4	9.3	33.2
Watershed development (thousands of acres of land treated)	0	0	0	8.1	13	21.1
Biogas (number of plants)	0	0	42	293	395	730

planning purposes), and more on smaller, but assured, grants from the European Commission (supplemented by government funds when possible). As a result, Sadguru's annual targets for the forestry program were deliberately lowered after 1994.

Apart from the above-noted exceptions, table 6.1 shows a steady increase in Sadguru's physical achievement over time. To what extent can this increase be attributed to learning processes in Sadguru? What are some alternative explanations for Sadguru's productivity? I focus on Sadguru's water resource development program to answer these questions.

Learning processes in water resource development

Sadguru's water resource development program has focused primarily on the production of two types of infrastructure: lift irrigation systems and checkdams. I argue below that learning by exploring and learning by doing have been important to the establishment and evolution of this program.

Forming a lift irrigation program   Table 6.2 provides a chronology of key events in the formation of Sadguru's water resource activities. The two directors of Sadguru began their work in 1974 in Panchmahals district of Gujarat state with a survey of local conditions and needs. They found that the most common demand in villages of this drought-prone region was for irrigation water. They also discovered that the government had constructed numerous water tanks in the region, but these tanks were not linked to irrigation facilities. Under the circumstances, Sadguru's directors decided to construct an experimental

Table 6.2 *The evolution of Sadguru's water resource program*

Year	Event
1974	Sadguru's directors conduct an initial survey in parts of Panchmahal (now Dahod) district and identify irrigation water as a basic need.
1976	Sadguru builds its first lift irrigation (LI) system with the assistance of a consulting engineer.
1976–80	Sadguru builds 4 more LI systems under the supervision of the consulting engineer and adds agricultural services to complement the LI program.
1981	Secretary of Rural Development, Government of Gujarat, encourages Sadguru to build more LI systems. Sadguru's LI department begins to grow.
1982–1984	Sadguru begins to devolve managerial responsibilities to village-level Lift Irrigation Cooperative Societies. A special Co-op cell is established in Sadguru to facilitate the formation of cooperatives.
1988	Sadguru begins receiving foreign funds from the Ford Foundation and Aga Khan Foundation. Sadguru hires its first water resource engineer.
1989	Sadguru's water resource engineer builds an experimental checkdam.
1990	Sadguru establishes a checkdam department and builds 10 more checkdams.
1991–97	Sadguru's Water Resource Program (i.e. LI systems and checkdams) grows rapidly from 11 checkdams to 128, and from 50 LI systems to 152.
1997	Sadguru establishes a federation of 40 Lift Irrigation Cooperative Societies.

irrigation system in Shankerpura village in 1976. This system used pumps to "lift" water from a government irrigation tank to a distribution chamber at a high point in the village. From this elevated position, water flowed downwards to outlets at various fields in the village. An irrigation consultant provided the technical expertise required for this pilot project, and a federal government initiative known as the Drought Prone Areas Program was used as the main source of funds. This experimental activity enabled a winter harvest in Shankerpura village, thereby encouraging the directors to build three more irrigation systems by 1980.

This initial phase in Sadguru's work was highly exploratory. Neither of the two directors had any previous experience with irrigation systems – the director had been a personnel manager in a private corporation for ten years, and the co-director had been a social worker. In addition, the directors were not aware of any previous attempts by other NGOs or agencies to undertake lift irrigation projects in their part of Gujarat state. The directors were also uncertain about how local communities would respond to the introduction of this new technology and how village members would react to management of the systems by outsiders. Due to the uncertainty and risk taking involved, this early experimentation with lift irrigation by Sadguru can be characterized as an example of learning by exploring. This process also involved learning by imitation: the NGO imitated practices known by the irrigation consultant.

Soon after Sadguru built its first four irrigation schemes, it was visited by Gujarat's Secretary for Rural Development who encouraged the NGO to expand its lift irrigation operations. With additional funds from the federal and state governments, Sadguru embarked on a phase of scaling up its irrigation activities in the early 1980s. By this time, lift irrigation had become the organization's "top most priority" (SSST 1981: 3). By 1985, Sadguru had built and was operating 30 lift irrigation systems in the region, and that number grew to 152 by early 1998.

During this expansion phase in the early 1980s, Sadguru found that many farmers were slow to take full advantage of the increased water supply. Sadguru's directors reasoned that unless farmers also had access to agricultural inputs such as seeds and fertilizers, as well as bank loans to purchase these inputs, the additional water provided by the irrigation systems would be underutilized (SSST 1981: 7). As a result, Sadguru put together a package of "total service" to rural communities which included "planning of crops, arrangement for the necessary finance for the inputs . . . , supply of irrigation, regular technical service, crop protection measures, [and] marketing" (SSST 1980: 4; 1981: 7). Sadguru even arranged for crop loans to be made available to farmers who had little financial collateral by initially taking on the assurance of loan repayment itself. The creation of this package of "total service" was a result of learning by doing: through trial and error, Sadguru learned that it could increase rural incomes by combining irrigation with access to rural credit and agricultural inputs.

Sadguru also realized at this time that scaling up its irrigation activities was going to be difficult if it were to continue looking after the operation and management of every irrigation system itself. The fledgling organization could handle the management of four irrigation systems (i.e. those built up until 1980), but if it were to expand, then it would need either to devolve some of its tasks to the village level or to add more staff. The NGO did both. Up until 1981, most of the administration of the irrigation systems, and all repairs and maintenance, were handled and paid for by Sadguru. Only the actual operation of irrigation pumps had been handed over to village members. In 1982, Sadguru began a process of training community members in the administration and management of lift irrigation systems. This process involved the creation of a Lift Irrigation Cooperative Society (LICS) in each village, and it was facilitated by the formation in 1984 of a new department in Sadguru known as the "Co-op cell." This department was created to handle the process of registering new irrigation cooperatives with the state government and providing training to executive members of each LICS in the management of accounts and the collection of users fees.

The work of constructing irrigation systems and turning over their management to cooperative societies was eventually routinized in an annual cycle:

village visits, site surveys and the formation of technical designs were set for late November and early December, construction was to be carried out from January until the start of monsoon rains in June, and training of village members in management and administration would begin during the construction phase but would continue through the first year of operation.

This arrangement of forming LICSs trained by the Co-op cell carried Sadguru into the 1990s, but as the organization continued to expand its irrigation activities, the Co-op cell found it difficult to keep track of new and old irrigation cooperatives (e.g. for occasional managerial support, and repair and maintenance of systems). At this time, Sadguru began to consider forming a federation of LICSs that could provide managerial and technical support to its member cooperatives. The first such federation of forty irrigation cooperatives was established in 1997 through the initiative and assistance of Sadguru's Co-op cell. Roles and responsibilities of this federation were worked out through a series of meetings held in 1997 and 1998. The formation of Sadguru's Co-op cell in 1984, and more recently of this federation of irrigation cooperatives, was a result of a process of learning by doing: Sadguru learned that in order to scale up its irrigation activities, it needed to expand its staff and to find ways of devolving some of its work to the village level. As such, this devolution of responsibility emerged through an empirical learning process rather than through an ideological emphasis on "participation."

From the early 1980s and into the 1990s, a formally departmentalized structure evolved in Sadguru, with specialized tasks in each department. The organization's 1983 annual report identified, for the first time, five distinct departments: general administration, agriculture (which included an emerging forestry program), irrigation, medical, and preschool education.[7] At that time, the irrigation department employed one consulting engineer (the same irrigation consultant that had been engaged in 1976) and four maintenance mechanics (SSST 1983: 2–3). As the organization increased its irrigation projects, between 1983 and 1986, it began to build its in-house expertise (in engineering and cooperative society formation) by hiring two civil engineering "supervisors" and two staff for its Co-op cell (SSST 1986: 5). By 1986, Sadguru's lift irrigation team had grown to a total of nine people.

The organizational structure that emerged was bureaucratic, with authority vested in hierarchy, and specialized roles at each level of the hierarchy designed to facilitate systematic and efficient implementation.[8] A cadre of "supervisors," of junior and senior ranks, was hired for supervising construction of irrigation projects. In addition, "program officers" (also at junior and senior ranks) were made responsible for developing annual workplans and project proposals for: designing irrigation systems (with technical specifications and cost-benefit ratios); coordinating with other departments in Sadguru; and interacting with government officials (e.g. to certify designs or acquire permits for lifting water from rivers). By 1996, Sadguru's lift irrigation department had grown to approximately twelve full time professional staff, while the Co-op cell had expanded to five employees, for a total of seventeen people involved in lift irrigation. This expansion occurred slowly, over a period of twenty years, as Sadguru developed its capacity for building and scaling up lift irrigation systems.

The formation of a specialized lift irrigation department in Sadguru, the creation of a new department known as the Co-op cell, and the establishment of a federation of irrigation cooperatives, are examples of learning by doing in Sadguru. In attempting to scale up its irrigation activities, Sadguru found it necessary to employ various levels of specialized staff and also to devolve responsibilities to the village level, first by creating irrigation cooperatives and later by federating them. By hiring specialized staff, the NGO was able to absorb new knowledge and skills that were instrumental to its growth and to the formation of standard operating procedures. This phase of learning by doing had been built upon an earlier phase of learning by exploring and by imitating in which Sadguru had experimented with lift irrigation systems and had engaged the services of a consulting engineer.

As shown above, learning by exploring, by imitating, and by doing have been important to the emergence and expansion of Sadguru's lift irrigation program. These types of learning also illustrate single-loop learning because they have been important in helping the NGO achieve its *existing* objectives and improve its performance with respect to those objectives.[9] Learning in Sadguru's lift irrigation program did not occur at a double-loop level because that learning did not involve changes to the governing factors or values underlying Sadguru's objectives and activities. As noted, Sadguru has always been a "basic needs" organization that sees poverty as being an outcome of material constraints, and it therefore strives to alleviate poverty by providing rural communities with access to material resources such as water and wood. This basic needs approach is a central component of the perceptual frame governing Sadguru's work in natural resource management – work which emphasizes building discrete village-level projects through a combination of technological and managerial interventions. Learning in Sadguru's lift irrigation program has been guided by this basic needs frame, and Sadguru has continuously focused on finding ways of improving rural access to material resources (in this case, irrigation water).

Forming a checkdam program Learning by exploring and by doing also characterized the creation of Sadguru's checkdam program. In 1988, Sadguru hired a young water resource engineer to head its irrigation department. Within a year of joining the organization, this engineer suggested that Sadguru's lift irrigation work might be complemented by constructing very small dams across rivers and their tributaries. In many cases these rivers were seasonal, that is, they dried up shortly after the monsoon season ended in September.

The water resource engineer argued that small dams could impound some of this monsoon water for irrigation and drinking purposes, thereby reducing soil erosion. (Small dams to control erosion are commonly referred to as check-dams.) These dams might also aid in recharging groundwater levels over time. The engineer felt that a series of checkdams located throughout a watershed could significantly improve the irrigation potential of this drought-prone region without the high construction and land inundation costs associated with large dams.

In 1989, after obtaining approval from Sadguru's directors, the water resource engineer proceeded to build an experimental dam in Shankerpura village (the same village which had received the first lift irrigation system). The dam was completed in 1990. The engineer and Sadguru's directors obtained technical guidance from a Bombay-based consultant and funds from the Aga Khan Foundation (Sadguru 1990: 14; 1991: 10). Local government agencies had refused to fund or technically certify the project because they felt it was too experimental. However, the dam was successful in storing monsoon runoff for drinking water and irrigation, and this success led Sadguru to form a special unit for building checkdams. This unit, in combination with Sadguru's lift irrigation unit, formed the NGO's water resource department. The checkdam program was also important to the expansion of Sadguru's lift irrigation program: Sadguru was no longer restricted to building irrigation systems only where government water tanks already existed because it could now build irrigation systems at reservoirs created by checkdams it constructed.

The pilot phase of Sadguru's checkdam program was followed by a period of learning by doing and rapid growth. Building on the experience with its first dam, Sadguru constructed ten new dams in 1990. The experimental dam had been built of timber in order to keep costs low, but all subsequent structures were constructed using longer lasting materials such as stone and concrete. As Sadguru gained experience in building checkdams, it developed a standard routine and schedule: village visits, site selection, and design were scheduled for September and October of each year, immediately after the monsoons (along with renovations of dams damaged in the rains); and intensive construction of new dams was arranged for January until the commencement of the monsoons in June (Khorakiwala 1997b).

The checkdam unit evolved in much the same way as the irrigation unit, by adding full time professional staff and devolving some tasks to the village level. In terms of staff, Sadguru eventually hired two engineers to aid the head of the checkdam unit (i.e. the water resource engineer who had pioneered the checkdam program) in planning and designing small dams, and it hired seven supervisors (at junior and senior levels) to oversee dam construction. To devolve tasks to the field level, the checkdam unit trained local masons in the building and repair of dams, and it also trained local individuals in the supervision of dam construction. One supervisor from a local village was contracted by Sadguru for each construction site, thus enabling each of Sadguru's own supervisors to oversee simultaneously three or sometimes even four sites. This arrangement allowed Sadguru to build as many as twenty or twenty-five dams in a single year while maintaining only six or seven permanent field staff.

In sum, Sadguru's checkdam program (like its irrigation program) emerged and expanded through a process of learning by exploring and by doing. First, the organization experimented with a water resource technology. It then found ways of replicating that technology by building up its own expertise, by developing standard operating procedures, and by devolving some of its activities to the village level. These learning experiences might also be characterized as being problem-initiated in the sense that they emerged as a response to problems of water supply and distribution as well as to problems of program expansion. As with the irrigation program, learning in the checkdam program occurred at a single-loop level: it was concerned primarily with the achievement of existing organizational objectives of fulfilling the "basic needs" of rural communities.

Alternative explanations for the growth of Sadguru's programs   I have presented the view that learning by exploring was important to the emergence of Sadguru's irrigation and checkdam programs, and that learning by doing was important to the growth of these programs. It is arguable, however, that these programs grew because of increases in staff and funding rather than a result of the increases in productive efficiency that arose from learning by doing. Productive efficiency refers to the ratio of outputs (e.g. numbers of lift irrigation systems produced) to inputs (e.g. expenditure and staffing) for a certain activity. Gains in productive efficiency arise when more of a desired output is obtained with a given set of inputs.

This alternative explanation holds true in the limited sense that Sadguru's growth was *facilitated* by an increase in staff and funding. However, Sadguru appears to have experienced an increase in productive efficiency through learning: the NGO's growth in programs has exceeded what would be expected from an increase in staff and funding. For example, Sadguru's total number of full-time staff increased from 35 in 1984, to 42 in 1990, and then doubled to 84 in 1996 (Sadguru 1996: 66; SSST 1984: 3). During this period when Sadguru's staff doubled, the NGO's total expenditure nearly tripled from approximately Rs. 25 million in 1990 to Rs. 70 million in 1996 (nearly US $ 2 million). But while the inputs of staff and funding increased by two- to three-fold from 1990 to 1996, Sadguru's outputs increased even more substantially: the NGO's annual production of lift irrigation projects and biogas plants approximately tripled, and it added new programs in checkdam building, watershed development, and training, all at a time when it was also building new offices and a training center. In addition, according to a 1997 evaluation by the European Commission, Sadguru had been able to reduce the price per cubic meter of water stored by checkdams by 55 percent during the 1994–97 period (Häusler et al. 1998: 53–55).[10] The same report also claimed that the cost per acre irrigated by lift irrigation projects rose by 52 percent from 1994 to 1997, but it attributed this jump in cost to increasing prices of pump sets and construction materials.

Furthermore, increases in staff and funding do not account for the growth in Sadguru's programs that has arisen from the devolution of organizational tasks to the field level. For example, I have noted that Sadguru has transferred the administration and management of irrigation cooperatives to local communities, and it has helped to create a federation of irrigation cooperatives. The processes of forming irrigation cooperatives and a federation evolved slowly over a period of two decades as Sadguru learned gradually to transfer some of its work to village-level groups. In summary, increases in staff and funding as well as learning processes (especially learning by doing) have been important to the growth of Sadguru's activities.

Double-loop learning: Sadguru's training institute and forestry program

Sadguru's water resource development program has provided examples of single-loop learning, but double-loop learning has also occurred. Double-loop learning – learning which involves a re-examination of organizational values and goals through changes in the cognitive capacities, relationships of power, and perceptual frames of an organization – appears to be more limited and less common than single-loop learning at Sadguru. This is not a surprising finding because, as Argyris and Schön (1996) have noted in general, organizations and individuals have considerable difficulty engaging in double-loop learning. In addition, since Sadguru's water resource programs appear to be working well and since there is considerable local demand for those programs, there is little reason to expect the organization to question its basic goals and values. Nonetheless, two examples of double-loop learning stand out: Sadguru's establishment of a "training institute" in 1995, and some ideological changes in the NGO's forestry program that also took place in 1995.

Establishing a training institute   Sadguru established a training institute in 1995, and this event represented a fundamental change in the organization. Training appeared as a main objective, for the first time, in Sadguru's annual report for the 1994 fiscal year (Sadguru 1995). The training institute was set up in order "to impart training for the strengthening of village institutions and also training other groups in the field of natural resources management"

(Sadguru 1998: n.p.). For nearly twenty years, Sadguru's work had been focused entirely upon the implementation of natural resource projects. But in the early 1990s, Sadguru's directors began to reconsider the direction of the organization, recognizing that a single organization could only have a very limited impact on the region. Building a training center seemed a sensible way of carrying Sadguru's legacy into the future:

> We want that many NGOs should enter into this field [i.e. natural resource management]. There is much potential and demand [for natural resource management work] but one NGO can't do it all. So we want to train [and] share our experiences with [the] government and NGOs. That's why the training center [has been established] . . . The training center was not in our original vision – it came later.[11]

Sadguru's expansion into training can be interpreted in terms of double-loop learning in that the directors questioned the wider impact and relevance of their work: even if Sadguru could improve material conditions in a few hundred villages, its impact would be minor in relation to the population of Gujarat. Concluding that they needed to find alternative means of extending the influence of their work, the directors began to see Sadguru as a model for other rural development organizations, and they settled upon providing training to other organizations as an important new objective. In addition, although the primary objective of Sadguru's training institute was to impart its expertise to others, a significant byproduct of the institute has been an increase in exposure of Sadguru staff to the experiences, skills, and perspectives of visiting trainees. This exchange has the potential to impact Sadguru's own work and learning in the long run, for example, through imitation of the work of others, or through outside challenges to Sadguru's development approach.

While the above instance of double-loop learning represents a change in perceptions in Sadguru about its work, that change is very circumscribed: Sadguru's directors raised concerns about the NGO's heavy emphasis on building more and more projects, but they did not question the "basic needs" approach which underlies that emphasis. Moreover, the directors' concern about their building program did not involve a challenge to Sadguru's approach to natural resource management, which has remained centered on the delivery of village-level technologies (e.g. lift irrigation systems) that are managed by citizen groups. In fact, the training institute was set up primarily to spread, rather than challenge, Sadguru's natural resource management agenda. Sadguru's expansion into training can thus be viewed as yet another way in which the organization has been able to expand its reach, to replicate its existing work, but without necessarily questioning the work itself or its relevance. From this perspective, Sadguru's expansion into training may even be interpreted as a form of single- rather than double-loop learning because it presented a new way of achieving existing organizational goals and objectives.[12]

Changing a forestry program   A more compelling example of double-loop learning occurred in 1995 when Sadguru hired a new department head for its forestry program. Several months after taking up his new position, this department head began to institute a series of fundamental changes in Sadguru's forestry program. The forestry program had been established in 1982 in order to help meet the fuel and timber needs of rural families, and it was seen by the NGO's directors as a way of reaching village members who had not benefited from irrigation projects. The department head hired in 1995 shifted the emphasis of the forestry program from planting trees for meeting the timber and fuelwood needs of *individuals and families* to activities that met *group* needs, with special attention to the needs of women. Fuelwood and fruit collection for household consumption is typically carried out by women who, as a result, are also more familiar with tree and plant species and their various uses. Staff of Sadguru's forestry department engaged groups of farmers, especially women farmers, in discussions on their forestry needs and assisted them in framing their needs within a larger perspective on development planning for their villages.

The *types* of learning involved here were learning by exploring and learning by imitating. Learning by exploring took place in the sense that the new department head did not know what the consequences of this group approach would be for Sadguru's forestry program, or how staff and village members would respond to it. Learning by imitating took place in the sense that the new department head borrowed this group approach from another NGO for which he had previously worked.

The discussions between Sadguru's forestry department and farmers reflected a change in the goals and basic practices of the forestry department. Instead of engaging in a service delivery (or basic needs) approach, in which saplings were provided to meet fuelwood and timber needs of individuals and their families, the forestry department moved to a capacity-building approach in which groups (particularly women's groups) were trained to collectively identify and articulate their needs and then to plan ways of meeting those needs. A tangible result of the exchange between women's groups and Sadguru has been a shift in the forestry program towards fruit-yielding (rather than wood-yielding) trees in order to meet household food needs and provide a marketable crop.

These changes in the forestry program can be described in terms of double-loop learning because they involved several changes in the governing factors underlying learning, particularly perceptual frames and relationships of power (see figure 6.1). These changes in governing factors led to changes in the goals, values, and practices underlying forestry. Perceptions of Sadguru's forestry staff shifted from seeing forestry as an activity for individuals only to seeing it as an activity for individuals, groups and communities. There was also a shift in relations of power between NGO staff and village women: women were recognized as being knowledgeable about tree species and as capable of planning forestry activities for their villages. In addition, there was a shift in the forestry program away from an emphasis on the provision of a basic need (i.e. wood for fuel or shelter) towards a focus on building the capacities of community members to plan and manage their own forest resources. But while double-loop learning resulted in significant changes in Sadguru's forestry program, these changes were circumscribed by departmental boundaries: the forestry department's shift in goals and practices did not extend to other departments or to a change in overall organizational goals or values.

Unlike the single-loop learning in Sadguru's irrigation and checkdam programs which focused on overcoming obstacles to achieving existing objectives (e.g. obstacles to water access and program expansion), the double-loop learning in Sadguru's forestry program led to fundamental changes in the NGO's approach to forestry. Such underlying change is unlikely to occur in the irrigation and checkdam programs which, given their success and long history in the organization, form the backbone of Sadguru's work and enjoy considerable local demand.

Learning processes in AKRSP (I)

I now turn to AKRSP (I) and show that learning processes there differ considerably from those in Sadguru. I begin by showing how learning by imitating was central to the early formation of AKRSP (I) during the mid-1980s. I then examine the extent to which there have been improvements in the productive efficiency of AKRSP (I)'s activities as a result of learning by doing. And finally, I look at the role of learning by exploring in introducing a new planning system and numerous innovations to AKRSP (I).

Forming a development program

Imitation: learning from the experience of others   Two organizations played central roles in influencing the formation of AKRSP (I) during the mid-1980s. The first of these organizations was an NGO in Pakistan known as AKRSP Pakistan (or AKRSP (P)). As its name suggests, AKRSP Pakistan was also a rural development NGO set up with the assistance of the Aga Khan Foundation network, but it commenced operations three years before AKRSP (I) in India in 1982. During its early years of operation, AKRSP Pakistan piloted an approach to natural resource management that emphasized two key factors: (1) the establishment of village-level organizations to manage all development interventions within villages; and (2) the use of "productive physical infrastructure" (i.e. a technological intervention, such as an irrigation channel, that would be economically productive) to enable increases in rural incomes and to provide an initial incentive for community organization (Aga Khan

Foundation 1987: 19; World Bank 1996: 31). AKRSP Pakistan's activities focused on the management of land and water resources for increasing rural incomes. Some of its early interventions included the construction of irrigation channels and link roads in remote mountainous areas, the planting of forest trees and orchards, agricultural experimentation, and the establishment of savings and credit programs (AKRSP Pakistan 1987).

The experiences of AKRSP Pakistan were introduced to India through the efforts of the Aga Khan Foundation network, and particularly through AKF's headquarters in Geneva. Although members of AKF Geneva were very sensitive to the contextual differences between Northern Pakistan and Gujarat, they carried to India a belief in village organizations and in "physical productive infrastructure."[13] Contact between AKF Geneva and AKRSP (I) was frequent during the 1980s, as AKF Geneva staff regularly visited India in order to provide technical and managerial guidance to AKRSP (I) and also to participate in the NGO's board meetings. By the time AKRSP (I) commenced operations in Gujarat in 1985, its Board of Directors had already determined that the NGO would work through "people's organizations" and would focus its activities on "water and land development".[14] AKRSP (I)'s early activities were thus similar to those in Pakistan: irrigation, tree planting, and demonstrations of new agricultural practices, all of which were implemented through village organizations (AKRSP (I) 1987). This approach to development, which emphasized village-level projects implemented through a combination of technological and managerial interventions, is what I have earlier referred to as natural resource management or NRM.

It would be misleading, however, to suggest that the similarity in programs between AKRSP (I) and AKRSP Pakistan was a result only of imitation. AKRSP (I)'s Board of Directors (which was comprised of well-known figures in Indian industry, government, and development) extensively deliberated the NGO's potential interventions and chose activities that they felt were most suitable to Gujarat's context. While the board was aware of AKRSP Pakistan's work and success, it also recognized that AKRSP Pakistan was working under very different circumstances than AKRSP (I). Gujarat differs considerably from the northern areas of Pakistan in the sense that the state government has a strong presence in development activity throughout Gujarat (whereas northern Pakistan had very little public development activity), and Gujarati villages are generally larger and more diverse in terms of caste and class composition than their northern Pakistani counterparts. Learning by imitating thus occurred only in the sense that AKRSP (I) borrowed from AKRSP Pakistan the concepts of the village organization and of productive physical infrastructure projects related to natural resources. These two concepts provided a basic framework upon which AKRSP (I) developed its activities, that is, the NRM approach to development.

One specific type of productive physical infrastructure which AKRSP (I) decided to build was the result of learning by imitating another organization – Sadguru. In 1981, AKRSP (I)'s first Chief Executive Officer, who was the Secretary of Rural Development for the Government of Gujarat at the time, visited Sadguru in order to examine the organization's lift irrigation activities. Having been impressed with Sadguru's work, he had arranged for additional government funds to be allocated to Sadguru. In 1984, he again visited Sadguru, but this time in order to examine lift irrigation as a possible activity for AKRSP (I). He returned to AKRSP (I) convinced that lift irrigation was a suitable activity for his organization and had even arranged for technical support to be provided by Sadguru. In 1985, when AKRSP (I) initiated the planning and construction of several lift irrigation schemes, it secured the services of Sadguru's Director and consulting engineer. AKRSP (I)'s CEO had learned from Sadguru that lift irrigation was an activity that could be implemented by an NGO and could lead to increases in rural incomes. He therefore tried, through imitation, to undertake lift irrigation projects in AKRSP (I). This imitation of Sadguru occurred at the level of single-loop learning as it was an imitation of a specific technology (i.e. lift irrigation) and did not affect the governing factors underlying AKRSP (I)'s work.

Productive efficiency and learning

Although learning by imitating was important to the initial formation of AKRSP (I), what evidence is there of subsequent learning in AKRSP (I)? In answering this question, I begin by examining the role of learning in affecting the productive efficiency (i.e. the ratio of outputs to inputs) of AKRSP (I)'s main activities over time.

Table 6.3 lists AKRSP (I)'s key activities and their respective outputs broken down into three-year periods from the calendar years 1985 to 1996.[15] While there was a consistent increase in AKRSP (I)'s production of checkdams and biogas plants over time, outputs in lift irrigation and watershed development fluctuated over time and even declined between 1994 and 1996. The organization's work on percolation tanks and forestry has remained fairly steady from 1990 to 1996. This unevenness in physical output is surprising given the fact that AKRSP (I)'s number of employees more than doubled from 1987 to 1996 (from 64 to 144 staff), and that its annual expenditure (in nominal terms) doubled from 1987 to 1991, and doubled once again from 1991 to 1996, reaching Indian Rs. 47.2 million (approximately US $ 1.3 million at the time).

It is not possible to comment on the productive efficiency of AKRSP (I)'s activities without details of inputs (i.e. expenditure and staffing) for each activity over time. Table 6.4 provides these details of physical output, expenditure, and staffing for each of AKRSP (I) key natural resource activities, as well as

Table 6.3 *Physical achievement in AKRSP (I), 1985–96*

	1985–87	1988–90	1991–93	1994–96	TOTAL
Lift irrigation (number of systems)	6	2	4	2	14
Checkdams (number of dams)	1	7	17	46	71
Percolation tanks (number of tanks)	1	4	7	7	19
Canal irrigation (number of canals)			1	2	3
Forestry (millions of saplings)	4.3	3	4	3.9	15.2
Watershed development (thousands of hectares of land treated)		3.2	7.5	5.1	15.8
Biogas (number of plants)	73	750	1784	3052	5659

estimations of expenditure and staffing per unit of output.[16] I have divided the activities in table 6.4 into two groupings based on increases in physical output over time: the first grouping includes those activities with little or only modest increases in output over time, and the second grouping (i.e. checkdams and biogas) includes activities with significant increases in output over time. It should be noted, however, that measurements of physical output do not provide a complete measure of organizational activity because they say little about the degree of citizen involvement in those activities and the organizational resources committed to enabling that participation.[17]

While physical output and financial expenditure in lift irrigation and forestry have oscillated up and down from 1988 to 1996, both programs witnessed an increase in field staff, thus suggesting that there may have been a decline in productive efficiency over time. The number of staff indicated as being involved in lift irrigation,[18] however, is actually a measure of all "water resource" personnel, and thus also includes staff hired for AKRSP (I)'s canal irrigation activities which commenced in the early 1990s; it is therefore difficult to draw any conclusions about changes in AKRSP (I)'s productive efficiency with respect to lift irrigation projects. AKRSP (I)'s forestry program, however, showed a steady increase in staff and expenditure since 1988, but without significant increases in output. Similarly, the watershed development program showed relatively flat output, but with increasing costs and numbers of staff. In both of these cases, the basic data provided in table 6.4 suggest that productive efficiency may

Table 6.4 *Physical achievement, expenditure, and staffing in AKRSP (I),*
1985–96

	1985–87	1988–90	1991–93	1994–96
Lift irrigation				
number of systems	6	2	4	2
expenditure (Rs. '000)	7058	3131	2891	3095
average number of staff	3	3	4	9
avg. expenditure per system	1176	1566	723	1548
avg. number of staff per system	0.5	1.5	1.0	4.5
Percolation tanks				
number of tanks	1	4	7	7
expenditure (Rs. '000)	3355	6939	6092	7172
average number of staff	6	7	8	8
avg. expenditure per tank	3355	1735	870	1025
avg. number of staff per tank	6.0	1.8	1.1	1.1
Forestry				
millions of saplings raised	4.3	3	4	3.9
expenditure (Rs. '000)	7223	4675	5722	7435
average number of staff	4	2	4	6
avg. exp. / million saplings	1680	1558	1430	1906
avg. no. staff / million saplings	0.9	0.7	1.0	1.5
Watershed development				
land treated ('000 of hectares)		3.2	7.5	5.1
expenditure (Rs. '000)		4519	7261	18214
average number of staff		3	4	9
avg. expenditure / 1000 ha		1412	968	3571
avg. number of staff/ 1000 ha		0.9	0.5	1.8
Checkdams				
number of dams	1	7	17	46
expenditure (Rs. '000)	706	2373	4332	13033
average number of staff	2	3	5	8
avg. expenditure per dam	706	339	255	283
avg. number of staff per dam	2.0	0.4	0.3	0.2
Biogas				
number of plants	73	750	1784	3052
expenditure (Rs. '000)	383	3613	8850	12504
average number of staff	1	2	5	7
avg. expenditure per plant	5.2	4.8	5.0	4.1
avg. number of staff per plant	0.014	0.0027	0.0028	0.0023

actually have dropped over time. Only for the percolation tank program was there a gradual increase in output, with costs and staffing remaining relatively constant, although this increase reached a plateau after 1993.

In short, of the first four activities listed in table 6.4, there is little evidence of sustained increases in productive efficiency over time (with the possible exception of the percolation tank program). But an examination of the last two activities – biogas and checkdams – does reveal increases in productive efficiency arising through learning processes.

It is apparent from table 6.4 that as the output of checkdams and biogas plants built by AKRSP (I) increased substantially over time, there were concurrent increases in funding. But the average expenditure per dam dropped over time, from approximately 339 thousand rupees to about 283 thousand rupees from the period 1988–90 to 1994–96. The average expenditure per biogas plant also fell during this period, from about 4.8 thousand rupees to 4.1 thousand rupees per plant. This evidence suggests that the biogas program did become more productively efficient over time, and that these gains would appear even greater were the financial figures adjusted downwards for inflation. Furthermore, these financial figures do not account for increases in the price of building materials (beyond increases due to inflation). Indeed, according to two AKRSP (I) reports, the organization has periodically experienced problems in expanding the biogas program due to increases in materials costs and also due to problems in finding a steady supply of quality materials (AKRSP (I)1997: 77; Alibhai 1989: 3).

A look at changes in the number of staff employed in AKRSP (I) in its biogas and water resource development programs also suggests that the growth of outputs has exceeded that of inputs over time. In the Junagadh field office, which has built most of AKRSP (I)'s checkdams, the total number of staff assigned to water resource development activities increased from an average of three members during the 1988–90 period, to eight members during the 1994–96 period. But the average number of water resource staff per dam built was cut in half during this time (i.e. from 0.4 staff per dam to 0.2 staff per dam). In biogas, staffing seems to have grown proportionately with output over the same time period, but if one compares only the last two periods (i.e. 1991–93 and 1994–96), the average number of staff per plant built dropped by about 20 percent. Moreover, the increase in total staff at this time occurred only in Bharuch district of southern Gujarat where AKRSP (I) previously had no full-time biogas staff. The number of staff in Junagadh district, where most of AKRSP (I)'s biogas plants have been built, remained unchanged during this period.[19]

These data on funding and staffing suggest that there have been gains in productive efficiency in AKRSP (I)'s biogas and checkdam programs over time, and particularly during the early 1990s. Further evidence from the biogas program indicates that processes of organizational learning were important to the formation and refinement of that program.

Learning by imitating and by doing in AKRSP (I)'s Biogas program
A series of reports generated by a consultant hired by AKF Geneva provide evidence that learning processes – especially learning by imitating and learning by doing – were important to the evolution and routinization of AKRSP (I)'s biogas program. This consultant was initially hired in late 1985 to conduct a feasibility study on starting a biogas program in Junagadh district of western Gujarat. In his report to AKF Geneva, the consultant suggested that AKRSP (I) take advantage of funds and technical skills available through the Government of India's National Biogas Program that was set up in the early 1980s as a response to fuel shortages and price increases arising from the oil crisis of the 1970s (Alibhai 1985: 40–45). While the consultant saw the potential for learning (by imitation) from the government's technical expertise, he was also weary of the high failure rate of government-built biogas plants which he attributed to poor construction quality and lack of follow-up maintenance. He felt that a carefully designed and monitored biogas program, built on well-trained masons (to ensure high construction quality) and regular follow-up on plant operation by AKRSP (I) staff, could be successful. Thus, when AKRSP (I) launched its biogas program in 1986, it learned from the government in two ways: it acquired technical training from the Gujarat Agro-Industries Corporation (the state agency responsible for the National Biogas Program in Gujarat), but was also aware of the government's dismal record with biogas plants arising from poor quality construction and maintenance.

Upon the recommendations of the consultant hired by AKF Geneva, AKRSP (I) commenced its biogas program with a series of mason training camps in five villages in Junagadh district of western Gujarat. Masons from the surrounding areas were provided with on-site training in constructing biogas plants, resulting in the building of 51 plants in these five villages by the end of 1986, and requests from farmers for 52 more (AKRSP (I)1987: 45). AKRSP (I)'s aim in training masons was to generate a pool of qualified local persons who could then assist the NGO in implementing its program while earning a stable income for themselves. AKRSP (I)'s experience with participatory village organizations was incorporated into the biogas program through the establishment of Biogas Users Associations which were responsible for monitoring the functioning of plants in their village, for motivating other village members to sign up for plants and assisting them in acquiring government subsidies, for procuring local materials needed for construction, and in some cases, for arranging for credit from banks (for costs of construction not covered by AKRSP (I) or the government).

The first few years of the biogas program, from 1986 to 1990, were focused on training masons, routinizing AKRSP (I)'s implementation and monitoring of the program, and in demonstrating that biogas plants could function reliably over time. During this period, the same biogas consultant initially hired by AKF Geneva continued to visit AKRSP (I) on a yearly basis in order to reevaluate the program, and also to create a biogas manual (written in Gujarati). This was a phase of learning by doing, in which a number of refinements were introduced. For example, AKRSP (I) had initially been experimenting with three different models of biogas plants and found that one of these models – known as the Deen Bandhu design – tended to fare better than the others (in terms of needing less maintenance and repair) when properly constructed. Through this trial-and-error process, AKRSP (I) decided to focus on building the Deen Bandhu model.

Another important step in developing and refining biogas operating procedures took place in 1988 and 1989, when the biogas consultant noted that the NGO was having problems in procuring construction materials (particularly bricks, but also cement) of adequate quality and on a regular schedule (Alibhai 1988; 1989: 3). As a result, AKRSP (I) eventually identified manufacturers to produce bricks specifically for the program, and also set up warehouses to stock certain materials. In addition, the consultant found that AKRSP (I) was losing its masons, either to the government's biogas program or to other jobs, because AKRSP (I) did not provide them with enough work. Part of the problem, he realized, concerned coordination – when the masons arrived in a village, the villagers had often failed to complete digging the pits in which the plants would be constructed. As a result, the masons were sometimes left without work for days. As a solution, the consultant suggested that AKRSP (I) work in three or four neighboring villages simultaneously, so that if the pits in one village were not ready on time, the masons could move on to the next one. Through experiences such as those above, AKRSP (I) eventually developed a routine for biogas construction in which adequate materials were secured in advance, pits were dug on a fixed schedule, and masons were rotated from village to village. In addition, AKRSP (I) eventually trained biogas extension staff, who were often women from local villages, to carry out basic trouble-shooting and repairs on malfunctioning biogas plants.

In an appraisal of AKRSP (I)'s biogas program in 1990, the biogas consultant found that AKRSP (I)'s plants had a "Very high success rate" of more than 95 percent. He also noted that the extension volunteers had been able to repair 49 of 52 breakdowns, with the remaining three being handled by AKRSP (I) (Alibhai 1990: 2,7). As a result of the demonstrated success of the program and due to requests for biogas plants from other villages, the biogas consultant undertook a study of other villages in Junagadh district to identify the potential for expansion.

The first few years of AKRSP (I)'s biogas program, from 1986 to 1990, can be seen as a startup phase that was focused on learning by doing and by imitating. A period of expansion followed, during which the organization made gains in productive efficiency: while output increased by about 70 percent from 1991–93 to 1994–96, AKRSP (I)'s expenditure and staffing rose by only 40 percent (not adjusting for inflation). The learning which occurred was at a level of single-loop learning: it led to improvements in a specific activity and to increases in productive efficiency, but it did not involve changes in the governing factors underlying AKRSP (I)'s basic approach to development (i.e. the NRM approach, with its emphasis on physical productive infrastructure and on village organizations).

Learning by exploring in AKRSP (I)

Although AKRSP (I) has learned to improved the productive efficiency of its biogas program, it has not been as successful in increasing productive efficiency in many of its other programs. Does this mean that AKRSP (I) has failed to learn from its experiences? The notion of productive efficiency – the ratio of outputs to inputs – is related to learning in only a very limited sense. An increase in productive efficiency in a particular activity points to the possibility that an organization has refined its routines or procedures for generating that output over time. But learning is not only about finding ways of generating a product faster, or increasing the *quantity* of a product (such as a biogas plant) at a lower cost and with less staff. Learning may also involve improving the *quality* of a product (which may mean producing it slower or at a higher cost), it may focus on a *process* rather than on a specific product, or it may involve producing different products, and may require considerable experimentation. I argue below that although AKRSP (I) has not learned to improve the productive efficiency of many of its activities, the NGO has frequently been involved in other kinds of learning. First, I examine the role of learning by exploring in leading to improvements in AKRSP (I)'s planning procedures, but without necessarily leading to increases in productive efficiency. I then show that exploration has also led to the introduction of many new activities and practices in AKRSP (I).

Improving planning through exploration   One of the key "problems" facing AKRSP (I) in the early 1990s was its failure to scale up its activities and to develop realistic projections for physical and financial progress on a yearly basis. In 1993, AKRSP (I) received a new Chief Executive Officer who was given three mandates from the NGO's Board of Directors: to improve performance with respect to targets, to reduce staff turnover, and to strengthen gender and equity aspects of the organization's work. It is significant that the first part of this mandate concerned *target* achievement and not *productive efficiency*. In other words, AKRSP (I) was under pressure to meet its annual targets, but not necessarily to do so more efficiently. It was also at this time (i.e. at the end of 1993) that AKRSP (I) was scheduled to receive its first installment of an 8-year grant from the European Commission, and was thus under pressure to demonstrate that it was capable of scaling up its work. I show below that through a process of learning by exploring, AKRSP (I) was able to improve its planning systems, which involved enhancing its ability to set realistic targets.

A key experimental step taken by AKRSP (I)'s Chief Executive Officer in 1994 was to decentralize planning processes to the field level. Annual planning, which included the setting of physical targets and budgets for the year, was until then managed by central office staff in consultation with the field offices (i.e. Spearhead Teams or SHTs). As a result of the CEO's decentralization effort, however, each SHT was made responsible for setting its own annual physical and financial targets. The role of the central office was to provide technical support and guidance as needed, and also to consolidate plans received from each of the SHTs. This system took two to three years to evolve, with the SHTs developing their first complete plans in 1996. This was also the first year in which AKRSP (I) was able to achieve most of the targets that it had set for itself. This success in meeting targets resulted partly from setting some targets *lower* than in 1995, especially in the forestry and watershed development programs.[20] Thus, although a lowering of targets does not imply learning in the sense of improving productive efficiency, it does indicate that AKRSP (I) staff had learned to better forecast their own capabilities, and could thus provide funders with realistic expenditure projections.

AKRSP (I)'s new planning process was based on an experimental planning approach referred to by NGO staff as the "watershed concept." AKRSP (I) had previously planned its interventions in rural communities on a relatively ad hoc village-to-village basis, and by 1996 the NGO was working in 402 villages (AKRSP (I)1997: 1). According to the CEO, because "a lot of [AKRSP (I)'s] work was so spread out . . . it [was] difficult to claim an impact this way, and [we had] no real focus other than farmers."[21] With the watershed concept, the new planning unit became the small watershed – a physical region distinguished by its water drainage patterns, and measuring approximately 5000 hectares in area.[22] The NGO's work was to be intensively focused on a limited number of watersheds, under the assumption that integrating the organization's interventions in a confined area would increase its impacts. It was expected, for example, that soil and water conservation activities would have a greater impact on reducing soil erosion and water loss from farms if they were combined with afforestation and biogas activities, not only in the same village but in all villages within the same watershed.

The 1996 planning process was thus based on micro-watersheds. For example, the Spearhead Team in Bharuch district marked out five watersheds in which to focus its work. Each watershed was then further subdivided into about ten micro-watersheds containing several villages in each. Budgets were proposed for each micro-watershed and then aggregated upwards. This planning approach helped field level staff make estimates at a scale with which they were comfortable. Micro-watershed "A1", for instance, contained fourteen villages, of which AKRSP (I) was already working in nine in 1995 (AKRSP (I) Netrang 1997). Thus, for 1996, the next step was to intensify work in those nine villages and also gradually to reach the five remaining villages. In this way, AKRSP (I)'s interventions could systematically expand across a watershed, as determined by plans developed at the SHT level.

In addition, each SHT was further subdivided into semi-autonomous "cluster offices". The Bharuch team, which consisted of 44 staff in 1995, was separated into the main office and three cluster offices, each located in a different region of the district and responsible for work in different watersheds.[23] The Dediapada Cluster, for example, was comprised of twelve staff members in early 1997 and was responsible for managing the work in two of the SHT's five watersheds. Each cluster was made responsible for a subset of the SHT's overall budget and targets.[24]

AKRSP (I)'s decentralization effort thus occurred at various levels with the central office handing over planning to the SHTs, which in turn subdivided their plans and managerial and implementation responsibilities into watersheds and clusters. Specific routines have emerged for planning purposes, with SHTs forming their annual plans shortly after the monsoon season (which ends in September) in order to receive central office approval prior to the new year in January. In addition to annual deliberations on budgets and targets, each SHT also holds quarterly planning meetings, and each department within the field offices (e.g. water resources, forestry, biogas, etc.) holds its own planning meeting prior to the SHT-level discussions.

One result of this decentralized process was that AKRSP (I)'s field staff became key planners for their SHTs. For an organization that values "participation," the new process gave field-level staff greater influence in determining their own work. Learning occurred in the sense that AKRSP (I) was now better able to set realistic targets and budgets than in the past and that the process of watershed-based planning became routinized in the organization. The primary type of learning involved was learning by exploring, particularly since the decentralization effort (based on the "watershed concept") was experimental and required from AKRSP (I) a certain degree of "flexibility, discovery, [and] innovation" (March 1991: 71). While this learning was not aimed at increasing the output of projects, it was important in two respects. First, AKRSP (I)'s improved ability to set realistic targets enhanced its relationship with funders who could now be assured of a reputation for supporting a "successful" organization (i.e. an organization that was meeting its annual physical and financial targets).

And second, the decentralization effort enabled field staff to set their own limits on targets, thereby enabling them to allocate sufficient time to garnering citizen involvement and to forming village organizations.

Innovation through exploration   Although tables 6.3 and 6.4 list AKRSP (I)'s primary physical activities, they provide a very incomplete picture of the range of activities that AKRSP (I) has explored. Table 6.5 provides a chronology of activities and practices added to and deleted from AKRSP (I)'s repertoire from 1985 to 1996.[25] What is surprising about the chronology in table 6.5 is the continuous stream of new activities or practices developed each year by AKRSP (I). The organization commenced operations in 1985 with a focus on lift irrigation, tree planting, and agricultural demonstration plots, and also began experimental trials with community wells and sprinkler irrigation systems. In the following year, AKRSP (I) expanded its activities to include a fledgling biogas program, a savings and credit program, assistance to farmers in marketing their crops, explored various irrigation technologies, and also began mobilizing communities to protect neighboring forest lands from illegal tree felling. During this time, the NGO was also trying to develop ways of mobilizing communities in order to form village organizations. As table 6.5 shows, new programs and activities continued to be added nearly every year. Some of these activities evolved into more or less permanent programs whereas others were eventually abandoned. For example, AKRSP (I) has always maintained water resource development program, although the components of that program (e.g. lift irrigation, checkdams, percolation tanks, canal irrigation, pedal pumps, and drinking water projects) have changed over time and across the regions in which it works. Other programs, particularly those involving farm animals (e.g. animal husbandry, cattle camps and fodder farms)[26] have been abandoned altogether.

While AKRSP (I) has explored many new activities, I have shown earlier in this chapter that it has not succeeded in increasing the productive efficiency of many of its activities. AKRSP (I)'s former CEO suggested that there may actually be tensions between experimentation and replication, in that "an organization may be good at innovating, but not at systematizing [its work] to the extent of scaling up" that work.[27] In addition, he noted that AKRSP (I) attaches considerable importance to community level participation, and that an increase in the *quantity* of activities (and possibly in productive efficiency) can compromise the *quality* of its work by reducing community-level involvement. For the former CEO, AKRSP (I) is not interested in simply scaling up its work; instead, it seeks to find a balance between quantity and quality, while also being an innovator.

AKRSP (I)'s constant experimentation with new activities can also be partly explained by the fact that one important organizational objective was to seek

Table 6.5 *Activities and practices added and dropped by AKRSP (I),*
1985–1996

Year	Activities and practices added	Activities and practices dropped
1985	lift irrigation, forestry, agricultural demonstration, community wells and well deepening, and the formation of village level organizations.	
1986	biogas, village-level savings and credit program, fodder farms, crop marketing, community forest protection, experimentation with sprinklers, drip irrigation and hydroponics.	well deepening was found to be technically and commercially non-viable in certain locations.
1987	checkdams, cattle camps, and renovation of existing percolation tanks.	
1988	watershed development (i.e. soil and water conservation), and animal husbandry (particularly artificial insemination of cattle for higher milk yields).	cattle camps established during the drought (1985–87) were no longer in high demand.
1989	participatory rural appraisal (pra), farmer-to-farmer extension ("extension volunteer") program, expansion of animal husbandry program to include training of villagers in veterinary services and in acquiring quality cattle feed.	
1990	Joint Forest Management, and Women in Development program.	
1991	canal irrigation (Participatory Irrigation Management program).	fodder farms established during drought years faced financial crises due to lack of demand and corruption among farm managers at the village level.
1993	new CEO places emphasis on gender and equity issues: AKRSP (I) commences gender sensitization training and begins to work more actively with women.	animal husbandry program faced difficulties with respect to community participation, conflict over pastureland use, and in setting up a reliable veterinary and milk marketing infrastructure.
1994	agriculture program adds organic farming and integrated pest management practices.	public wasteland development (i.e. afforestation of public forest and grazing lands adjacent to villages) faced problems in certain areas with intra-community conflicts and uncooperative public officials.
1995	children's environmental awareness program; water resource program adds drinking water & homestead irrigation technologies; a drive to increase membership of women in village organizations begins; village organization maturity index developed.	
1996	decentralization of planning and budgeting procedures using a "watershed concept."	

out new and innovative ways of approaching rural poverty that could later be replicated, not just by AKRSP (I), but by other NGOs and government agencies. A former senior member of AKRSP (I) explained that rather than seeking to scale up its work, "AKRSP was more interested in researching, through action, alternative [approaches to the] management of natural resources."[28] The NGO's board of directors referred to this experimental work as "action research" designed to draw lessons for "future programmes and to make available the experience of cost-effective development to government and non-government organisations working in the same field."[29] This action research was apparent not only in AKRSP (I)'s constant experimentation with new activities and practices, but also in its selection of geographical regions in which to work. Three districts of Gujarat were selected by AKRSP (I)'s board, each with a distinct set of problems – one district faced frequent droughts, another had salinity problems in groundwater and soils, and the third district was an extremely poor "tribal" region with high soil erosion. A reason for selecting these diverse districts was to develop a range of models of natural resource management that could then be applied to a variety of contexts.

The innovations that arose from action research (which include many of the activities listed in table 6.5) were divided by one member of AKRSP (I) into two broad categories: *product* innovations and *process* innovations.[30] Product innovations referred to new activities that were physical products or technologies, such as checkdams and pedal pumps. Process innovations referred to new approaches or methodologies, such as participatory rural appraisal, methods for increasing community participation (in terms of time, labor, or funds), gender sensitization techniques, or new approaches to collaborating with the government (e.g. Joint Forest Management or Participatory Irrigation Management). These innovations can be characterized as being a product of learning by exploring – they were experimental activities that were somewhat unpredictable in terms of their eventual consequences.

Some of AKRSP (I)'s product and process innovations can also be viewed in terms of learning by imitating. For example, a number of AKRSP (I)'s innovations were introduced by international consultants hired by the Aga Khan Foundation Geneva. AKRSP (I)'s biogas activities, its watershed development program, and its work on participatory rural appraisal all began through visits by consultants who had worked on similar activities elsewhere. The consultants can thus be seen as intermediaries in an imitation process: they serve as mediums through which activities and innovations in development are transmitted from one organization to another. Learning by doing also played a role in the formation of new activities. As AKRSP (I) developed experience in villages, it discovered that it needed to develop new activities to complement existing ones. For example, as the NGO began working on irrigation issues, it found that it also needed to provide support to farmers on issues related to agriculture, which in turn led to the formation of credit and marketing programs to enable farmers to purchase agricultural inputs and to sell their crops.

The distinction between product and process innovation is also important for understanding the *level* at which learning occurs, that is, at a single-loop or double-loop level. AKRSP (I)'s product innovations (i.e. physical or techno-logical activities such as biogas plants, checkdams, etc.) have served primarily to augment AKRSP (I)'s array of activities, and do not seem to have actually changed thinking within the organization about development. Whether AKRSP (I) was building biogas plants or a checkdam in a village, it was still working to-wards building village organizations focused on natural resource management. As such, the learning which led to the introduction of these new activities (i.e. learning by exploring) and in scaling up some of these activities (e.g. learning by doing in the case of biogas) can be said to have occurred at a single-loop level.[31]

Some of the "process innovations" introduced through learning by exploring, however, have led to double-loop changes. For example, AKRSP (I)'s exper-imentation with participatory rural appraisal methodologies led to important changes in the relationships between organization members and village mem-bers: through PRA techniques, village members became the "experts" from whom AKRSP (I) staff sought information. Although AKRSP (I) had previ-ously espoused the idea of "participation", it was able to learn through PRA that community members are experts in their own right and capable of participating in the planning of projects, and not just in their implementation. AKRSP (I)'s experimentation with PRA can be considered a form of double-loop learning because it facilitated a transformation in how NGO staff perceived and re-lated to community members. In addition, through its pioneering work on Joint Forest Management and Participatory Irrigation Management, AKRSP (I) has attempted to change state-level policies on natural resource management and also to alter relationships of resource control and power between state agencies and local communities.

In brief, AKRSP (I) has been engaged in both single-loop and double-loop levels of learning. Single-loop learning (in the form of learning by doing, im-itating, and exploring) has been important to scaling up and improving the productive efficiency of AKRSP (I)'s biogas program, as well as to introducing product innovations to the NGO. Double-loop learning (in the form of imitation and exploration) played a central role in the initial formation of AKRSP (I)'s activities and developmental approach, as well as in the development of process innovations in AKRSP (I). Both of these levels of learning, as detailed below, have also been influenced by funders.

Funder influences on learning and accountability

Learning in NGOs is a result not only of their own internal efforts but also of influences from their environment. Inter-organizational relationships in particular, such as those between NGOs and their funders, affect learning and change. Moreover, configurations of power and accountability play an important role in guiding learning. In this section, I briefly examine the role of funders in influencing learning in NGOs. In particular, I explore the role of the AKF network in: (a) impacting standard activities and procedures in the case NGOs; (b) influencing information and accountability systems in NGOs; and, (c) promoting new thinking in NGOs.

Changes in standard activities

Intermediary funders serve as a key link between NGOs and international donors, transmitting global discourses on development to NGOs while simultaneously packaging their activities in terms understandable to bilateral donors. The AKF network has played a pivotal role in the evolution of both AKRSP (I) and Sadguru, particularly in influencing the emergence of standard activities and procedures in these organizations. The NGOs have been given access to resources, information, technologies, and ideas (through funds, technical expertise, and consultants) that would have otherwise been difficult for them to acquire. Consultants on participatory rural appraisal, for example, were hired by AKF upon the request of AKRSP (I)'s chief executive officer in the late 1980s. Biogas as well as soil and water conservation activities were introduced through a string of visits by the same consultants over a number of years. Through the AKF network's insistence, AKRSP (I) also began devoting more attention to issues of gender in the early 1990s, and AKRSP (I) now provides gender sensitization training not only to its own staff and village organizations, but also to other NGOs and government agencies. The initial adoption of gender programming in AKRSP (I) may have been affected by learning processes, although it was more likely a result of funder pressures. I have noted earlier that AKRSP (I) initially formed a Women in Development program in response to demands from funders. The initial adoption of this program can be seen as being a result of coercive pressure (from funders) rather than a product of learning, although learning processes may eventually have played a role in the evolution of the program.

The influence of funders on NGO activities and learning can also be *constraining*. At the same time that links between AKRSP (I), Sadguru and the AKF network have led the NGOs to develop specific types of expertise, those relationships have also limited the work of the NGOs in new directions. The activities of the NGOs have always been heavily technology-based with a large part of their development interventions centering on scientific practices or technologies (e.g. irrigation systems, checkdams, biogas plants, and forestry practices) that are capable of either generating income or reducing stress on local natural resources.[32] Village organizations and users groups are generally formed around these activities. AKF's assistance to the case NGOs has been focused on the improvement or scaling up of such interventions, particularly through the provision of funds and technical and managerial support. This emphasis on technologies and techniques of natural resource management, and their replication, has necessarily been accompanied by less attention to other development approaches and priorities. For example, although both AKRSP (I) and Sadguru have succeeded in influencing state-level policies on natural resource management, this is not a central focus of their work, although it was an important part of AKRSP (I)'s work in the past.[33] The AKF network (AKF Geneva and AKF India more specifically) has played only a weak role in encouraging the NGOs to influence policies on natural resources, and has sometimes even discouraged it. As such, while funders can be instrumental to introducing new ideas and approaches to NGOs, they can also exert a constraining influence on NGO activity.

Information and accountability

The influence of funders on NGOs is not limited to standard activities. Funders also play central roles in affecting information and accountability systems in NGOs. As detailed in chapters 4 and 5, there is an *interdependence* between NGOs and funders based on relations of capital exchange in which funders provide money or "economic capital" to NGOs in exchange for "symbolic" forms of capital such as information and reputation. Control over information is a lever of power both for NGOs and for funders. It enables NGOs to secure funds and to control what funders know about them. At the same time, funders employ various strategies to increase their control over this information including, for example, an insistence on standardized reporting formats, an emphasis on easily measurable inputs and outputs, and a centralizing of information generation within monitoring departments in the NGOs.

For the cases of Sadguru and AKRSP (I), these information systems were established not only to satisfy funders needs for information but also to help the NGOs monitor and adjust their work. The information gathered as part of the "logical framework" introduced by AKF and the EC, however, has actually been of little use to NGO staff. The CEO of AKRSP (I) has observed that "the coerced adoption of information systems to suit the needs of donors reproduces a key deficiency" in the usability of that information for NGO staff. But he is also keen to note that his organization is "aware of this deficiency" and has adopted "compensatory systems" such as a series of internal quarterly reviews carried out by each field office.[34] Similarly, Sadguru has its own decentralized system of data collection and analysis managed by individual departments (e.g. forestry, water resources, etc.) that gather information "regularly and constantly" for use by field-level workers.[35] In essence, there are two parallel information systems in AKRSP (I) and Sadguru: monitoring systems set up by funders and systems internal to the NGOs. The systems set up by funders are of limited use to the NGOs, but are necessary for funds to flow.

The existence of these dual information systems points to larger concerns about accountability and learning. Funder requests for information are necessary for purposes of accountability: members of the AKF network must show bilateral donors how their funds are being spent, and those donors need to justify their spending to their governments. Interactions over funding are relationships of "upward" accountability, with AKRSP (I) and Sadguru being accountable to the Aga Khan Foundation, AKF being accountable to the European Commission, and the EC being accountable to its member governments. Information flows up this chain: information from villages is collected by NGO staff who write reports for funder consumption, and funders send evaluation teams and monitoring missions to NGOs.

To be sure, some degree of limited "downward" accountability does exist.[36] AKRSP (I)'s Chief Executive has acknowledged that while procedures for village members to evaluate NGOs are uncommon, consultation with communities, both in terms of short-term projects and longer-term strategy, is common in AKRSP (I). In addition, he noted that "it has to be recognised that evaluation teams and missions do talk to village groups and people to get their views, and in this limited sense hold AKRSP (I) accountable to villagers."[37] Sadguru's Director has similarly noted that while there are no formal systems for downward accountability, "there are strong informal system[s] in which we get constant feed back on our programmes from the villagers" and that high demand for Sadguru's programs is indicative of programmatic success as well as accountability.[38]

While there appear to be some forms of informal and limited downward accountability in the NGOs, there is little downward accountability at higher levels of the chain: the NGOs do not assess the AKF network, and AKF does not evaluate the EC. Although AKF periodically conducts evaluations or reviews of its own work, the organization lacks a transparent policy for making this material available to NGOs or its own staff. On the one hand, evaluations of AKF Canada have been regularly conducted by the Canadian International Development Agency and are publicly accessible and thus available for deliberation (e.g. Smillie and Catmur 1988; Universalia 1995). On the other hand, a review of the AKF network commissioned by AKF Geneva in 1995 is unavailable even to many of the organization's own staff.

Accountability and information systems also influence organizational learning. Learning that is made possible by upward accountability mechanisms occurs higher up in the chain, removed from the sources of information in the field. The monitoring units in both AKRSP (I) and Sadguru are primarily occupied with meeting the monitoring and evaluation needs of managers and funders, and are consequently unable to devote much attention to assisting field level workers with their information requirements. This is a system in which information is collected and designed for use by "uppers" and neglects the needs of "lowers." Chambers (1994a) has argued that such systems are inimical to learning and change for, in such cases, the "uppers" acquire and interpret information in ways that fit their preconceptions while "lowers" generate information to fit what they believe uppers want to hear and will reward:

The outcome of uppers' dominance and defenses, and lowers' responses, can be stable systems of power and misinformation.

[M]ultiple sources of feedback to those in power often mislead, tending to show things better than they are, and so justifying further funds to complete the feedback loop of a self-sustaining myth. (Chambers 1994a: 22–23)

It is important to recognize, however, that these relationships of power between uppers and lowers differ from case to case. The AKF network's relationship with AKRSP (I) has always been very different from its relationship with Sadguru. Although AKRSP (I) is officially independent of the AKF network and has its own board of directors, AKF Geneva has a permanent membership on the board, and all board members continue to be approved by the Aga Khan (Aga Khan Foundation 1998b: 11). On the other hand, AKRSP (I)'s membership in the AKF "family" also provides it with a certain degree of financial security. From this perspective, AKRSP (I)'s relationship with AKF is a golden handcuff, for the NGO is on one hand tied to AKF, while on the other hand it is secure in funds. Sadguru, by comparison, is not part of the AKF family and does not share the same history of genesis, nor the accompanying security, with the AKF network.

In sum, funders like AKF can influence learning and behavioral change in NGOs by introducing them to new technologies and activities, but they also limit learning and change through their own specific information requirements and accountability systems. A bias towards the needs of funders or "uppers" can lead to information systems that are inimical to field-level learning, and to accountability systems that neglect the needs of NGOs and "lowers."

Promoting new thinking in NGOs: a strategic review of AKRSP (I)

The above observations notwithstanding, it would be unfair to portray the AKF network as inattentive to the field-level challenges facing NGOs. Indeed, AKF has been actively involved in promoting new thinking in the NGOs, and especially in AKRSP (I) through a strategic review process.

In 1996, AKF Geneva proposed a review of AKRSP (I) in order to assess the relevance of the NGO's work to its changing environment, and to articulate a vision for AKRSP (I)'s future – an activity which, in academic terms, can be thought of as a formalized double-loop learning process. This proposal came on the heels of a recently completed strategic review process of AKRSP Pakistan. The review of AKRSP Pakistan (which is a slightly older and more established organization than AKRSP (I)) commenced a phase of devolution for AKRSP Pakistan in which the NGO would eventually be divided into a number of smaller and financially independent organizations. For example, deliberations were underway to spin off the savings and credit department of AKRSP Pakistan into an independent development bank. Similarly, it was envisioned that the sections of AKRSP Pakistan that promote non-agricultural enterprises could be spun off into an "enterprise support company". This division of AKRSP Pakistan into a group of independent but integrated organizations was also seen as a means of leading the NGO to financial sustainability, that is, independence from foreign financial support.

A rethinking of AKRSP (I)'s strategy and vision followed from this review of AKRSP Pakistan. Members of AKF Geneva and AKF UK saw themselves as playing the necessary role of forcing AKRSP (I) to take a hard look at itself. As the Programs Manager at AKF UK put it:

There is a lack of vision for AKRSP (I). Is it merely to continue getting donor funds and doing more of the same [work] in other areas? . . . [A strategic review] can be painful for an organization. Therefore it needs outside influence in the review process. For example, in AKRSP Pakistan, hiving off parts [of the organization] was a difficult decision. One of AKF's key roles is to get organizations like AKRSP to look at this [vision] and to force the agenda a bit. Otherwise there's a tendency to sit on one's laurels.[39]

AKF's determination to conduct a strategic review of AKRSP (I) was also motivated by rapid changes in Gujarat's economy, including a substantial growth in petrochemical industries and in foreign investment in the regions in which AKRSP (I) operates. The Director of Rural Programs for AKF's headquarters in Geneva expressed concern that "we don't know that in ten years anything we're doing [in Gujarat] will be relevant at all" due to changes in the local labor economy and in the depletion and pollution of natural resources.[40] Through a strategic review, AKF Geneva encouraged a reassessment of AKRSP (I)'s goals and work in light of these changing economic and environmental conditions. In the terminology of organizational learning, AKF Geneva was promoting a form of double-loop learning because the review required a fundamental reevaluation of goals and practices. A strategic review was not, however, seen as necessary by all AKRSP (I) staff. AKRSP (I)'s Chief Executive Officer, in particular, expressed reservations about the process, arguing that the review was "thrust upon us" and that "AKF felt it necessary; we didn't."[41] He did, however, eventually buy into the strategic review. Nearly two years after the above statement, AKRSP (I)'s head reflected candidly on his earlier position:

It is amazing how quickly things seem dated. The strategic review is now "owned" by us, and we involved AKF entirely in its lengthy and participatory process.

Reflecting now, distanced in time from the situation, a lot of our earlier resistance to the Strategic Review was to do with the issue of control . . . There was a strong fear that external consultants would be imposed [by AKF Geneva and AKF India], and control of the exercise would go out of our hands, resulting in a vision we did not own . . .[42]

In the end, the strategic review was carried out in 1998 under AKRSP (I)'s terms, involving no international consultants, and in close collaboration with AKF India and one external Indian consultant.[43] The strategic review concluded that AKRSP (I)'s current NRM activities were still appropriate for certain parts of Gujarat, but that the NGO needed to pay closer attention to region-specific needs and to intensify its existing work on issues of gender and equity. Reflecting on the review and the relevance of the NRM approach, AKRSP (I)'s Chief Executive Officer explained that while the NRM approach may still have considerable relevance in some districts (such as Bharuch in south Gujarat), it was important that his organization also look at issues of salinity, common property resources, and wildlife sanctuaries in other areas of the state (such as the Saurashtra region of central-western Gujarat).[44] The review also recommended that AKRSP (I) build linkages between village organizations and "Panchayati Raj Institutions" (i.e. local political councils), and that the NGO increase its interaction with government agencies in order to access more funding and to influence policy (AKRSP (I)1998).

More generally, AKRSP (I)'s experience points to the significance of a strategic review as a mechanism of organizational change, particularly since it can assist an organization to look beyond its everyday routines. Northern funders can play important roles in supporting such reviews as part of a capacity-building process. At the same time, an externally forced process can undermine itself by compromising cooperation and enthusiasm. In the case of AKRSP (I), improved relationships between the NGO and its key funder led to a collectively "owned" process that was then able to move forward.

Conclusions

The broader purpose of this chapter has been to demonstrate how learning can enable organizational change in NGOs and yet how it is simultaneously constrained. Learning at a single-loop level, for example, can lead to scaling up of programs (such as Sadguru's lift irrigation and checkdam activities). Yet learning within programs is often structured and circumscribed by historical factors and experiences (such as by Sadguru's focus on basic needs which continues to guide its approach to natural resource management). In other words, while learning can lead to change in an organization and its environment, learning is also a circumscribed process in the sense that what an organization learns is often bounded by a set of governing factors – the cognitive capacities of organizational members, relationships of power within and between organizations, and the perceptual frames through which organizations interpret their world. As Argyris (1992: 7–12) has noted, learning which alters this basic frame (i.e. double-loop learning) is rare in individuals as well as in organizations.

In the cases examined in this chapter, single-loop learning was common, whereas double-loop learning was less widespread and less systematically employed. This is true in most organizations. Single-loop learning is likely to dominate in contexts where existing programs appear to be doing well (but can be improved), where routines are well established or are in the process of becoming standardized, where the environment appears to be relatively stable (i.e. it is not undergoing rapid or obvious change), and where organizations are so confident of their success that they fail to register or attend to changes in their environment (Levitt and March 1988; March 1988). Double-loop learning, on the other hand, is likely to be triggered by less predictable factors. In the experience of Sadguru's forestry program, it was triggered by a change in leadership. Double-loop learning can also be triggered by other factors including (but not limited to): a change in local economic and environmental conditions (e.g. an influx of industry into a rural region causing a shift in the local economy and thereby affecting employment, natural resource use, and pollution); a failure of existing programs to achieve wider goals despite meeting targets and objectives (e.g. a failure to alleviate poverty in a region despite the provision of basic services); a decline in demand for an organization's services; exposure to the work and worldviews of outside organizations and individuals; a periodic organizational self-assessment (e.g. a five-year strategic review); and, a systematic analysis by the organization of alternative development approaches and scenarios.

While both of these levels of learning are important for organizations, it is noteworthy that single-loop learning is largely based upon exploiting success, particularly in the short-run, whereas double-loop learning is more reflective and dependent upon examining possible failures, especially for ensuring long-term relevance.

Relationships between NGOs and funders are also central to learning, for they not only affect the standard activities of NGOs but also their accountability systems and strategic visions. Excessive upward accountability systems can compromise field-level learning and downwards accountability. In addition, it is surprising that while Northern NGOs and funders often require their Southern counterparts to engage in self-assessments and to build complex information systems, many Northern NGOs have invested very little in their own learning systems (Smillie and Hailey 2001). Many Northern NGOs have very small (if any) research departments, they offer limited opportunities for staff training, and they are rarely willing to hire external advisers and management consultants to facilitate organizational development and change. This "failure to invest in their own learning and self-reflection stands in marked and odd contrast with their willingness to build the same capacities in their Southern counterparts" (Smillie and Hailey 2001: 79). Clearly, there is much to be learned by Northern organizations from the NGOs they support.

7 Challenges ahead: NGO-funder relations in a global future

You know the story about the flute and the bassoon. They used to meet once a year, and one year the bassoon criticized the flute for its high sounds, and the flute also made fun of the bassoon for its deeper, heavier sounds. So they went away and both came back the next year as clarinets.

Director of Rural Programs, AKF Geneva[1]

This book has provided an in-depth look at the dynamics of organizational change in two prominent Southern NGOs. It has sought to demonstrate that NGO behavior is both a result of local experience and a response to much broader global forces. Throughout the book, I have stepped back from the rich particularities of the cases in order to discuss larger questions concerning the international context in which NGOs emerge and operate, the structured nature of information struggles between NGOs and funders, and the circumscribed and slow nature of organizational change through learning. The task of this concluding chapter is to weave together these preceding analyses into a wider discussion on the fabric of organizational change and the future of NGO-funder relationships.

Although the populations of NGOs around the world have exploded over the past two to three decades, these numbers tell us little about what these organizations do or how they interact within an ever globalizing development setting. We do know that the proliferation of NGOs has been partly fueled by increases in international funding to them. AKRSP (I) and Sadguru have been on the vanguard of this funding shift in India, being the first NGOs to receive "bilateral" funds directly from the European Commission. Such grants are normally provided to governments rather than to NGOs. It is also well known that funders attempt to influence the behavior of NGOs (and even states) through conditionalities attached to funds. But we know little about how NGOs respond to the demands exerted by funders or to the challenges raised by shifts in global development discourses.

A key goal of this book is to shed light on how NGOs respond to these larger transnational forces. More specifically, there are four overarching themes that run throughout the work and which I revisit below: *discourses* on development and environment, *interdependence* between NGOs and funders, *reporting* and monitoring systems, and processes of *organizational learning*. Development discourses and reporting systems, because of their pervasiveness, can have a homogenizing effect on NGOs – effectively transforming flutes and bassoons into clarinets. Processes of organizational learning, on the other hand, provide a means for NGOs to continually adapt their activities to local needs and thus retain their unique characters over time.

Global discourses on environment and development

International funders and Northern NGOs play important roles in introducing and spreading various development ideas and practices to NGOs. Development discourses – such as those concerning environment, sustainable development, gender, participation, and professionalism – are transmitted to NGOs through a variety of mechanism including consultants and funding conditionalities. As I have shown, however, NGOs are not passive recipients of new development practices and ideas, but are actively involved in challenging, testing, and re-shaping these discourses. All discourses represent a historically produced, or socially constructed, way of thinking about and practicing development.

The cases detailed in this book provide grounding for understanding the effects of changing development discourses on organizational behavior and change – not only in terms of charting the historical evolution of certain NGO activities but, more importantly, in terms of making sense of how NGOs conceptualize or think about their activities. The first chapter of this book introduced excerpts from a grant proposal written by an intermediary funder that described poverty in western India as being a result of "environmental degradation." The solution to this problem, it was argued, lay in a combination of technological intervention and better management of existing resources. This solution, which links technological and managerial expertise in discrete village-level projects, underlies the *natural resource management* or "NRM" approach to development that has become the hallmark of Southern NGOs like AKRSP (I) and Sadguru. But while NRM is becoming an increasingly popular and standardized approach to development, it is *not* necessarily a logical and inevitable solution to problems of poverty and development. Rather, it is a specific and historically produced way of thinking about and practicing development and has, over time, come to form the invisible bedrock underlying the behavior of some NGOs and their funders. There are other ways of viewing and addressing development problems – e.g. by emphasizing change in natural resource and agricultural policies that encourage resource depletion, or by attending to political inequalities in which poorer classes lack access to government decision makers – but it is NRM that forms the basic organizing framework through which issues of poverty and development are understood and addressed by members of organizations such as AKRSP (I) and Sadguru.[2]

The broader relevance of this experience is twofold. First, there is evidence that the NRM approach to development is spreading across India well beyond the experiences of AKRSP (I) and Sadguru, and that public agencies and international funders are playing central roles in this diffusion process. For example, both NGOs have facilitated the spread of NRM through their involvement in a nation-wide watershed development program supported by the central government. The guidelines for this program were developed with considerable input from AKRSP (I)'s first chief executive officer, and Sadguru has been specially designated as a key training resource for the program. Both NGOs also serve on district-level government advisory committees for the watershed program. In addition, with funding from the European Commission and the Norwegian government, Sadguru has established a large "training institute" where it provides government agencies, other NGOs, and rural communities with workshops and training programs on natural resource management.[3] In the fiscal year ending in March 2001 alone, a total of 105 NGOs and 104 government organizations participated in programs or workshops held at its training institute (Sadguru 2001: 47). AKRSP (I) also hires out its expertise to others, especially on topics of gender sensitization, participatory rural appraisal, and forest and water resource management. In 2000, its staff offered about two dozen training programs to government departments, NGOs, and academic institutes, which it markets as "AKRSP (I) Services" (AKRSP (I) 2001: 83).

Through the mechanisms outlined above (i.e. training provision, and the national watershed development program), the NRM approach to development shows signs of becoming increasingly institutionalized: it is being transformed into a legitimized way of practicing development by a growing set of NGOs, government agencies, and funding organizations. This process of homogenization is what DiMaggio and Powell (1983) have referred to as "institutional isomorphism." Isomorphism results in organizations resembling one another over time. Even AKRSP (I) and Sadguru have become more alike over time (in terms of their NRM approach and their reporting and monitoring systems), particularly since they were coupled together by the AKF network in 1993 in order to attract European Commission funding.

The wider relevance of this experience rests in the observation that the primary rewards of homogenization lie in the conferring of legitimacy upon organizations, thus providing access to resources controlled by other organizations (such as funds held by international funders and government agencies).[4] Viewed from this perspective, the spread of natural resource management in Gujarat state and to other parts of India is linked in significant ways to relationships between organizations and the legitimacy conferred through the adoption of specific resource management practices. In particular, NGO-funder relationships play an important role in supporting and reinforcing the NRM approach to development.

A second key point raised in this book is the analytical insight that NGO behavior is embedded in development discourses. Thus, in order to make sense of organizational change over time, it is helpful to examine shifts in development discourse over time. Conditions surrounding the founding of an organization are particularly important. Sadguru, for example, remains committed to a "basic needs" perspective on development that prevailed during its initial, formative stages in the early 1970s. Subsequent changes in the global development environment are, of course, also crucial, with international consultants and funders playing important roles in introducing to NGOs new technologies (e.g. biogas, watershed development, and lift irrigation) and techniques (e.g. participatory rural appraisal, and farmer-to-farmer extension). Consultants and funders also serve as agents of homogenization, as carriers of the broader discourses in which these technologies and techniques are embedded (e.g. participation, professionalism, environment, sustainable development, and gender and development). The commonality of such discourses among NGOs worldwide is a testament to the effectiveness of international funding as a diffusion mechanism.

It would be inaccurate, however, to suggest that the approaches to development adopted by NGOs are primarily determined by global ideas or trends. Strategies of sustainable development and ideas about participation and gender equity have made their way to NGOs through funders and consultants, but NGOs are also involved in developing their own local ideas and practices while testing, contesting, and sometimes even appropriating ideas received from others. Techniques of participatory rural appraisal, as I have shown, have been tested and improved by AKRSP (I), and have been then re-transmitted to global levels through the very same consultants that introduced them in the first place. Empirical evidence of such "reverse" influences from local to international levels indicates that while global development discourses shape NGO behavior, the experiences of NGOs can also modify (albeit incrementally) those discourses. The rhetoric of sustainable development discourse, on the other hand, has been embraced by many NGOs, including AKRSP (I) and Sadguru, as a means of legitimizing their work, but without necessitating actual changes in that work. Such evidence underscores the socially constructed nature of global development discourses, and their centrality in conferring organizational legitimacy.

In brief, NGOs can be seen as being molded by global development discourses by virtue of being embedded in them, but also as simultaneously improvising within those very same structures. This dynamic process, in which organizational behavior and change are shaped by global forces as well as by local experiences and learning processes, is what I have referred to (in chapter 1) as a dialectical relationship between structure and agency. The structured dimension of this process, as reviewed below, is also evident in how NGOs report to their funders.

Interdependence and reporting

A substantial portion of this book has been devoted to conceptually framing the *interdependence* between NGOs and their funders, especially as manifested in systems of monitoring and reporting (see chapters 4 and 5). This interdependence is characterized by an exchange of economic capital for symbolic capital. In such a relationship, funders provide NGOs with financial support and, in turn, they rely on NGOs for information which demonstrates that their funds have resulted in "successful" projects. In other words, the reputations of funders are dependent on positive assessments (by NGOs themselves as well as by hired evaluators) of NGO work. These relations of capital exchange form a basic structure that guides interactions between NGOs and funders.

The more general import of this model lies in the new perspective it offers for understanding a set of central problems in interactions between NGOs and funders. A substantial literature on NGOs, and on inter-organizational relations more broadly, has focused on the importance of funding, control over funding, and conditionalities associated with funds in influencing organizational behavior. It is natural to assume that the "piper calls the tune" in asymmetric relationships between organizations. The cases in this book challenge this assumption by demonstrating that funding (or economic capital) is only one source of influence, with other non-financial resources such as reputation, status, and authority (or symbolic capital) being equally crucial. Systems for gathering, interpreting, evaluating, and disseminating information on projects are important subjects of enquiry, since it is these systems that manufacture reputation. Intermediary funders, like AKF and many other Northern NGOs, are key nodes in this model of interdependence, since they enable capital exchange to occur by channeling funds from bilateral agencies to Southern NGOs, while simultaneously collecting and packaging information from Southern NGOs for donor consumption. They add value to both directions of the exchange, by negotiating with donors and managing fund flows from North to South, while also ensuring that quality information flows in the reverse direction.

A more nuanced understanding of the processes through which information is produced and regulated is enabled through a closer look at the cases of AKRSP (I), Sadguru, the European Commission, and AKF. While these limited cases obviously cannot hope to uncover the range of plausible mechanisms, they do shed light on some of the possibilities. In particular, funders such as AKF and the EC structure the flow of information from NGOs through special reporting formats and analytical tools such as the "logical framework." While useful for planning purposes, these efforts to organize and control information have resulted in a framing of NGO activities in largely quantitative, simplified, and depoliticized terms. This experience is not unique to the organizations detailed in this book, but appears to be fairly common among international donors that are keen to show the tangible results of their investments. The wide use of logical frameworks and their derivatives among donors, as well as the competitive nature of development contracting, have led Edwards and Hulme (1996: 968) to express concern over a "tendency to 'accountancy' rather than 'accountability'" and a trend towards the treatment of information as a "public relations activity."

At the same time, however, there is evidence that NGOs attempt to resist donor efforts to structure their information systems and behavior. A number of strategies of resistance were observed in the cases in this book: the symbolic generation of information, a bias towards sharing product (rather than process) information with funders, and the use of professional staff to legitimate their work in terms that funders are likely to accept. The lesson of more general interest here is that information systems within NGOs can serve as a means of "buffering" internal decision processes and activities from unwanted external interference.

Ironically, it is precisely through such efforts to resist funder control that NGOs can end up perpetuating or reproducing tensions with funders. By providing funders with large amounts of product data (i.e. easily measurable and quantifiable information on targets) and very little process data (i.e. harder to measure and qualitative information about the complexities of community mobilization, about gender, class, and caste tensions, and about long-term processes of social and political change), the NGOs in this book have inadvertently reinforced the dominance of product data in assessments of success and failure. In particular, two types of tensions between NGOs and funders are thus perpetuated: (1) a *product–process tension* in which the rhetoric of NGOs and funders emphasizes the importance of process issues, while standard reporting is heavily biased towards products; and, (2) an *insider–outsider tension* in which NGO members (the "insiders") see funders (the "outsiders") as being out of touch with ground realities. Insider-outsider tensions are inevitable if funders are not provided with the type of information which might help them to understand the complexities and ambiguities engulfing development interventions on the ground.

The main point here is counter-intuitive: it is not just funder demands for information but also NGO *resistance* to those demands that reinforces tensions between NGOs and funders. These tensions are highly structured in the sense that they are embedded within a framework of capital exchange where only certain kinds of information (i.e. simplistic and depoliticized product data that unambiguously demonstrate "success") are convertible into funds. While the details of these tensions are likely to vary across NGOs and funders, this research provides an analytical framework for thinking about funding and information flows as being part of a structured exchange. And while the interactions between NGOs and funders cannot be reduced only to exchanges of money and information, especially since NGOs and funders are also often linked by a shared commitment to poverty alleviation, it is quite possible for the tensions which arise from relations of capital exchange to eclipse common goals and collaborative intentions.

Organizational change through learning

The profoundly structured nature of NGO-funder exchange is even evident in processes of organizational learning. The learning model developed in this book distinguishes between learning that is concerned primarily with improving organizational performance (i.e. single-loop learning) and learning that leads to more fundamental change in the governing factors underlying organizational behavior (i.e. double-loop learning). Single-loop learning, while common in most organizations, is highly structured in the sense that it is guided and constrained by a number of factors: cognitive capacities of individuals within organizations, relationships of power between and within organizations and, most importantly, the perceptual frameworks or worldviews that influence how organizational members interpret their environment. The practical import of this analysis is that change through learning – even in very innovative NGOs – can be slow and constrained by multiple factors. For scholars and practitioners who work with NGOs and possibly try to facilitate change in them, it is important to recognize how learning occurs and what its limitations may be.

Relationships with funders play an important role in enabling as well as impeding learning. As the cases in this book demonstrate, international funders have played pivotal roles in introducing NGOs to new ideas and technologies of natural resource management through international consultants, and they have sometimes even been responsible for initiating strategic reviews of NGOs that lead to a deeper reflection on the relevance of NGO activities in a rapidly changing environment. But funders can also impede learning in NGOs (particularly at a double-loop level) by insisting on reporting and monitoring systems that emphasize product data rather than process data, and which are designed primarily to meet their own information needs for demonstrating "success" rather than those of the NGOs. More generally, this imperative to regularly show success (rather than to learn from failure), combined with a culture of highly centralized control over information, has made it difficult for Northern funders to transparently reflect upon their own work. This experience is not limited to the organizations discussed in this book, but is part of a much broader trend in the "contracting" of NGOs by donors which place an "emphasis on outputs rather than on longer-term learning and development" (Lewis 2001: 64–65).

The circumscribed and incremental nature of learning also has implications for the longer-term capacity of NGOs to reflect upon and modify their own work. To the extent that the learning facilitated by funders is limited to very structured monitoring systems (biased towards quantitative measurement) and the hiring of external consultants or technical experts to advise NGOs, it can lead to a homogenizing of NGO practices. The expertise offered by funders and consultants is not value-neutral but is subject to prevailing global development discourses, personal values, and relationships of power. As "experts," consultants and funders occupy positions of symbolic power: they potentially regulate not only the sort of information that carries global legitimacy, but they also guide how that information is collected, interpreted and used, especially through reporting and evaluation protocols. Learning protocols, however, can nurture innovation and creativity in NGOs, particularly if those systems promote experimentation by field-level staff rather than by outside experts, along with regular and open assessment of failures in the field. As such, learning systems can be seen as both structuring organizational behavior, and also facilitating organizational change in new directions.

Challenges ahead: the future of reporting and learning

The above discussion raises a number of very practical questions regarding learning processes and information systems in NGOs. If the current information and monitoring systems in organizations like AKRSP (I) and Sadguru are designed to meet the short-term needs of funders, then what would be the characteristics of systems oriented towards a longer-term perspective on social change? How can information systems better facilitate not only upward accountability (from NGOs to funders) but also downward accountability (from funders to NGOs to village communities)? And what new measures of success are necessary in order to replace the current positivist emphasis on quantitative assessments of NGO work? These questions will have to be answered if the critique of information systems and learning processes which I have offered is to be translated into practice.

This book provides the beginning of a response to these questions. In particular, it offers three normative directions. First, monitoring and learning systems that emphasize long-term social change will require less of a focus on the physical and financial component of reporting, and much more attention to the design of simpler, qualitative, and less onerous information systems. This will require international funders to relax their demands for narrowly focused (but resource intensive) reports designed to show quick results to their home constituencies. This challenge will remain difficult for donor governments and Northern NGOs, particularly in an economic climate of state retrenchment in which short-term results are often demanded for surviving budgetary cuts.

Second, these concerns about reporting raise larger normative questions about accountability and are indicative of a deep mismatch in NGO-funder systems of accountability. Physical and financial reports, while serving the necessary function of providing basic data on NGO operations, emphasize upwards accountability to funders, with only limited indication of the quality of NGO work and almost no attention to downward accountability to local communities. These are external approaches to accountability, enforced through punitive threats such as the loss of funding. While important, this external and upwards approach has only limited potential for encouraging NGOs and funders to take internal responsibility for shaping longer-term performance for impacting problems of poverty.

Similar concerns surround the use of performance assessments or evaluations. There is a tendency to equate evaluation with assessment of performance. While it makes sense to conduct evaluations in order to assess progress towards objectives, should this be the sole, or even the primary, purpose of evaluation? Performance assessments tend to focus attention on projects or programs, while overlooking the NGO or organization itself. Evaluations have the potential for facilitating broader organizational change, particularly through capacity building and organizational learning. Evaluations which reward success while punishing failure are unlikely to engender learning since they encourage NGOs to exaggerate successes, while discouraging a scrutiny of mistakes. External evaluators such as donors can thus improve NGO accountability (upwards and downwards) not merely by assessing performance, but by building NGO capacity to conduct self-evaluations, and by encouraging the analysis of failure as a means of learning. In order for this to occur, however, donors will need to make funding less contingent on simplistic assessments of success, and more closely linked to criteria of capacity-building and learning.

Third, and finally, responsibility for changing the myopic nature of reporting and learning lies not only with donors but also with NGOs. Southern NGOs carry a weighty responsibility for looking more closely and openly at their failures and, in so doing, to educate their donors about the complexities of social change. While the temptation to feed donors information only on successful activities may satisfy short-term fund disbursement needs, this occurs at a cost to longer-term and innovative solutions to alleviating poverty and inequity.

The challenges facing NGOs and funders are thus about the very structure of their interdependence. Rethinking and reworking these relationships will likely be an incremental and difficult process. Yet it will be necessary if we are to intentionally maneuver change in a world where planned action is itself limited.

Notes

I THE MAKING OF NGOs: THE RELEVANCE OF FOUCAULT AND
BOURDIEU

1 The EC maintains separate procedures for fund transfers to governments and to NGOs.
Bilateral funds, intended for governments, are much larger than funds allotted to
NGOs. In this particular case, the grant to the NGOs was large enough to qualify
as bilateral, and as a result, it also needed special approval from the Government of
India.

2 This approach to history is called "genealogy" by Foucault (Foucault 1984c). He
cautions, however, against viewing power as being vested in individuals, groups, or
social classes. For him, power is something fluid that is expressed through those who,
for a time, have access to it: "Power must be analysed as something which circulates,
or rather as something which only functions in the form of a chain. It is never localised
here or there, never in anybody's hands, never appropriated as a commodity or piece
of wealth . . . [I]ndividuals are the vehicles of power, not its points of application"
(Foucault 1980: 98).

3 It is clear that development activities in a country, such as India, are not determined
solely by *exogenous* organizations such as the World Bank. Indeed, *indigenous* support
for development activities in India can be traced to India's independence movement
from the 1920s through the 1940s, to India's central government initiatives since
independence from the British in 1947, and to a growth in NGO activity since the
1970s. But while there is a great deal of indigenous support for development activities
in India, international organizations such as the World Bank also play an important
role in shaping how development is understood, especially by providing funding and
expertise (to governments) with an emphasis on economic growth and modernization
activities.

4 My usage of discourse differs here from that of Foucault. The notion of "dominant"
or "competing" discourses is quite foreign to Foucault. For him, a discourse refers to
a body of knowledge and practice (e.g. on medicine, madness, or sexuality). These
discourses are part of a very stable "discursive formation" – an ensemble of practices, texts, institutions, and relations of power – which changes only incrementally
over hundreds of years. The present discursive formation can be characterized by the
entrenchment of "scientific" and "rationalist" systems of thought, with its roots trace-
able to post-Enlightenment Europe. By tracing the histories of some of these systems
of thought (e.g. medicine), Foucault shows that scientific knowledge and practices
(such as theories concerning disease, or medical procedures such as controlled

experiments) are not based on "objective truths" but on historical accidents and the exercise of power. Within such a discursive formation, there is no such thing as a dominant discourse because all discourses are embedded within this larger discursive system. My usage of discourse, however, which includes the notion of "dominant" or "competing" discourses is more closely aligned to the concept of "ideology" employed by the Italian political theorist and activist Antonio Gramsci (see Hall 1996 for an overview).

5 The relationship between structure and agency has also been theorized by the British sociologist Anthony Giddens, for whom social structure tends to include two elements: "the *patterning of interaction*, as implying relations between actors or groups; and the *continuity of interaction* in time" (Giddens 1979: 62–5, emphasis in original). Both Giddens and Bourdieu emphasize the importance of including change over time in their theoretical models. Giddens' notion of "resources" is incorporated into Bourdieu's theory as "capital." And what Bourdieu calls "double structuration," Giddens refers to as the "duality of structure." For additional details on similarities and differences in their work, see Harker et al. (1990: 201–4).

6 See Adams 1979, as cited in Edwards (1989: 118).

2   THE NGOs AND THEIR GLOBAL NETWORKS

1 The industrialist was Arvind Mafatlal of the Mafatlal (now Stanrose) Group of Companies. His inspiration was the "humanitarian saint," Ranchhod Dasji Maharaj.

2 Both directors are of equal rank and use the title of "Director." I henceforth refer to one of them as "Co-Director" simply for the purpose of distinguishing between them.

3 The US dollar figure is calculated at the 2001 exchange rate of about US$ 1 = Indian Rs. 40, but is considerably greater in real terms.

4 For example, the first Chairman of the Board was Dr. V. Kurien, who was also the head of the National Dairy Development Board of the Government of India. He was succeeded by Dr. I. G. Patel, formerly Director of the London School of Economics. The present chairman is Nasser Munjee, Executive Director of Housing Development and Finance Corporation (HDFC).

5 This difference in emphasis between AKRSP (I) and Sadguru is more complex than portrayed here. For example, while AKRSP (I) does often emphasize the *process* of community organization through its activities, it has also established a number of village organizations "simply to manage a technological intervention, such as canal irrigation societies" especially in Junagadh district (personal communication, CEO of AKRSP (I), April 14, 1999). At the same time, while Sadguru emphasizes the technological dimensions of its projects, it "does not impose technology on villages" (personal communication, Director of Sadguru, April 19, 1999). Indeed, many (if not most) of Sadguru's recent irrigation projects have been built in response to direct requests from village members. The formation of a village-level organization or user group is a standard component of Sadguru's work.

6 While both AKRSP (I) and Sadguru have received funds in the past from the Canadian International Development Agency and the British Department for International Development, there has been very little contact with either of these organizations since the early 1990s, and they are therefore not described in this chapter. Similarly,

both AKRSP (I) and Sadguru receive funds for biogas development from a Canadian organization known as Partners in Rural Development (Partners) via a Delhi-based NGO called Action for Food Production (AFPRO). Interactions with Partners and AFPRO have been very limited and are not discussed here.

7 Other actors in the social development area of the AKDN include the Aga Khan University based in Pakistan, and several development NGOs in South Asia and East Africa known as the Aga Khan Education Services, Aga Khan Health Services, and Aga Khan Planning and Building Services. AKF plays a central role in securing funding for the various social development activities of the AKDN.

8 AKF's overall policy direction is determined by a Board of Directors that is chaired by the Aga Khan. The central office in Geneva is headed by a General Manager who oversees a very small team of about a dozen professional staff, of which two are responsible for rural development. Country offices, such as AKF India, are headed by a CEO assisted by a small team of professional staff.

9 The acronyms AKDN, AKF, and AKRSP (I) are often confused with one another because they share the same first two words: Aga Khan (AK). It is necessary to distinguish between these three entities. AKDN is an umbrella notation for a vast set of organizations headed by the Aga Khan. AKF is one component of this large network and is made up of a central office in Geneva and various country units (e.g. in Canada, India, etc.). For purposes of clarity and specificity, each AKF office is henceforth referred to by attaching its location name (e.g. AKF Geneva, AKF Canada, AKF India), while references to AKF as a whole are denoted simply as "AKF" or as the "AKF network." AKRSP (I) receives most of its funding through AKF, but is not formally a part of AKF or the AKDN, although it is unofficially considered a part of the "family."

10 The Foundation's role in JFM was handed over in early 1997 to a Delhi-based organization, the Society for Promotion of Wastelands Development.

11 Gujarat is a relatively prosperous state in India and has become a low priority region for NORAD. NORAD's funds for Rajastan, however, are increasing. Having worked in border villages on the Gujarat side, Sadguru has expanded into Rajastan with funds from NORAD and the Rajastan Government.

3 NGO BEHAVIOR AND DEVELOPMENT DISCOURSE

1 Although development as an international industry is relatively young, development within different regional and local contexts predates the 1940s. In the Indian sub-continent, for example, Gandhian "constructive work" activities were common in the 1920s and 1930s [Alliband, 1983; Ramachandra Guha, personal communication, February 14, 1998] and Christian missionary and welfare activity can be traced back to the arrival of St. Francis Xavier of Portugal in the early 1540s (Sahay 1980: 15–52).

2 Lift-irrigation involves the use of pumps to "lift" off water from a river or reservoir to higher ground, from where it can be distributed by gravity through pipelines to outlets near farmers' fields.

3 The work of Jan Breman, an anthropologist who has been studying the political economy of south Gujarat since the 1970s, has shown that economic growth in the region has led to increased class and caste differentiation. Moreover, he shows

that migration and labor patterns are embedded in a larger regional economy that is unlikely to change through technocratic rural development activity (see Breman 1996).

4 The Foreign Contribution Regulation Act (FCRA) of 1976 enabled the government to monitor the flow of foreign funds to NGOs (Fernandes 1986, as cited in Sen 1999: 338). It was enacted shortly after a State of Emergency was declared by the government of Indira Gandhi.

5 While there have not been any comparative studies of these two perspectives on village organizations, there is no evidence to suggest that one approach has fared better than the other, in terms of economic or social change.

6 Interview, Former CEO of AKRSP (I), February 15, 1997.

7 Lewis (1998) uses the term "reverse agenda" to describe the role of NGOs in the United Kingdom in shaping official UK government development policy.

4 INTERDEPENDENCE AND POWER: TENSIONS OVER MONEY AND REPUTATION

1 My use of the term "capital" is very general and should not be confused with more specific uses of the term (e.g. capital as investible resources only). I also do not distinguish between different forms of capital "exchange" (e.g. generalized reciprocity, barter, spot sales, transfers, etc.) at this stage.

2 The financial figures presented in this section were obtained from annual reports, various financial records, correspondence records between the NGOs and their funders, and from personal communication with financial officers in each NGO. The reporting periods used in calculating annual expenditure are different for both organizations. AKRSP (I) produces its annual report based on the calendar year (e.g. 1996), while Sadguru bases its report on the fiscal year ending on March 31 (e.g. April 1, 1996 – March 31, 1997 is the 1996 fiscal year, and it is referred to as FY 1996). The data in figures 4.1, 4.2, and 4.3 should be taken as approximations only. The purpose of these figures is only to demonstrate trends.

3 Funds from the EC are passed on to AKF UK and then onwards to AKF India (with approval from headquarters in Geneva) and then finally to AKRSP (I) and Sadguru. The AKF network (and AKF Geneva in particular) insists that all communication (reports as well as correspondence) between the NGOs and the EC be routed through them. In addition to preventing miscommunication, this protocol allows the AKF network to retain a central role in controlling the relationships between the EC and the NGOs.

4 Interview, Former Program Executive, AKRSP (I), Ahmedabad, Gujarat, January 3, 1996.

5 Interviews, Director, Sadguru, May 8, 1996 and May 22, 1996 respectively.

6 Interview, Former CEO, AKRSP, Ahmedabad, Gujarat, February 15, 1997.

7 Interview, Programs Manager, AKF UK, Ahmedabad, Gujarat, March 21, 1996.

8 Personal communication, Director, Sadguru, April 19, 1999.

9 Interview, AKRSP (I), CEO, Ahmedabad, Gujarat, March 18, 1996.

10 This is not the case between AKF and Sadguru for, as Sadguru's Director remarked, "AKF will never disown AKRSP. But not so with Sadguru" (Interview, Chosala, Gujarat, April 17, 1997). These words, uttered in 1997, anticipated events in 2001

in which AKF and Sadguru were unable to agree to terms on continuing their relationship beyond the EC grant. AKF's relationship with AKRSP (I), however, continues on.

11 Interview, Programs Manager, AKF UK, London, June 3, 1996.
12 Interview, Program Officer, AKF Geneva, Geneva, January 6, 1997.
13 Interview, Program Officer, AKF Geneva, Geneva, January 6, 1997.
14 Interview, Program Officer, AKF Geneva, London, June 3, 1996.
15 Interview, CEO, AKRSP (I), Ahmedabad, Gujarat, January 29, 1997.
16 Interview, Counselor (head of EC Delegation to India), New Delhi, December 27, 1995.
17 Interview, Project Officer A, EC Delegation to India, New Delhi, May 28, 1996.
18 Interview, Program Officer, AKF Geneva, Geneva, January 6, 1997.
19 Interview, Director, Rural Programs, AKF Geneva, Geneva, January 9, 1997.
20 Interview, Former Program Executive A, AKRSP (I), Ahmedabad, Gujarat, January 3, 1996.
21 Interview, Resident Consultant, EC Delegation to India, New Delhi, May 28, 1996.
22 Interview, Project Officer A, EC Delegation to India, New Delhi, May 28, 1996.
23 Interview, Director, Sadguru, Chosala, Gujarat, May 22, 1996.
24 Interview, Adviser, NORAD, New Delhi, May 28, 1996.
25 Interview, Director, Sadguru, Chosala, Gujarat, May 22, 1996.
26 Interview, CEO, AKRSP (I), Ahmedabad, Gujarat, March 18, 1996.
27 Interview, Former Program Executive A, AKRSP (I), Ahmedabad, Gujarat, April 3, 1996.
28 Interview, Program Officer for Social Forestry, Ford Foundation, New Delhi, October 6, 1995.
29 Interview, Program Officer for Water Resources, Ford Foundation, New Delhi, January 24, 1997.
30 This conceptualization of the link between information and reputation, which I denote as information/reputation, is directly related to and inspired by Michel Foucault's conceptualization of the link between knowledge and power, which he denotes as power/knowledge (Foucault 1984b; Rabinow 1984: 9; Shumway 1989: 112). For him, knowledge and particularly the right to create and decide what counts as knowledge is a form of power. Development professionals decide what information about a development activity is to be collected and scrutinized in order to separate "successes" from "failures". In doing so, they set up norms for the assessment and understanding of "development."

5 INFORMATION STRUGGLES: THE ROLE OF INFORMATION IN THE REPRODUCTION OF NGO-FUNDER RELATIONSHIPS

1 This usage of the terms product and process data differs from its use in a US context where process data are contrasted with outcome data – with the former being concerned with data about the process of service delivery (e.g. numbers of clients served) and the latter focusing on outcomes of services (e.g. number of people placed in permanent jobs).
2 Interviews with Senior Program Officer for Lift Irrigation (May 13 1996) and Senior Supervisor for Social Forestry (May 10, 1996), Sadguru, Chosala, Gujarat.

3 Interview, Senior Program Executive, AKRSP (I), Ahmedabad, Gujarat, February 28, 1997.
4 Interview, CEO, AKRSP (I), Ahmedabad, Gujarat, March 18, 1996.
5 Interview, Program Manager for Bharuch, AKRSP (I), Netrang, Gujarat, February 24, 1997.
6 Interview, Program Organizer for Forestry in Bharuch, Netrang, Gujarat, March 14, 1996.
7 Interview, Senior Program Officer A for Monitoring, Sadguru, Chosala, Gujarat, May 6, 1996.
8 Interview, CEO, AKRSP (I), Ahmedabad, Gujarat, March 18, 1996.
9 Interview with Senior Program Executive, AKRSP (I), Ahmedabad, Gujarat, February 28, 1997 and personal communication with Senior Program Officer A for Monitoring, Sadguru, Dahod, Gujarat, November 9, 1995.
10 Personal communication, Senior Program Executive, AKRSP (I), January 13, 1999.
11 Interview, Project Officer B, EC Delegation, New Delhi, March 27, 1997.
12 Legitimacy is conceptualized here as a *condition* achieved through the exchange of resources such as information/reputation or money. For NGOs to be legitimated by funders (through the receipt of funds), they must provide reputation (which is conferred through information that demonstrates success) to those funders.
13 Interview, Senior Program Officer for Monitoring, Sadguru, Chosala, Gujarat, May 6, 1996.
14 Interview, Director, Sadguru, Chosala, Gujarat, May 8, 1996.
15 Consultants have been responsible for introducing AKRSP (I) and Sadguru to a number of activities and procedures, such as biogas energy development, watershed development, and participatory rural appraisal. See chapter 3 for more details.
16 The Ford Foundation's task environment differs significantly from that of AKF and the EC, particularly because Ford has its own endowment and emphasizes "process" activities in its work. It would be useful to examine NGO-funder relations in light of such differences in task environments. Such an analysis, however, is beyond the scope of the present book.
17 Feldman and March (1988: 422) make a similar argument, stating that "Organizational departments assigned information-processing responsibilities are unlikely to remain neutral with respect to the uses of information. Partly, people who gather and use information will tend to be people who believe that information gathering is important." In a study of organizational change in the US Army Corps of Engineers, Mazmanian and Nienaber (1979: 183–91) provide evidence that changes in personnel and organizational structure led to changes in the Corps' projects and policies.
18 Interview, Program Officer, AKF Geneva, Geneva, January 6, 1997.

6 LEARNING IN NGOs

1 It is useful to distinguish between information and knowledge. Knowledge arises from the processing or analysis of information (Edwards 1997), as well as from the conducting and analysis of action.
2 Learning is only one of many processes yielding organizational change (e.g. changes in organizational routines can be brought about through new laws which mandate

procedural changes). Moreover, learning is not always an intentional process, and it does not always lead to improvements in an organization's performance (Levitt and March 1988: 333; Scott 1992: 110).

3 Neither Argyris and Schön (1978; 1996) nor Levitt and March (1988) explicitly differentiate *types* of learning from *levels* of learning. I find it useful to introduce these distinctions in order to establish a relationship between the concepts developed by Argyris and Schön and those formed by March and colleagues. Hedberg (1981), however, refers to single-loop and double-loop learning as "low-level" and "meta-level" learning, respectively.

4 This view of individual and organizational behavior – in which behavior is highly structured or constrained and yet amenable to change – is inspired by the work of the French social theorist Pierre Bourdieu, and in particular by his concept of *habitus*: a capacity for improvising in highly structured environments. See Bourdieu (1977), Postone et al. (1993: 4), and Mahar et al. (1990). This view is also related to Weick's (1979: 147–169) argument that organizations "enact" their environments. He claims that organizations do not simply "perceive" their environment but are involved in actively inventing and creating what they see and thus to what they respond.

5 Foreign direct investment to India has increased from about US $0.15 billion in 1991–92 to approximately US$ 2 billion in 1995–96. Of the latter figure, about US$ 1.4 billion went to the industrial sector (Indira Gandhi Institute of Development Research 1997: 30, 135).

6 Sadguru and its main funders call these outputs "physical achievements." The NGO provides quarterly reports to the Aga Khan Foundation and to the European Commission on "physical and financial progress," and those reports are the sources of data for this table. The first period, FY 1976–81, is six years rather than four. I have chosen to use four-year periods following FY 1981 in order to create breaks at 1990 and 1994. Sadguru began to receive substantial foreign funding in 1990, and its grant from the European Commission commenced in 1994.

7 The medical and preschool departments which operated independently of the irrigation and agriculture programs were eventually dropped from Sadguru's activities. This wide-ranging combination of activities was characteristic of the "integrated rural development" approach of the early 1980s.

8 The term "bureaucratic," used here in its Weberian sense (not in its common pejorative sense), refers to the specialization of tasks in an organization, along with the establishment of standard operating procedures and centralized control. For more on the term bureaucracy, see Weber (1947 trans.: 324–37) and Scott (1992: 38–45).

9 A primary objective of Sadguru has long been to improve rural living conditions by increasing income-earning opportunities for the rural poor via "environmentally sound land and water resources programmes" (Sadguru 1998: n.p.). While the wording used to describe this objective has changed somewhat over time, the objective itself has not.

10 Arguably, there may have been economies of scale (e.g. in terms of the cost of materials, or in terms of reproducing designs) as Sadguru built more projects. But scale economies may have been partially offset by increasing costs for labor and transport as the NGO expanded to villages further from its office. Since the mid-1990s, for example, Sadguru has expanded its operations into the neighboring states of Rajastan and Madhya Pradesh.

11 Interview, Co-director of Sadguru, Chosala, Gujarat, May 8, 1996.
12 My point here is not to suggest whether or not Sadguru *should* engage more in double-loop learning, but only to make evident that learning at this level is difficult and circumscribed in significant ways.
13 Interviews: former Program Officer of AKF Geneva, London, January 15, 1997, and Director of Communications, AKF Geneva, Geneva, January 8, 1997.
14 Key initial deliberations are detailed in minutes of two board meetings held on October 15, 1984 in Bombay and on November 28, 1984 in Anand, Gujarat.
15 AKRSP (I) commenced operations in 1985. Table 6.3 is divided into three year periods in order to create a break at 1994 – the year when AKRSP (I) began to receive large amounts of funding from the European Commission. AKRSP (I) is also engaged in numerous other activities such as the formation of savings and credit groups, and the implementation of smaller scale water resource technologies including roof rainwater harvesting structures, pedal pumps, group wells, and percolation wells. Table 6.3 lists only AKRSP (I)'s primary and more long-established technical activities.
16 Table 6.3 also included canal irrigation as a key activity. I have very limited data on AKRSP (I)'s canal irrigation work, and have thus omitted it from table 6.4.
17 There is a difference between increasing the *quantity* of activities and improving the *quality* of those activities. As AKRSP (I)'s Senior Program Executive noted, since 1997, AKRSP (I) has substantially increased the number of staff devoted to enhancing the capacities of village organizations. Improvements in the capacity and diversity of village organizations can thus be seen as organizational outputs. Measures of productive efficiency entirely miss these types of outputs (Personal communication, Senior Program Executive, AKRSP (I), May 4, 1999). The distinction between the quality and quantity of outputs is taken up again later in this chapter.
18 In arriving at these numbers of staff, I counted only those members of the Bharuch district field office designated as "water resource" or "engineering" staff, and have also included two-thirds of all "surveyors" or "field specialists". It was not possible to disaggregate various kinds of water resource staff from the data available. I chose to include only those staff in the Bharuch office since most of AKRSP (I)'s lift irrigation projects (12 of 14) until 1996 were built in this district.
19 Of the total 5659 biogas plants constructed by the end of 1996, 4708 were in Junagadh district, 693 in Bharuch district, and 258 in Surendranagar district (which did not have any full-time biogas staff according to AKRSP (I)'s 1996 annual report).
20 This conclusion that some targets were lowered is drawn from a comparison of targets in AKRSP (I)'s 1996 annual report to its workplan for 1995 and the overall workplan for years 1994–2001 submitted to the European Commission (AKRSP (I)Aga Khan Foundation 1994a; Aga Khan Foundation 1994b: Annex 1; 1997: 3). For example, AKRSP (I) aimed to raise over 2.1 million tree saplings in 1995, and only 0.75 million in 1996 (although it ended up raising 1.1 million saplings). AKRSP (I)'s watershed development targets were similarly reduced from 2400 hectares in 1995 to 1535 hectares in 1996.
21 Interview, CEO of AKRSP (I), Ahmedabad, Gujarat, March 18, 1996.
22 A watershed is a physical drainage basin determined by topography and runoff drainage patterns. Large watersheds consist of entire river basins, such as for the Mississippi River in the USA or the Ganges-Brahmaputra Rivers in South Asia.

These large watersheds can be further subdivided into smaller units, with each smaller watershed distinguished by its drainage patterns. The Government of India has set 5,000 hectares as a norm for small watershed size (for purposes of funding allocation). AKRSP (I)'s watersheds vary in size.

23 The formation of clusters was not an abrupt change. AKRSP (I) already had some "satellite" offices that were used as work spaces by staff in different regions of each district. But the decentralization effort provided these offices with greater control over the planning and management of their work.

24 This information was collected from several members of the Bharuch SHT during a meeting of the Dediapada Cluster, on February 2, 1997 in Dediapada, Gujarat.

25 Most of the details in this chronology are extracted from annual reports for each year and should be regarded as approximations only. The reasons provided for abandoning certain activities have been inferred from the annual reports as well as from interviews with three AKRSP (I) staff in Ahmedabad, Gujarat: Senior Program Executive, February 28, 1997; CEO, February 27, 1997; former Program Executive, March 1, 1997.

26 Cattle camps were compounds set up during the droughts of 1986–88 where farmers could bring their cattle in order to provide them with fodder and water. Fodder farms were stockpiles of fodder established not only for the existing drought but also to safeguard against future droughts.

27 Interview, former CEO of AKRSP (I), Ahmedabad, Gujarat, February 15, 1997. This statement is very similar to one made by James March in the first part of this chapter under the heading "Types of Learning". What AKRSP (I)'s former CEO calls innovation and replication, March calls exploration and exploitation.

28 Interview, former Program Executive, AKRSP (I), Ahmedabad, Gujarat, January 3, 1996.

29 AKRSP (I) (1992: n.p.). An early reference to action research can be found in the Minutes of the Meeting of the Board of Directors of AKRSP (I) India, held on 28th November 1984 at Anand, Gujarat, p.4.

30 Interview, Senior Program Executive, AKRSP (I), Ahmedabad, Gujarat, March 23, 1997.

31 There are, of course, exceptions. For example, AKRSP (I)'s adoption of drinking water technologies (i.e. a new activity) can be seen as having occurred through double-loop learning: it was the result of a shift away from water resource projects that emphasized income generation (e.g. irrigation) to projects that emphasized an important household need or a "quality of life" issue (Personal communication, Senior Program Executive, AKRSP (I), May 4, 1999).

32 There are some notable exceptions to this observation, such as savings and credit programs in AKRSP (I).

33 AKRSP (I)'s Senior Program Executive has pointed out that influencing state-level policies on natural resource use was a key activity of AKRSP (I) prior to 1993, and that this was a "major reason why physical target[s] were under achieved" at that time. He also noted "that AKF's role in policy influencing has been very weak" (Personal communication, May 4, 1999).

34 Personal communication, CEO of AKRSP (I) April 14, 1999. The types of information to which AKRSP (I)'s CEO refers are described in the first part of Chapter 5.

35 Personal communication, Director of Sadguru, April 19, 1999.

36 The terms "upward" and "downward" accountability draw from Edwards and Hulme (1996).
37 Personal communication, CEO of AKRSP (I), April 14, 1999.
38 Personal communication, Director of Sadguru, April 19, 1999.
39 Interview, Programs Manager, AKF UK, Ahmedabad, Gujarat, March 21, 1996.
40 Interview, Director of Rural Programs, AKF Geneva, Geneva, January 9, 1997.
41 Interview, CEO of AKRSP (I), Ahmedabad, Gujarat, February 27, 1997.
42 Personal communication, CEO of AKRSP (I), December 23, 1998.
43 Personal communication, CEO of AKRSP (I), April 14, 1999.
44 Personal communication, CEO of AKRSP (I), April 14, 1999.

7 CHALLENGES AHEAD: NGO-FUNDER RELATIONS IN A GLOBAL FUTURE

1 Interview, Director of Rural Programs, AKF Geneva, Geneva, January 9, 1997.
2 This is not to suggest that one approach is "better" than another, but only to point out that there are various ways of addressing problems of environmental degradation and poverty, and that NRM, as practiced by AKRSP (I) and Sadguru, is only one of these ways.
3 Training has become one of Sadguru's five key objectives.
4 The legitimacy granted to an expert or professional – what Bourdieu calls symbolic capital – confers power and thus access to resources.

References

Adams, A. 1979. An Open Letter to a Young Researcher. *African Affairs* 78, no. 313 (Oct. 1979): 451–79.

Aga Khan Development Network. undated. *The Aga Khan Development Network.* Aiglemont, France: The Information Department, Secretariat of His Highness the Aga Khan.

Aga Khan Foundation. 1983. *Multi-Year Programme Strategy for the AKF Network, December 1, 1983.* Unpublished, Switzerland: Aga Khan Foundation.

1987. *Current Projects: Pakistan, 1987.* Pakistan: Aga Khan Foundation.

1992. *AKF International Strategy 1991–1999.* Switzerland: Aga Khan Foundation.

1993. *Community Management of Natural Resources in Gujarat: A Proposal to the European Community on behalf of the Aga Khan Rural Support Programme (India) and Sadguru Water and Development Foundation:* Aga Khan Foundation.

1994a. *Community Management of Natural Resources, Gujarat, India Overall Work Plan (1994–2001).* New Delhi: Aga Khan Foundation.

1994b. *Community Management of Natural Resources, India: Work Plan for Year Two (January–December 1995).* New Delhi: Aga Khan Foundation.

1995. *Management of Environmental Resources by Communities: Programme Proposal.* New Delhi: Aga Khan Foundation.

1996a. *AKF(I) Programme Strategy 1996–2001: A Draft.* New Delhi: Aga Khan Foundation.

1996b. *Annual Report 1995.* Geneva: Aga Khan Foundation.

1997. *Annual Report 1996.* Geneva: Aga Khan Foundation.

1998a. *Annual Report 1997.* Geneva: Aga Khan Foundation.

1998b. *Project Brief: Aga Khan Rural Support Programme (India).* Switzerland: Aga Khan Foundation.

Aga Khan Rural Support Programme (India). 1987. *Annual Progress Report: January–December 1986.* Ahmedabad, India: Aga Khan Rural Support Programme (India).

1992. *Annual Progress Report 1991–92.* Ahmedabad, India: Aga Khan Rural Support Programme (India).

1994. *Annual Progress Report 1993.* Ahmedabad, India: Aga Khan Rural Support Programme (India).

1995. *Annual Progress Report 1994.* Ahmedabad, India: Aga Khan Rural Support Programme (India).

1996. *Annual Progress Report 1995.* Ahmedabad, India: Aga Khan Rural Support Programme (India).

1997. *Annual Progress Report 1996*. Ahmedabad, India: Aga Khan Rural Support Programme (India).

SHT-Netrang. 1997. *Budget 1996*. Netrang, India: Aga Khan Rural Support Programme (India).

1998. *Strategies to Position AKRSP(I) in the Year 2010: A Concept Paper*. Ahmedabad, India: Aga Khan Rural Support Programme (India).

2001. *Annual Progress Report 2000*. Ahmedabad, India: Aga Khan Rural Support Programme (India).

Aga Khan Rural Support Programme (Pakistan). 1987. *The Aga Khan Rural Support Programme: Profile of the District and some Village Projects*. Gilgit, Northern Areas, Pakistan: Aga Khan Rural Support Programme (India).

Alibhai, Karim. 1985. *Feasibility of Small-Scale Biogas Plants in Project Areas of Junagadh District in Saurashtra Region of Gujarat State*: Aga Khan Foundation Geneva.

1988. *Report IX (Biogas)*: Aga Khan Foundation Geneva.

1989. *Biogas at AKRSP (India)*: Aga Khan Foundation Geneva.

1990. *Biogas and Gir Periphery Programmes of AKRSP (I)*: Aga Khan Foundation Geneva.

Alliband, Terry. 1983. *Catalysts of Development: Voluntary Agencies in India*. West Hartford, Connecticut: Kumarian Press.

Archer, Robert. 1994. Context: Markets and Good Government. In *Governance, Democracy and Conditionality: What Role for NGOs?*, ed. A. Clayton, Oxford: INTRAC.

Argyris, Chris. 1982. *Reasoning, Learning, and Action*. San Francisco: Jossey-Bass.

1992. *On Organizational Learning*. Cambridge, MA: Blackwell.

Argyris, Chris, and Donald A. Schön. 1978. *Organizational Learning*. Reading, MA: Addison-Wesley.

1996. *Organizational Learning II: Theory, Method, and Practice*. Reading, MA: Addison-Wesley.

Bernstein, Henry. 1992. Agrarian Structures and Change: India. In *Rural Livelihoods: Crises and Responses*, eds. H. Bernstein, B. Crow, and H. Johnson, Oxford: Oxford University Press.

Biggart, N. W. 1977. The Creative–Destructive Process of Organizational Change: The Case of the Post Office. *Administrative Science Quarterly* 22: 410–26.

Boserup, Ester. 1970. *Women's Role in Economic Development*. New York: St. Martin's Press.

Bourdieu, Pierre. 1977. *Outline of a Theory of Practice*. Translated by Richard Nice. Cambridge: Cambridge University Press.

1979. *Algeria 1960*. Translated by Richard Nice. Cambridge: Cambridge University Press.

1984. *Distinction: A Social Critique of the Judgment of Taste*. Cambridge, MA: Harvard University Press.

1987. (French edn.). *Choses dites*. Paris: Les Editions de Minuit.

Breman, Jan. 1996. *Footloose Labour: Working in India's Informal Economy*. Cambridge: Cambridge University Press.

Campbell, Jeffrey Y., Subhabrata Palit, and Shree Bhagwan Roy. 1994. Putting Research Partnerships to Work: The Joint Forest Management Research Network in India.

Paper presented at the Fifth International Symposium on Society and Resource Management, Fort Collins, Colorado, June 7–10, 1994.

Cernea, Michael M. 1988. *Nongovernmental Organizations and Local Development.* Washington, DC: World Bank.

Chambers, Robert. 1994a. All Power Deceives. *IDS Bulletin* 25 (2):14–26.

1994b. Participatory Rural Appraisal (PRA): Analysis of Experience. *World Development* 22 (10): 1253–68.

Clark, John. 1995. The State, Popular Participation, and the Voluntary Sector. *World Development* 23 (4): 593–601.

Clayton, Andrew, ed. 1994. *Governance, Democracy and Conditionality: What Role for NGOs?* Oxford: INTRAC.

Commission of the European Communities. 1993a. *Project Administration Agreement between the Commission of the European Communities and the Aga Khan Foundation for the Administration of the Community Management of Natural Resources in Gujarat, Project.* New Delhi: Commission of the European Communities.

1993b. *Project Cycle Management: Integrated Approach and Logical Framework.* Brussels: Commission of the European Communities.

Crow, Ben. 1992. Rural Livelihoods: Action from Above. In *Rural Livelihoods: Crises and Responses*, eds. H. Bernstein, B. Crow, and H. Johnson, Oxford: Oxford University Press.

Cyert, Richard M., and James G. March. 1963. *A Behavioral Theory of the Firm.* Englewood Cliffs, NJ: Prentice-Hall.

Dichter, Thomas W. 1999. Globalization and Its Effects on NGOs: Efflorescence or a Blurring of Roles and Relevance? *Nonprofit and Voluntary Sector Quarterly* 28 (4 Supplement): 38–58.

DiMaggio, Paul J., and Walter W. Powell. 1983. The Iron Cage Revisited: Institutional Isomorphism and Collective Rationality in Organizational Fields. *American Sociological Review* 48 (April): 147–60.

Drabek, Anne Gordon. 1987. Development Alternatives: The Challenge for NGOs – An Overview of the Issues. *World Development* 15 (Supplement): ix–xv.

Edwards, Michael. 1989. The Irrelevance of Development Studies. *Third World Quarterly* 11 (1): 116–35.

1994. International NGOs and Southern Governments in the "New World Order": Lessons of Experience at the Programme Level. In *Governance, Democracy and Conditionality: What Role for NGOs?*, ed. A. Clayton, Oxford: INTRAC.

1997. Becoming a Learning Organisation, or, the Search for the Holy Grail? In *Strategies of Public Engagement: Shaping A Canadian Agenda for International Co-operation*, ed. D. Gillies, Montreal and Kingston, Canada: McGill-Queen's University Press.

Edwards, Michael, and David Hulme. 1996. Too Close for Comfort? The Impact of Official Aid on Nongovernmental Organizations. *World Development* 24 (6): 961–73.

Edwards, Paul N. 1996. *The Closed World: Computers and the Politics of Discourse in Cold War America.* Cambridge, MA: MIT Press.

Escobar, Arturo. 1995. *Encountering Development: The Making and Unmaking of the Third World.* Princeton, New Jersey: Princeton University Press.

Fals-Borda, O., and A. Rahman, eds. 1991. *Action and Knowledge: Breaking the Monopoly with PAR.* New York: Apex.

Feldman, Martha S., and James G. March. 1988. Information in Organizations as Signal and Symbol. In *Decisions and Organizations*, ed. J. G. March, 410–28. Cambridge, Massachusetts: Basil Blackwell.

Ferguson, James. 1990. *The Anti-Politics Machine: "Development," Depoliticization, and Bureaucratic Power in Lesotho.* Cambridge: Cambridge University Press.

Fernandes, W. 1986. The National NGO Convention: Voluntarium, the State and Struggle for Change. *Social Action* 36 (4): 431–41.

Fillingham, Lydia Alix. 1993. *Foucault for Beginners.* New York: Writers and Readers.

Fisher, Julie. 1998. *Nongovernments: NGOs and the Political Development of the Third World.* West Hartford, Connecticut: Kumarian Press.

Foucault, Michel. 1980. Two Lectures: 7 January 1976, 14 January 1976. In *Power/Knowledge: Selected Interviews and Other Writings 1972–1977*, ed. C. Gordon, 78–108. New York: Pantheon.

1984a. Madness and Civilization. In *The Foucault Reader*, ed. P. Rabinow, 123–67. New York: Pantheon.

1984b. Disciplines and Sciences of the Individual (Discipline and Punish). In *The Foucault Reader*, ed. P. Rabinow, 170–238. New York: Pantheon.

1984c. Nietzsche, Genealogy, History. In *The Foucault Reader*, ed. P. Rabinow, 76–100. New York: Pantheon.

Fowler, Alan. 1997. *Striking a Balance: A Guide to Enhancing the Effectiveness of Non-Governmental Organizations in International Development.* London: Earthscan.

Frank, Andre Gunder. 1967. *Capitalism and Underdevelopment in Latin America.* London: Monthly Review.

Freire, Paulo. 1973. *Education for Critical Consciousness.* New York: Seabury Press.

Gardner, Katy, and David Lewis. 1996. *Anthropology, Development and the Post-Modern Challenge.* Edited by R. Wilson and T. H. Eriksen, *Anthropology, Culture and Society.* London: Pluto Press.

Ghosh, Jayati, and Krishna Bharadwaj. 1992. Poverty and Employment in India. In *Rural Livelihoods: Crises and Responses*, eds. H. Bernstein, B. Crow, and H. Johnson, Oxford: Oxford University Press.

Giddens, Anthony. 1979. *Central Problems in Social Theory: Action, Structure and Contradiction in Social Analysis.* Berkeley: University of California Press.

Government of India. 1951. *First Five Year Plan 1951–56.* New Delhi: Planning Commission, Government of India.

1978. *Draft Five Year Plan 1978–83.* New Delhi: Planning Commission, Government of India.

1985. *Seventh Five Year Plan, 1985–90, Volume II.* New Delhi: Planning Commission, Government of India.

1992. *Eighth Five Year Plan, 1992–97.* New Delhi: Planning Commission, Government of India.

Grant, Nadine. 1989. *A Study of the Impact of Sadguru Water and Development Foundation's Social Forestry Programme on Women.* Dahod, India: Navinchandra Mafatlal Sadguru Water and Development Foundation.

Guhan, S. 1988. Aid for the Poor: Performance and Possibilities in India. In *Strengthening the Poor: What Have We Learned?*, ed. J. P. Lewis, Washington: Overseas Development Council.

Hall, Stuart. 1996. Gramsci's Relevance for the Study of Race and Ethnicity. In *Stuart Hall: Critical Dialogues in Cultural Studies*, eds. D. Morley and K.-H. Chen, 411–40. London: Routledge.

Hampshire, Jonathan. 1991a. *Aga Khan Rural Support Programme India: Review of Programme Planning, Budgeting and Monitoring Systems*. West Sussex, United Kingdom: Information Technology & Agricultural Development Ltd.

———. 1991b. *Sadguru Water and Development Foundation: Programme Planning, Budgeting and Monitoring Assessment*. West Sussex, United Kingdom: Information Technology and Agricultural Development Ltd.

Hannan, Michael T., and John Freeman. 1977. The Population Ecology of Organizations. *American Journal of Sociology* 82 (5): 929–64.

Haribhakti Consulting. 1995. *Budgeting Process and Delegation of Financial Powers in Aga Khan Rural Support Programme (India): Draft Report*. Bombay: Haribhakti Consulting Pvt. Ltd.

Harker, Richard. 1990. Bourdieu: Education and Reproduction. In *An Introduction to the Work of Pierre Bourdieu: The Practice of Theory*, eds. R. Harker, C. Mahar, and C. Wilkes, 86–108. New York: St. Martin's Press.

Harker, Richard, Cheleen Mahar, and Chris Wilkes, eds. 1990. *An Introduction to the Work of Pierre Bourdieu: The Practice of Theory*. New York: St. Martin's Press.

Häusler, Sabine, Piet van den Boom, Aard Hartveld, J. P. L. Srivastava, and Sanjiv Phansalkar. 1998. *Mid Term Review: Community Management of Natural Resources (CMNR) India*: Commission of The European Union.

Hedberg, Bo. 1981. How Organizations Learn and Unlearn. In *Handbook of Organizational Design*, eds. P. C. Nystrom and W. H. Starbuck, 3–27. Oxford: Oxford University Press.

Huber, George P. 1996. Organizational Learning: The Contributing Processes and the Literatures. In *Organizational Learning*, eds. M. D. Cohen and L. S. Sproull, 124–62. Thousand Oaks, California: Sage.

Hudock, Ann. 1999. *NGOs and Civil Society: Democracy by Proxy?* Cambridge, MA: Blackwell.

Hulme, David, and Michael Edwards, eds. 1997. *NGOs, States and Donors: Too Close for Comfort?* New York: St. Martin's Press in association with The Save the Children Fund.

Indira Gandhi Institute of Development Research. 1997. *India Development Report 1997*. Delhi: Oxford University Press.

Khanna, Renu, and Shyamala Hiremath. 1990. *Review of Five Year Plan of Sadguru Water and Development Foundation*: Norwegian Agency for Development Cooperation.

Khorakiwala, Tasnim. 1997a. *Greening of the Panchmahals: Sadguru's Social Forestry Programme 1996*. Dahod, Gujarat, India: Navinchandra Mafatlal Sadguru Water and Development Foundation.

———. 1997b. *Harvesting Water for Basic Livelihood: Checkdam*. Dahod, Gujarat, India: Navinchandra Mafatlal Sadguru Water and Development Foundation.

Levinthal, Daniel A., and James G. March. 1993. The Myopia of Learning. *Strategic Management Journal* 14: 95–112.

Lévi-Strauss, Claude. 1976. *The Story of Asdiwal*. Vol. 2, *Structural Anthropology*. Chicago: University of Chicago Press.

Levitt, Barbara, and James G. March. 1988. Organizational Learning. *Annual Review of Sociology* 14: 319–40.

Levy, Frank, Arnold J. Meltsner, and Aaron Wildavsky. 1974. *Urban Outcomes: Schools, Streets, and Libraries.* Berkeley: University of California.

Lewis, David. 1998. Development Policy and Development NGOs: The Changing Relationship. Paper presented at the CVO 20th Anniversary Conference, 17–18 September, 1998, at London School of Economics.

——— 2001. *The Management of Non-Governmental Development Organizations.* London: Routledge.

Lipton, Michael, and John Toye. 1990. *Does Aid Work in India? A Country Study of the Impact of Official Development Assistance.* London: Routledge.

Mackintosh, Maureen. 1992. Questioning the State. In *Development Policy and Public Action,* eds. M. Wuyts, M. Mackintosh, and T. Hewitt, 61–89. Oxford: Oxford University Press.

Mahar, Cheleen, Richard Harker, and Chris Wilkes. 1990. The Basic Theoretical Position. In *An Introduction to the Work of Pierre Bourdieu: The Practice of Theory,* eds. R. Harker, C. Mahar, and C. Wilkes, 1–25. New York: St. Martin's Press.

Manzo, Kate. 1991. Modernist Discourse and the Crisis of Development Theory. *Studies in Comparative International Development* 26 (Summer) (2): 3–36.

March, James G. 1988. *Decisions and Organizations.* Cambridge, MA: Basil Blackwell.

——— 1991. Exploration and Exploitation in Organizational Learning. *Organization Science* 2 (1): 71–87.

——— 1992–93. Learning and the Theory of the Firm. *Economia E Banca – Annali Scientifici* 5–6: 15–35.

March, James G., and Johan P. Olsen. 1988. The Uncertainty of the Past: Organizational Learning under Ambiguity. In *Decisions and Organizations,* ed. J. G. March, 335–58. Cambridge, MA: Basil Blackwell.

March, James G., and Herbert A. Simon. 1958. *Organizations.* New York: John Wiley.

Matthews, Eric. 1996. *Twentieth-Century French Philosophy.* Edited by C. Butler, R. Evans, and J. Skorupski, *Opus.* Oxford: Oxford University Press.

Mazmanian, Daniel A., and Jeanne Nienaber. 1979. *Can Organizations Change?: Environmental Protection, Citizen Participation, and the Corps of Engineers.* Washington, D.C.: The Brookings Institution.

Meyer, John W., and Brian Rowan. 1977. Institutionalized Organizations: Formal Structure as Myth and Ceremony. *American Journal of Sociology* 83 (2): 340–63.

Mohanty, Manoranjan, and Anil K. Singh. 1996. *Foreign Aid and NGOs.* New Delhi: Voluntary Action Network India (VANI).

Moser, C. O. N. 1989. Gender Planning in the Third World: Meeting Practical and Strategic Needs. *World Development* 17 (11): 1799–1825.

Najam, Adil. 2000. The Four-C's of Third Sector-Government Relations: Cooperation, Confrontation, Complementarity, and Co-optation. *Nonprofit Management and Leadership* 10 (4): 375–96.

Nederveen Pieterse, Jan. 1991. Dilemmas of Development Discourse: The Crisis of Developmentalism and the Comparative Method. *Development and Change* 22 (1): 5–29.

Nyborg, Ingrid, Robert Mitchell, Sindhu Phadke, and Jan Erik Studsrød. 1993. *Mid-Term Evaluation of the Sadguru Water and Development Foundation's Five-Year*

Plan: Norwegian Agency for Development Cooperation, Aga Khan Foundation, Sadguru Water and Development Foundation.

Perera, Jehan. 1997. In Unequal Dialogue with Donors: The Experience of the Sarvodaya Shramadana Movement. In *NGOs, States and Donors: Too Close for Comfort?*, eds. D. Hulme and M. Edwards, New York: St. Martin's Press in association with The Save the Children Fund.

Pfeffer, Jeffrey. 1987. A Resource Dependence Perspective on Intercorporate Relations. In *Intercorporate Relations: The Structural Analysis of Business*, eds. M. S. Mizruchi and Michael Schwartz, 25–55. New York: Cambridge University Press.

Pfeffer, Jeffrey, and Gerald R. Salancik. 1978. *The External Control of Organizations: A Resource Dependence Perspective*. New York: Harper and Row.

Poate, Derek. 1989a. *AKRSP(I): Monitoring, Reporting and Impact Assessment*. West Sussex, United Kingdom: Information Technology & Agricultural Development Ltd.

——— 1989b. *Sadguru: Monitoring, Reporting and Impact Assessment*. West Sussex, United Kingdom: Information Technology & Agricultural Development Ltd.

Postone, Moishe, Edward LiPuma, and Craig Calhoun. 1993. Introduction: Bourdieu and Social Theory. In *Bourdieu: Critical Perspectives*, eds. C. Calhoun, E. LiPuma, and M. Postone, Chicago: University of Chicago Press.

Rabinow, Paul, ed. 1984. *The Foucault Reader*. New York: Pantheon.

Rahnema, Majid. 1997. Participation. In *The Development Dictionary: A Guide to Knowledge as Power*, ed. W. Sachs, Hyderabad, India: Orient Longman.

Rathgeber, Eva M. 1990. WID, WAD, GAD: Trends in Research and Practice. *Journal of Developing Areas* (July):489–502.

Robinson, Mark. 1994. Governance, Democracy and Conditionality: NGOs and the New Policy Agenda. In *Governance, Democracy and Conditionality: What Role for NGOs?*, ed. A. Clayton, Oxford: INTRAC.

Robinson, M., J. Farrington, and S. Satish. 1993. NGO-Government Interaction in India: Overview. In *Non-Governmental Organizations and the State in Asia: Rethinking Roles in Sustainable Agricultural Development*, eds. J. Farrington and D. Lewis, London: Routledge.

Ruttan, Vernon W. 1989. Improving the Quality of Life in Rural Areas. In *Aid and Development*, eds. A. O. Krueger, C. Michalopoulos, and V. W. Ruttan, Baltimore: Johns Hopkins University Press.

Sadguru Water and Development Foundation. 1990. *The Rural Development Programme in Panchmahal-Gujarat: A Brief Progressive Report up to 31-3-1990*. Dahod, Gujarat, India: Navinchandra Mafatlal Sadguru Water and Development Foundation.

——— 1991. *Annual Report for the Year Ending 31st March 1991*. Dahod, Gujarat: Navinchandra Mafatlal Sadguru Water and Development Foundation.

——— 1993. *Annual Report for the Year Ending 31st March 1993*. Dahod, Gujarat, India: Navinchandra Mafatlal Sadguru Water and Development Foundation.

——— 1995. *Annual Report for the Year Ending 31st March 1995*. Dahod, Gujarat, India: Navinchandra Mafatlal Sadguru Water and Development Foundation.

——— 1996. *Annual Report for the Year Ending 31st March 1996*. Dahod, Gujarat, India: Navinchandra Mafatlal Sadguru Water and Development Foundation.

——— 1997a. *Annual Report for the Year Ending 31st March 1997*. Dahod, Gujarat, India: Navinchandra Mafatlal Sadguru Water and Development Foundation.

1997b. *Progress Report for the Calendar Year 1996*. Dahod, Gujarat, India: Navinchandra Mafatlal Sadguru Water and Development Foundation.

1998. *Annual Report for the Year Ending 31st March 1998*. Dahod, Gujarat, India: Navinchandra Mafatlal Sadguru Water and Development Foundation.

2001. *Annual Report: Year Ending 31st March 2001*. Dahod, Gujarat, India: Navinchandra Mafatlal Sadguru Water and Development Foundation.

Sahay, Keshari N. 1980. *Christianity and Culture Change in India*. New Delhi: Inter-India Publications.

Sánchez Triana, Ernesto. 1998. How Rent Seeking, Learning and Path Dependence Shape Environmental Institutions: The Case of the Cauca Valley Corporation in Colombia. PhD Thesis, Civil and Environmental Engineering, Stanford University, Stanford, CA.

Scott, W. Richard. 1992. *Organizations: Rational, Natural, and Open Systems*. 3rd edn. Englewood Cliffs, NJ: Prentice Hall.

1995. *Institutions and Organizations*. Edited by D. Whetten, *Foundations for Organizational Science*. Thousand Oaks, CA: Sage.

Sen, Siddhartha. 1993. Non-Profit Organizations in India: Historical Development and Common Patterns. *Voluntas* 3 (2): 175–93.

1999. Some Aspects of State-NGO Relationships in India in the Post-Independence Era. *Development and Change* 30: 327–55.

Shri Sadguru Seva Sangh Trust. 1978. *Brief Note on the Activities of Shri Sadguru Seva Sangh Trust / Mafatlal Group in Panchmahals (Gujarat)*. Dahod, Gujarat, India: Shri Sadguru Seva Sangh Trust (SSST).

1980. *The Rural Development Programme in Panchmahals, Gujarat: Progress up to 30-10-80*. Dahod, Gujarat, and Bombay India: The Surat Cotton Mills, The Standard Mills, Shri Sadguru Seva Sangh Trust (SSST).

1981. *The Lift Irrigation Schemes in Panchmahals*. Dahod, Gujarat, India: Shri Sadguru Seva Sangh Trust (SSST), Rural Development Programme, the Surat Cotton Mills, the Standard Mills Ltd.

1983. *The Rural Development Programme in Panchmahals, Gujarat: Progress up to 31-12-1983*. Dahod, Gujarat: The Surat Cotton Mills, The Standard Mills Ltd., Shri Sadguru Seva Sangh Trust (SSST).

1984. *The Rural Development Programme in Panchmahals, Gujarat: Progress up to 30-10-1984*. Dahod, Gujarat: The Surat Cotton Mills, The Standard Mills Ltd., Shri Sadguru Seva Sangh Trust (SSST).

1986. *The Rural Development Programme in Panchmahals, Gujarat: Progress up to 31-7-1986*. Dahod, Gujarat: Stanrose Group of Companies, Shri Sadguru Seva Sangh Trust (SSST).

Shumway, David R. 1989. *Michel Foucault*. Edited by D. O'Connell, *Twayne's World Authors Series: French Literature*. Boston: Twayne.

Smillie, Ian, and David M. Catmur. 1988. *Aga Khan Foundation Canada and Aga Khan Foundation Network: An Evaluation*. Ottawa: Canadian International Development Agency and Aga Khan Foundation Canada.

Smillie, Ian, and John Hailey. 2001. *Managing for Change: Leadership, Strategy and Management in Asian NGOs*. London: Earthscan.

Smith, Steven Rathgeb, and Michael Lipsky. 1993. *Nonprofits for Hire: The Welfare State in the Age of Contracting*. Cambridge, MA: Harvard University Press.

Society for Participatory Research in Asia. 1991. *Voluntary Development Organisations in India: A Study of History, Roles and Future Challenges*. New Delhi: Society for Participatory Research in Asia (PRIA).

Stinchcombe, Arthur L. 1965. Social Structure and Organizations. In *Handbook of Organizations*, ed. J. G. March, 142–93. Chicago: Rand McNally.

Sukhatme, Vasant. 1989. Assistance to India. In *Aid and Development*, eds. A. O. Krueger, C. Michalopoulos, and V. W. Ruttan, Baltimore: Johns Hopkins University Press.

Tendler, Judith. 1975. *Inside Foreign Aid*. Baltimore, Maryland: Johns Hopkins University Press.

Thompson, James D. 1967. *Organizations in Action*. New York: McGraw-Hill.

Tripathi, P. M., M. Kala, B. Mishra, and R. Patni. 1991. *Role of NGOs in Development: A Study of the Situation in India*. New Delhi: Association of Voluntary Agencies for Rural Development (AVARD).

Universalia. 1995. *AKFC Organizational Evaluation Report*. Montreal, Canada: Universalia.

Wallerstein, Immanuel. 1974. *The Modern World-System I: Capitalist Agriculture and the Origins of the European World-Economy in the Sixteenth Century*. New York: Academic Press.

Watts, Michael J. 1993. Development I: Power, Knowledge, Discursive Practice. *Progress in Human Geography* 17 (2): 257–72.

Weber, Max. 1947 trans. In *The Theory of Social and Economic Organization*, eds. A. H. Henderson and T. Parsons, Glencoe, Illinois: Free Press.

Weick, Karl. 1979. *The Social Psychology of Organizing*. 2nd edn. Reading, Massachusetts: Addison-Wesley.

Weir, Andrew, Doris Buddenberg, Kiran Bhatia, and Neal Mountstephens. 1995. *Joint Monitoring Mission 1995: Draft Report, Community Management of Natural Resources (ALA/93/33)*. New Delhi: The Commission of the European Communities, The Aga Khan Foundation.

Weir, Andrew, and Parmesh Shah. 1994. *Report of the Baseline Monitoring Mission: Community Management of Natural Resources (ALA/93/33)*. New Delhi: Commission of the European Communities, The Aga Khan Foundation.

Wolch, Jennifer R. 1990. *The Shadow State: Government and Voluntary Sector in Transition*. New York: The Foundation Center.

World Bank. 1989. *Sub-Sahwan Africa: From Crises to Sustainable Growth*. Washington, DC: The World Bank.

1996. *The Aga Khan Rural Support Program: A Third Evaluation*. Washington, DC: The World Bank.

World Commission on Environment and Development. 1987. *Our Common Future*. New York: Oxford University Press.

Young, Dennis R. 1999. Complementary, Supplementary, or Adversarial?: A Theoretical and Historical Examination of Nonprofit-Government Relations in the United States. In *Nonprofits and Government: Collaboration and Conflict*, eds. E. T. Boris and C. E. Steuerle, 31–67. Washington, DC: Urban Institute Press.

Index

accountability (*also see* learning), 158–59
action research, 141
   process innovation, 141–42
   product innovation, 141–42
Ahmedabad, 24, 83
Aga Khan, 28–29, 53
Aga Khan Development Network (AKDN),
   29, 30, 61
Aga Khan Education Service, 61
Aga Khan Foundation (AKF), 1, 9, 21, 23, 27,
   28–30, 41, 42, 45, 61, 71, 74–75, 112,
   123, 155
   AKF Geneva, 23, 30, 31, 42, 55, 61, 66, 67,
     129
   AKF India, 31, 55, 61, 62, 65, 66, 71, 82
   European Commission and (*see* European
     Commission)
   history, 29
   funding, 29, 49, 55, 59
   relations with NGOs, 64–67
Aga Khan Health Service, 61
Aga Khan Rural Support Programme (India)
   (AKRSP (I)), 7, 21
   Corpus fund (*see* endowment)
   endowment, 23, 30, 53
   funding, 24, 53–56, 60–61
   gender and development (*also see*
     discourse), 24, 51, 143, 148
   history, 23–24, 39–40
   monitoring systems, 97–98
   planning procedures, 83–84
   spearhead teams, 24, 83, 84, 98, 137–38
   village organizations, 24–26, 27, 39, 50,
     129, 134, 142
Aga Khan Rural Support Programme
   (Pakistan) (AKRSP (P)), 128–29, 147
agency (*also see* structure), 14–19, 20, 101
Argyris, Chris (*also see* learning levels), 10,
   107, 109, 125, 149

Baseline Monitoring Mission (BMM), 85, 86,
   87, 91–93, 94, 97, 99

basic needs, 34, 35, 37, 39, 50, 113, 122, 124,
   126, 154
Bharuch District, 24, 26, 133
Biogas, 87, 113, 130, 133–36, 143
Biogas Users Association, 134
Bombay, 45
Boserup, Ester, 43
Bourdieu, Pierre, 3, 10, 15, 16–18, 19, 20,
   101
   capital, 3, 16, 17–18, 19, 20
   habitus, 3, 16–17, 18, 20
   reproduction, 4, 16, 18–19
BRAC, 30
Bretton Woods, 34
Bruntland Commission, 43
Buffering, 95, 99, 156

Canadian International Development Agency
   (CIDA), 1, 24, 55, 145
capital (*also see* resource and Pierre Bourdieu)
   economic, 52–53, 66
   exchange, 4, 52, 63, 75–76, 101–102, 103,
     112, 144, 155, 156
   symbolic, 52–53, 66, 73, 75
Chambers, Robert, 45, 146
civil society organizations, 1, 47–48, 50
conditionality, 43, 45, 50, 51, 64, 77, 114, 151
consultants, 42–43, 45–46, 51, 66, 100
core technologies, 95
Council for Advancement of People's Action
   and Rural Technology (CAPART), 48

data (*also see* information), 87
   baseline, 79, 80, 82, 94–95, 96
   physical and financial, 82–85
   process, 78, 79–80, 85, 87–90, 98–99,
     102–104, 157
   product, 78, 80, 81, 85, 98–99, 102–104,
     157
decoupling, 96–97, 98, 100, 103
Department for International Development
   (DFID), United Kingdom, 24, 55

discourse, 3, 4, 19
  anti-development, 13
  changes in, 19, 50, 51, 154
  constrained by, 51
  definition of, 10–11, 34
  development, 11–14, 19, 33, 34, 38, 41, 50,
    152–54
  Foucault and changes in, 15
  gender, 44–45
  global, 19, 33, 51, 113, 143, 151, 158
  participatory development, 38–39
  sustainable development, 43–44, 51, 154
District Rural Development Agencies
  (DRDA), 32, 38
Drought Prone Areas Program, 119

economic reform, 47
Edwards, Michael, 17–18
European Commission (EC), 7, 9, 21, 23, 24,
  27, 28, 46, 55, 59, 61, 112, 118, 125, 137,
  151, 155
  Aga Khan Foundation and, 28, 30, 48, 55,
    56, 66, 85
  Community Management of Natural
    Resources (CMNR), 7–9, 28, 32, 55, 61,
    67, 87, 91
  relations with NGOs, 67–68, 70
  reporting requirements, 28, 62, 71–73,
    82–83, 95
European Community, 47
European Union, 3

Ferguson, James, 12
Five Year Plan, 36, 48
Ford Foundation, 21, 23, 24, 28, 30–31, 42,
  56, 59, 61, 71, 100
  relations with NGOs, 69–70
Foucault, Michel (also see discourse), 3, 10,
  11, 12, 15–16, 19, 20
Freire, Paulo, 38
funder and NGO relations: (also see Aga Khan
  Foundation, European Commission, Ford
  Foundation, Norwegian Agency for
  Development Cooperation), 52, 63–64,
  79, 81, 149, 157–58
Funding
  constraints, 15, 61, 104, 142
  flows, 18, 32, 48, 50, 53–59, 74–75, 145,
    156
  pressures as a result of, 49–50, 98

Gandhi, Indira, 38
good governance, 47
Government agencies, 32
Green revolution technology, 35, 37, 38

Gujarat, 9, 21, 23, 31, 38, 39, 40, 55, 65, 69,
  114, 129
  map of

India–Canada Environment Facility (ICEF),
  46, 49
Indian Administrative Service, 48
industrialization, 35, 114
information
  flows, 18, 32, 74–75, 77, 78, 79–81, 102,
    103, 155, 156
  reputation and (see reputation)
  reporting requirements and, 78, 81–82,
    84–85, 94–95, 102
  systems, 77, 78, 102, 103, 112, 113,
    144–45, 156, 158–59
Integrated Rural Development (IRD), 36
International Labour Organisation (ILO), 23,
  59, 61
International Monetary Fund (IMF), 13, 47

Joint Forest Management (JFM), 24, 30, 31,
  40, 56, 69, 70, 85, 90, 141, 142
Junagadh District, 24, 26, 133, 134, 135

learning
  accountability and, 145–46, 149
  definition of, 107
  stimulus–response model, 114–16
learning by doing, 108, 109–10, 117
  in AKRSP (I), 134–36, 141–42
  in Sadguru, 118–24, 125
learning by exploring, 108, 109–10, 117
  in AKRSP (I), 137–39, 141
  in Sadguru, 118–24, 127
learning by imitating, 108–10, 117
  in AKRSP (I), 128–30, 134–36, 141
  in Sadguru, 119, 122, 127
learning cycle, 110–14
  cognitive capacities, 110–12, 117, 149, 157
  relationships of power, 110, 112, 117,
    127–28, 149, 157
  perceptual frames, 110, 112–14, 117, 122,
    127–28, 149, 157
learning levels
  double-loop, 5, 109, 110, 117, 149, 157–58
    in AKRSP (I), 142, 147
    in Sadguru, 122, 125, 127–28
  single-loop, 5, 109–10, 116–17, 148, 149,
    157–58
    in AKRSP (I), 130, 136, 141–42
    in Sadguru, 122, 124, 125, 126
Lévi-Strauss, Claude, 14
Logical Framework Analysis (LFA), 85,
  86–93, 94, 96, 102, 144, 155–56

Madhya Pradesh, 21
March, James (*also see* learning by doing and
    learning by exploring), 10, 107, 108
McNamara, Robert, 36
modernization, 12–13, 35
monitoring (*see* reporting)

Natural Resource Management (NRM), 8–9,
    10, 34, 46–47, 95, 129, 136, 141, 142,
    148, 152–53, 157
  as dominant development approach, 9–10
  training programs, 46, 125–26, 153
Navinchandra Mafatlal Sadguru Water and
    Development Foundation (*see* Sadguru)
Nehru, Jawaharlal, 35
Norwegian Agency for Development
    Cooperation (NORAD), 21, 23, 28, 30,
    31–32, 42, 59, 61, 62, 100
  relations with NGOs, 75

objectivism (*see* Structure)
Organisation for Economic Cooperation and
    Development (OECD), 48

Panchmahals District, 36, 118
Participatory Action Research (PAR), 38
Participatory Irrigation Management (PIM),
    24, 30, 31, 40, 46, 69, 70, 141, 142
Participatory Rural Appraisal (PRA), 27,
    42–43, 45–46, 51, 66, 86, 104, 141–42,
    143, 153, 154
Partners in Rural Development, 56
Pieterse, Nederveen, 12
Platinum Jubilee Investment Ltd, 61
productive efficiency, 124–25, 130–33, 136,
    139, 142
professionalization, 39, 40–41

Rajastan, 21, 31
reporting
  see AKRSP (I) monitoring systems
  see data
  see European Commission Reporting
      Requirements
  see information
  see resource interdependence
  see Sadguru reporting systems
reputation (*also see* information), 4, 52, 65,
    66, 67, 75, 76, 92, 101, 144, 155
resistance, 1, 2, 15, 64, 65, 78, 101, 102–103,
    156–57

resistance strategies, 95
  professionalization, 95, 99–101, 102, 156
  selectivity, 95, 98–101, 102, 156
  symbolism, 95, 96–98, 99–101, 102, 103,
      156
resource (*also see* Capital)
  dependence, 4, 53, 60–63, 71
  inputs and outputs, 71–73
  interdependence, 2, 4–5, 52, 53, 60, 64,
      65–66, 67, 75, 112, 144, 155–57, 159
  interstructuring and, 60, 62, 66
  reverse influence, 45–47, 154
  rules, 96

Sadguru, 7, 21
  endowment, 23, 55, 56, 59
  funding, 23, 53, 56–59, 60
  gender and development (*also see*
      discourse), 24
  history, 21–23, 36
  reporting systems, 82–83, 97
  village organizations, 26–27, 39
    Lift Irrigation Cooperative Cell (LICC),
        26, 120–21, 122
    Lift Irrigation Cooperative Societies
        (LICS), 39, 49, 50, 51, 120–21
Sartre, Jean-Paul, 14
Schön, Donald (*also see* Learning levels), 107,
    109, 125
Shankerpura Village, 119, 123
Shri Sadguru Seva Sangh Trust (SSST) (*also
    see* Sadguru), 21
Sir Dorabji Tata Trust, 62
Sir Ratan Tata Trust, 62
Stanrose-Mafatlal Group of Companies, 59, 61
strategic review, 146–48, 157
structure (*also see* agency), 14–19, 20, 101
subjectivism (*see* agency)
Surendranagar District, 24, 26

Tulsi Trust, 62

United Nations (UN), 13, 44
  Conference on the Human Environment, 43
  Environment Programme (UNEP), 43
United States Agency for International
    Development (USAID), 35, 44, 73

watershed development, 46, 49, 56, 63, 87,
    124, 130, 131, 141, 153
World Bank, 13, 19, 35, 36, 44, 46, 47

9 780521 671576